MOVING

THROUGH

FEAR

MOVING

THROUGH

FEAR

CULTIVATING THE
7 SPIRITUAL INSTINCTS
FOR A FEARLESS LIFE

Jeff Golliher

JEREMY P. TARCHER
a member of Penguin Group (USA) Inc.
New York

JEREMY P. TARCHER/PENGUIN
Published by the Penguin Group
Penguin Group (USA) Inc., 375 Hudson Street, New York, New York 10014,
USA * Penguin Group (Canada), 90 Eglinton Avenue East, Suite 700, Toronto,
Ontario M4P 2Y3, Canada (a division of Pearson Penguin Canada Inc.) *
Penguin Books Ltd, 80 Strand, London WC2R 0RL, England *
Penguin Ireland, 25 St Stephen's Green, Dublin 2, Ireland (a division of
Penguin Books Ltd) * Penguin Group (Australia), 250 Camberwell Road,
Camberwell, Victoria 3124, Australia (a division of Pearson Australia Group Pty Ltd) *
Penguin Books India Pvt Ltd, 11 Community Centre, Panchsheel Park,
New Delhi–110 017, India * Penguin Group (NZ), 67 Apollo Drive,
Rosedale, North Shore 0632, New Zealand (a division of Pearson
New Zealand Ltd) * Penguin Books (South Africa) (Pty) Ltd,
24 Sturdee Avenue, Rosebank, Johannesburg 2196, South Africa

Penguin Books Ltd, Registered Offices: 80 Strand,
London WC2R 0RL, England

Most Tarcher/Penguin books are available at special quantity discounts for bulk purchase for sales
promotions, premiums, fund-raising, and educational needs. Special books or book excerpts also
can be created to fit specific needs. For details, write Penguin Group (USA) Inc. Special Markets, 375
Hudson Street, New York, NY 10014.

Library of Congress Cataloging-in-Publication Data

Golliher, Jeffrey.
Moving through fear : cultivating the 7 spiritual instincts for a fearless life / Jeff Golliher.
p.   cm.
ISBN 978-1-58542-838-0
1. Fear—Religious aspects—Christianity.   2. Spirituality.
3. Spiritual life—Christianity.   I. Title.
BV4908.5.G657   2011   2010039506
248.8'6—dc22

Printed in the United States of America

1   3   5   7   9   10   8   6   4

BOOK DESIGN BY AMANDA DEWEY

For
Nene

CONTENTS

Do not let your hearts be troubled,
and do not let them be afraid.

—The Gospel According to John, 14:27b

LIVING IN THE REAL WORLD: THE CHOICE OF FREEDOM OR FEAR

Writing is always a labor of love, but an abiding love for the subject of fear is not among the reasons that I've written this book. My labor has been for the love of freedom that we find by moving through our fear, and for the love of the world that fear would like to claim as its own. I have no deep-seated interest in fear itself. I don't like fear very much; I don't like to be afraid; and apart from the occasional entertainment of scary movies, I can't imagine why anyone would like it.

Let me quickly state that some fear is good and essential. Our very survival depends upon a healthy fright/flight response. It can focus our attention when we need it, wake us up from the slumbering existence we know all too well, and, most important, save our lives. And as terrible as real threats to our survival obviously are—bad news from the doctor or stockbroker; the mere presence of vindictive, mean-spirited people; the possible collapse of the economic system; terrorism; environmental destruction generally; and climate change specifically, to name a few off the top of my head—they help us to remember the truly sacred parts of life that we habitually take for granted or ignore, despite the fact that they matter the most.

But most of our fear is not like that. Most of the fear that we carry around in our hearts, heads, bodies, and souls serves no useful, helpful, or adaptive purpose, and it can be harmful. No immediate threat to our survival or well-being is involved. Some of this fear might have had a legitimate basis sometime in the past, but the threat has gone, while the fear remains. This kind of fear can create a world unto itself. At first, it creeps into the fabric of our lives in small and subtle ways. Perhaps it only wounds our egos and self-confidence, which is not always a bad thing. Yet, if we carry this kind of fear around for very long, its impact becomes considerably more profound. It can alter the normal functioning of our bodies; for example, our breathing, stress responses, digestion, and who knows what else. Gradually, it changes how we see ourselves, live in the world, and relate to God or the possibility of God. Adaptable creatures that we are, this kind of fear can become a familiar way of life, so familiar that we learn to regard it as "normal." We may tell ourselves that we have no substantial fears or that we've moved through our fear, when, in truth, we're filled with it and nearly oblivious to its hugely relevant but unknown presence.

Most everyone I know struggles with harmful fear, not just one particular fear, but all kinds of fear, large and small, most of which are not acknowledged as fear. To make matters worse, a large portion of our harmful fear is anything but individual—although we usually locate it within our private selves and confine it there, believing that "the problem" is solely ours. In fact, the source of this fear lies largely in society, politics, and religion. It is manufactured and manipulative. It magnifies the fear we already have and adds to it, and its overriding purpose is to create allegiances, followings, constituencies, and mass political movements.

Although the claim is made that this kind of fear leads to freedom in this world and saves our souls in the next, it's more truthful to say that it simply serves the bottom line. The outcome is that we learn to see the world through that lens and to adopt it as ours, which is one of the reasons we harbor so much unacknowledged fear. We're told that these "movements" will move us through our fear, when they actually trap us within it. Rather than sharpening our senses or giving us a clearer sense of reality, they befuddle our faith and divert our attention from the very real destructive forces that we could turn in a more creative direction. This kind of fear has become integral to our way of life. It is so accepted and acceptable by large portions of the public and so ingrained in our culture that we, as a people, are in danger of no longer recognizing it for what it is—just plain fear.

That's why it's so peculiar when people say that the experience of fear offers a clearer vision of reality than we usually have. In a sense, they are right to say this, but only when and where the principle truly applies, and only up to a certain point. After that, fear can be one of the greatest obstacles in life that we ever face. As legitimate as some of our fear may be, to live in a world ruled by it is to move further and further from anything remotely resembling "the real world."

I'm not trying to be cute or simply playing with words. Like I said, some fear is obviously good and essential, but to surrender our lives to a world shaped or governed by fear is to risk losing ourselves and the world too. If we surrender to that kind of fear, then we will tell ourselves that we're acting for the common good, when, in fact, we don't know what we're doing or why we're doing it. We fail to see the consequences of our actions, or we don't think about them at all. Rather than protecting us from danger, the fear that rules our lives makes us a danger to ourselves—and not only to ourselves. Stuck in our fear and afraid of what we might lose, we hand our lives and integrity over to our primal instincts, taking whatever we can as fast as we can, while ignoring those who suffer, as if they don't exist or have no right to exist. We become a danger to whole communities, including our families and friends, to people whom we've never met, and even to the great body of life, alive with Spirit, that we once knew as "God's green earth." That describes both our failure to live in the real world, and our relentless assault on it.

This is what I mean by finding, discovering, and living in the real world. Recall just one time in your life when you were trapped in fear, and then freed from it. Let yourself remember what it was like to be free again, to feel heartfelt love and friendship, to have done the right thing because you knew, in your soul, that it was the right thing to do. Remember what it's like to smile a real smile that you can't hold back, to have a real sense of community in your life, to be who you really are, and to say what you really think. Once we remember that, and realize that it's neither a fantasy nor a passing dream, then we're well on our way to recovering what the real world really is and claiming it as our own.

Needless to say, the nature, purpose, and meaning of fear are deeply spiritual matters. For example, I would be among the first to proclaim that "the fear of the Lord is the beginning of wisdom" (Psalms 111:10a), having learned this invaluable lesson in survival on more than one occasion. And I would quickly add an equally important spiritual truth found in another biblical passage: "There is no fear in love, but perfect love casts out fear" (I John 4:18a). We'll return to the thorny "fear of God" issue at some length later on, as it is central to what I've written here. For now, let me only say that fear touches the most tender, vulnerable, and deeply personal part of our souls, which makes it exceedingly personal, but no less destructive. Of course, fear touches our souls. Up to a point, it can save our souls. After that, our fear is feeding on them.

John Newton's (1725–1807) inspiring words—in the hymn "Amazing Grace"—describe the interplay between fear and freedom in a profoundly moving way:

Amazing grace! how sweet the sound,
that saved a wretch like me!
I once was lost but now am found,
was blind but now I see.
'Twas grace that taught my heart to fear,
and grace my fears relieved;
how precious did that grace appear
the hour I first believed.

What I hear Newton saying is that the love of God sets us free: The same love that helps us to perceive our moral blindness also opens our eyes to the world's sacred nature. Grace relieves us of the terrible and tragic belief that we're the very center of things. It helps us to realize that our responsibility, as creatures made in God's image, is to resist letting fear become the center of our lives. We weren't created for the purpose of being enslaved by fear.

As things are now, we're stuck somewhere near the beginning of wisdom—free, but not free; afraid, but still wise enough to remember that we can move through our fear, and with the grace of God, do what needs to be done. The principal message of this book is that our God-given spiritual instincts—awe, love, intent, conscience, community, rest, and faith—are the best and most reliable answer to fear that we have, or ever will have.

What you will read here is a highly personal account of how any of us can move through our fear and become who we are meant to be. The introductory chapter discusses the peculiarity of fear with a touch of humor. Humor is good, especially in relation to fear. It provides some needed balance to our usual fixation on fear's merciless power. The second chapter lays out the five key insights into the movement through fear on which the book is based.

Then, each of the main chapters—the heart of the book—puts

flesh and blood on the five insights. These chapters explore our spiritual instincts in some detail, beginning with brief introductory sections that describe each instinct and tie one chapter to the next. Keep in mind that all of our spiritual instincts are interrelated and yet distinct. It would be misleading to speak of one instinct in complete isolation from the others, nor should we want to. Our spiritual instincts make us people. They give us our humanity, which makes them profoundly personal. For that reason, personal stories, essays, and spiritual practices follow the introduction to each chapter.

The practices should not be overlooked. They are based on spiritually sound, deeply reflective principles. But unlike forms of prayer and meditation that strengthen our inner resources separate from the world around us, these practices not only show us how to cultivate our spiritual instincts in the midst of everyday life, but also how to move through our fear, rather than surrender our lives to it.

I should also say that this book is not about moving through particular kinds of fear. My concern is with the movement through any and every fear. This could be seen as a grandiose claim, but it's not. Whatever our specific fears might be, they undermine the integrity of our lives by making us forget the most basic truths about life. That's how fear feeds on our souls. Temporary escapes, now and again, can provide some relief, but they're not enough to turn this around. What we need is to nurture our souls every day with the solid food that all our spiritual instincts readily provide. They are our most cherished resource for living. They shape every experience we have and guide us through a lifetime. Ultimately, they are who we become. These spiritual instincts—awe, love, intent, conscience, community, rest, and faith—are the deciding factor in whether we remain stuck in our fear or choose to live the kind of lives that "freedom" really means.

I.

THE POWER AND PECULIARITY
OF FEAR

Still round the corner there may wait
A new road or a secret gate;
And though I oft have passed them by,
A day will come at last when I
Shall take the hidden paths that run
West of the Moon, East of the Sun.

—J. R. R. TOLKIEN, *The Return of the King*

The Power of Fear

As harmful and debilitating as fear can be, we have no choice but
to respect its power. Fear is powerful. That's the first thing that
comes to mind when we think about fear. Its power is raw and,
in some ways, truthful. When the fear response kicks in, nothing
seems to be hidden. The feeling is of losing control or being out of
control. Time seems either to speed up or to slow down. Yet our
attention becomes intensely focused and our sense of "reality" is
heightened. We're ready for action—or we're ready to run.

Still, the power of fear is not what it seems. It reveals a whole dimension of ourselves that we actually do hide—from ourselves: an unused, untapped, unacknowledged energy that exists within us all. The secret to this power is that its source does not lie outside of us. It is solely ours, and behind it (or within it) is the possibility of something immensely good and deeply spiritual. Just imagine that we could take all the energy that we give to our unwanted fear and put it to a better use. This is more than possible. This is within the grasp of anyone, simply by cultivating and using the spiritual instincts that God has given to us.

Like everyone, I first learned about the power *and* peculiarity of fear when I was a kid. The lesson that I learned, probably the first great lesson of my life, was that I didn't like to be afraid *and* I wanted to be free from it. Even back then, I knew what I wanted—at least in that one part of my life. I also learned another, less than helpful lesson: that we're *not* supposed to realize how pervasive fear is, much less to talk about it out loud. This inevitably means that we learn the art of hiding our fear from others *and* from ourselves; and if we happen to become skillful in the art of hiding, we eventually deceive ourselves into believing that the fear is not there. Lessons like that complicate our lives unnecessarily *and* tragically, often to the point where we risk losing one of our greatest gifts—the simple joy of life. After we've grown up *and* if we're fortunate, it might occur to us that what was once learned can be unlearned. We do not have to live under the thumb of fear, *and* we can do something about it.

The people I grew up with might be surprised to hear me talk like this. My mom and dad were exceptionally peaceful people, which meant that my sister and I were raised in a basically serene household. I have no vivid memory of loud voices at home, with the exception of frequent laughter, nor do I remember anyone being particularly angry or instilling any kind of harmful fear in me or anyone else. I'm not saying that it never happened, but if it did, it left no lasting impression. Yet it would be absurd to claim that fear was completely absent from our home, as there are different kinds of fear, both helpful and harmful. For example, my father, who was employed in the furniture business until he retired, had a healthy and understandable fear of fire. My mother was afraid of thunder and lightning. Today, I'm careful, but I love a warm fireplace in the wintertime, and I thoroughly enjoy a summer storm.

Despite all that (or because of it), there's no great secret about why I've written this book. I've been aware of the powerful impact that fear has on all of us for almost as long as I can remember. I'm talking about the ordinary but otherwise harmful fears that we take for granted, as if they're a "normal" part of life: the fear of thinking our own thoughts or expressing them, the fear of "the other," the fear of what other people might think, the fear of being blamed or accused, of being judged (rightly or wrongly), of being alone or not being alone, of not having enough or losing what we have. These are only a few noteworthy highlights in a list that's usually quite long.

Although it's regrettable to say this, one of the first places I experienced these "ordinary" kinds of fear was in church, not my church, but "the church" nonetheless. A few of my colleagues wince when I make comments like this—it hits very close to home. I can understand their feelings. Yet I also know that a book about fear must be honest if it has any chance of being helpful. I should add that although the church was the first place that I experienced harmful fear, it was not the only place, not by a long shot. Dressed up in different clothes and modified slightly by a different choice of words and tone, the fearful message I first heard from that one pulpit, nearly fifty years ago, could have been delivered from almost any public platform in the country. It's a very old, familiar, and manipulative kind of fear, generated by the nearly seamless, often shadowy blend of religious, political, economic, and sometimes educational attitudes and opinions that have become all too commonplace. These days, they've become especially loud in some quarters, and popular. That's a scary thought.

Basically, what I heard (what we all hear) was that if I didn't have the same fears as everyone else and accept certain negative, fear-ridden opinions about one group of people or another as true, then I would be a bad person and receive my deserved punishment in this life or the next. I would get what was coming to me. When all is said and done, the logic behind it was a mixture of secular and sacred salvation that's won, not by a Savior on the cross, but by acquiescence to sheer emotional manipulation. It's fear cast in the guise of faith, and it has virtually no relation to what was once called "true religion"—a crusty yet traditional and thoroughly insightful phrasing that needs to be resurrected.

Concerning the second lesson—that we're not supposed to be aware of the extent that fear has been ingrained in our nervous systems—I suspect that the relatively serene atmosphere of my childhood home was the reason I never learned this lesson very well. There was no reason to learn it, for which I am truly grateful. At church, I kept the part about God and love close to my heart, while jettisoning the part about fear. They're not the same, and they're easy to separate with some prayerful reflection and effort.

Ever since, I've done my best to be free from the often fear-ridden world that we create for ourselves, and I cannot deny that it has been a struggle. Fifty years ago (I'll tell you about this in some detail later), I first perceived how afraid we are as a people, how much we deny it, even to ourselves, and what a confusing mess we make because of it. I was in church then; I was a mere child, and I was shaken. I believe most children would have had basically the same response. Right then and there, I confronted that treacherous conflict between the two *seemingly* contradictory teachings that I mentioned before: on the one hand, that "the fear of God is the beginning of wisdom," and on the other hand, that "perfect love casts out fear." How can both of these teachings be true?

I would not underestimate how tenacious this ambiguity can be, even if you don't consider yourself a religious person. The tension between "the fear of God" and "the love of God" permeates nearly every part of our lives, and it makes fear one of the worst and most tenacious of all the obstacles we face in life. However, things are not always as they seem to be. These two teachings are better understood as two successive stages in a lifelong process that we usually fail to recognize, much less pursue, so we live within the confusion. The problem is that the fate of the soul is played out there—within the confusion—and the confusion is powerful indeed. The result is that we become trapped in our fear and frozen within ourselves.

Fear is powerful. I have no doubt about that. I also know of few "ordinary" words that are more profoundly spiritual, more powerful, and more potentially life-changing than these: *"I don't want to be afraid anymore,"* or *"I've been afraid of one thing or another nearly all my life, and I didn't even know it."* If you've ever said something like that yourself, wanted to say it, or heard someone else say it, you know that the words don't come easily. They reveal weaknesses and vulnerabilities that we'd rather keep to ourselves. Spoken with true conviction and the willingness to follow through, those honest, spoken-from-the-heart words are infinitely more powerful than fear. They can turn our lives around completely. To me, they are the sound of Joshua's army, announcing an assault against the walls of Jericho saying, "You are not the most powerful force in the world." I'm not exaggerating. I've seen this happen, time and time again, in the lives of many people whom I know well.

Imagine what it's like *to say "no" to your fear*—and really mean it. I'm serious, and I'm serious about imagining it. It's entirely possible that we haven't heard ourselves speak this way before, or if we have, it was much too long ago. This is a powerful moment, and a subtle one. The key is to say "no" without triggering the fear response within yourself—to say "no" without preparing to fight in the usual sense of the word. It's not the word itself that matters, but the thought behind it. What I'm suggesting is that the movement through fear is not really a heroic fight against an enemy that can be defeated, as if all we have to do is muster the courage and do what needs to be done. It seems that way in the heat of fearful moments, and courage definitely plays a large part. But the kind of courage that we really need is the mindfulness to move through our fear without absorbing its energy. Otherwise, we might believe that we've defeated our fear, when, in fact, we only become the kind of person who makes others afraid.

The art of saying "no" to fear without putting up a fight is a subtle process that I'll address again in the next chapter. Here, I'm suggesting that this art can be learned, and once it is learned, two things happen simultaneously: In the very moment that the wall of fear begins to fall, we realize how trapped we had been all along. We know this is true because we can feel it within ourselves. An inner stillness seems to come out of nowhere. If that isn't enough, we know exactly what we're saying and why we're saying it. Even that seems strange and new—our words really express what we want to say. This is when we understand, as if for the first time, that there's a great deal about ourselves and about life that we haven't accounted for or understood. Not only that, there's a great deal more that we haven't been told, and even more that we've been told to be afraid of. In that fateful moment, we're beginning to take back the power that we've unwittingly given away—for fear has no power in itself, only the power that we give to it.

This is only the beginning. It has probably never occurred to us that we could speak like this. We might not have said anything at all, not until we were backed into a corner or so fed up with being afraid that we can't live with ourselves anymore. But we have spoken, and now we sense a power that propels us to say it again, and again—*never again*. This power really does come from inside ourselves, and we wonder what it means. We should wonder; it's only natural that we would wonder—what is this unknown power within us?—and yet, it may take a long time to understand even a small part of what this power is.

That's why I love to hear people say "no" to fear. By saying "no" to fear, we're saying "yes" to life and opening ourselves to the possibility of actually becoming who we are meant to be. The purpose of this book is to help us to do exactly that. Because our whole being—body, mind, and spirit—is involved, I call it a "spiritual" book. God created us as an act of love, and the love of God really does cast out fear. Rather than accepting our ordinary but harmful fears as a part of life or as God's will, we need to realize the terrible impact that they actually have. Namely, they undermine the spiritual instincts that God has given us to cultivate and use: awe, love, intent, conscience, community, rest, and faith. I can't imagine anything more harmful than that.

I'll expand on that point in the next chapter; but for now, let me make only one comment about our spiritual instincts: They are *ours*. As creatures made in God's image, we are born with the capacity to develop these instincts. Even more, it is our birthright to cultivate them—in ourselves, in each other, in our children, and through them, in our children's children. This is how our humanity is passed down through the generations. If we don't acknowledge our birthright and accept it, then we lose the joy of life, while becoming oblivious to who we are, what needs to be done, frozen when right action is needed, and unwilling to become who we really are—perhaps believing that we're doing something wrong by even trying. The result is that we remain stuck in our fear and complicit in a world that desperately wants to keep things the way they are.

As powerful as our fear may be, it is not more powerful than our spiritual instincts. The principal message of this book is that the spiritual instincts that we already have, but may not recognize or use, are our best and most reliable answer to fear. There are no tricks or gimmicks about this. When we give ourselves even half a chance, we will know what to do and how to do it; and if that's not enough, then the Spirit will provide whatever else we need. I sometimes wish that I had some simple instructions—an easy-to-read, step-by-step guide, perhaps in pamphlet form. I don't have that; I cannot offer it; and it would be a mistake to pretend that instructions of this kind would be helpful.

Of course, there are exceptions. There always are exceptions. Some fear is easy to deal with. Imagine an abandoned but vicious dog in your neighborhood that persistently terrorizes you and your family. What could you do? You call the police or the dog-catcher. You ask for help, someone comes to the rescue, and "your work" is done for you. But most of our fear, particularly harmful fear, cannot be dealt with by appealing to the authorities. Our fear may feel like a vicious dog, but it's not one. To deal with fear in this way only compounds the problem for ourselves and others, usually with tragic results. We might, for example, hold loved ones, parents, neighbors, or whole groups of people accountable for something within ourselves that we are afraid to see. Rather than cultivating our spiritual instincts and trusting them to carry us through our fear, we look for the devil out in the world, which means we avoid the real issue—which is us. Blaming someone else and avoiding the truth about ourselves is a really peculiar thing to do, but we do it all the time. The key word here is "peculiar."

The Peculiar Nature of Fear

It's both obvious and understandable that when we think of fear, its power would come to mind first. We're remembering the presence of danger. What's not so obvious is that this is the very same power that claims our attention and awareness long after the danger has passed and the lessons have been learned. The fact that this happens so routinely has a terrible impact on our understanding of what fear is really like—and on what our lives are like. It distorts our vision, more than it reveals anything that's really helpful. It's like throwing gas on a fire. The shooting flame is all we see, and then we look upon everything else about our lives from a misleading point of view. The outcome is that we strengthen the very power that holds us in its grip and trip ourselves up before we ever begin. What should be obvious, but usually isn't, is that it would be better to begin at another place; that is to say, if we really want to move through our fear.

I realize how silly it would be to suggest or imply that simply making a point about fear will help to set us free. It's easy to say "Do this or do that." I may feel good about what I've said, but everything, including my own life, remains very much the same. My purpose is actually not to make a point, but to pry open a door that remains tightly shut because of the firm grip that the power of fear has on our awareness. If I can open it even a little here, and then explain how to keep it open—by cultivating our spiritual instincts—then I will have done my job.

To pry open that door, I want to set a tone for the book as a whole that's not based exclusively on the power of fear, but on how we perceive it when we're not afraid. Besides, fear actually does have characteristics other than its power. The first that comes to mind is that *fear is incredibly peculiar.* I would argue that fear is considerably more peculiar than it is powerful. If you believe that fear is powerful simply because it's a biologically driven response to a perceived threat, then think again. Human experience is more complicated—and more peculiar—than that, and I'll give you several reasons why.

The first reason is that fear has a close relationship with love. Even that is peculiar. Fear—and sometimes love—can play astonishing tricks on our imaginations. This may help psychotherapists and screenwriters make a living, and it may make our lives richer, more interesting, and creative, but most of the fear that we routinely experience doesn't help us live—not in any way, shape, or form. It makes our lives more frustrating and painful.

In this regard, I feel obligated to acknowledge that many reasonable people would say that fear helps me, a priest, make a living too—given the confusing, if not conflicting, messages that they hear about the "fear of God." Although some of those same reasonable people may have a cynical streak, they make a good point; and to be completely fair, I could say the same about love. Love helps me making a living—given the "love of God." I'll return to the subject of religion, love, and fear again and again; but for now, let me only say that the "fear of God," as the word "fear" is commonly understood, is not the whole story about God or religion. Yet our fear is joined to love at the hip. Pay close attention to your heart and you'll discover that fear follows love, and the possibility of love, like a shadow.

This tells me that we don't know nearly as much about love or fear as we would like to believe. The evidence for this would be plain to see if we paid more attention. For example, we routinely say (and believe) that the opposite of love is hate. There is some truth in it, at least on the surface: That's the way the world seems to work; and as far as language goes, it is how the dictionary defines the meaning of the words. However, people who listen closely to their hearts and the Spirit will tell you something very different. They will tell you that fear, rather than hate, is the very opposite of love. Nearly twenty years ago, Marianne Williamson emphasized this very point in her wise reflections on *A Course in Miracles*. Children understand the primary reality of love before they learn how prejudiced, sometimes mean-spirited, and threatening the world can be. If they remember as adults what they once knew in their childhood, then they will tell you that love is the greatest of all our desires (who doesn't want to love and be loved?) and that fear is the greatest roadblock to its fulfillment. I'll put this another way: In one moment, fear can save our lives; and in the next moment, it can cause us to lose the one thing— love—that makes life worth living. Of all the reasons that fear is peculiar, this is the greatest.

I can think of other reasons too. It's peculiar that one person may be completely terrified by the very thing that another person finds enjoyable. It's peculiar that the instinct of fear may have a genetic basis, but the way it's expressed varies greatly. It's peculiar that the fear of any one person can loom so large in one moment that you would think the whole world is going to end; and then, in the next moment, the same fear vanishes into thin air. All this brings me back to love. Love—real love—doesn't do that. Love has its ups and downs; but, as Saint Paul said, love is kind, it endures all things, and it remains steadfast (1 Corinthians 13:4–7).

The conclusion we should draw is that fear is not so powerful after all. I'm saying this simply to establish the fact that the peculiar nature of fear, rather than its power, is a much better place to start if we want to gain some understanding of how it actually works in our lives. It gives some perspective; it makes us smile a little; and it helps us understand what a profound Mystery that fear really is, like love.

Again, my purpose is to pry open a door by piling up evidence about the peculiar nature of fear—so bear with me. Here's yet another reason that should be blatantly obvious to everyone: There are occasions when our fear is entirely justified; but for the most part, they are exceedingly rare. Why is this peculiar? Because whether we realize it or not, we're afraid of one thing or another nearly all the time. I have to conclude that we make very little headway in differentiating between true (objective) fears and false (baseless) fears. If we did, we would be nearly free from fear and really happy. Instead, we do our best to manage all our fears rolled into one. "Management," in this area of life, often involves drugs—prescription and otherwise. I don't use drugs myself, but many people do. Most doctors say that anxiety-reducing prescription drugs are effective and worthwhile. I know this is true; nevertheless, I only half believe it. I'm not against them, but I don't believe it enough to vote or campaign for them. The whole idea of it, from a spiritual point of view, sounds way too peculiar for me to believe completely.

Drugs or no drugs, our efforts to "manage" fear essentially mean that we try to carve out a space in our lives—a comfort zone—where we experience as little emotional pain as possible. We try to find a workable balance where our fears manage us a little, and we manage them a little. I'm not only talking about outright fear and panic, but also the low-level anxiety that arises from the expectation of fear, which may be the worse of the two. In this way, we get through the day without being bothered very much by our fear. We might not even notice it. This is how we manage our emotions—creating the illusion of feeling safe and secure—while doing our best to live a productive life in an uncertain, fear-ridden world. We may find a measure of freedom, but this has next to no relation to anything spiritual traditions mean by the word "free." If you're reading this book, you may be living within that comfort zone in this very moment, and you know what I'm talking about.

Any way you look at it, our lives are occupied by fear, consciously and unconsciously, more than we readily admit. It shapes our lives in ways we would never believe possible or acknowledge as "fear-ridden." The fact of the matter is that we grow accustomed to it—or should I say something like "oblivious"? Adaptable people that we are, we may even learn to like it, which only shows us the extremes to which we can go. For example, a certain social and professional competence is based on how well we, as individuals, adapt to our fear and perform the balancing act that we regard as "normal." This competence encourages us to turn our backs to the truth about our lives and to the decisive moments of truth (when we say "no" to fear) that we usually do our best to avoid—despite the fact that those otherwise lost opportunities would set us free. That's really peculiar.

Any reasonable person would have to believe that fear is peculiar because we are. We're the peculiar ones—every one of us. Every person that I've ever met is peculiar, which makes our fear deeply personal. We know something about our fears, but not as well as they apparently know how to pull our strings and push our buttons. Even more peculiar are the ordinary ways in which our fears are manifested in everyday life. Think of our quirky habits of avoiding fear, usually expressed through ordinary likes and dislikes, the embarrassing ways that we hide our fear as if our lives depended on it, and those really stupid streaks of recklessness that we confuse with fearlessness—like a teenager driving a car too fast.

During my high school years, I routinely put the pedal to the metal on one particular stretch of road. I did it for the thrill, or so I thought. Teenagers do that sometimes—their hormones flow out of control, and so do their cars. In one part of my brain, I wanted to believe that I was fearless. In another part, I knew that it was reckless. Nevertheless, I convinced myself that I knew exactly what I was doing. Other people, those who know us well, aren't sure whether we're coming or going. They see us more clearly than we see ourselves. When I'm in a good mood, I can laugh about things like this. But it's not so funny when I think of the peculiar people who have made their way into positions of political power. They tell themselves that they're grown-up. They look like they've grown up, but we know there's a reckless teenage soul hiding behind the expensive hair and clothes, looking for a "fearless" thrill. That's a real reason to be afraid, so I try not to think about it.

Having said that, I realize that anyone reading this book deserves to know a great deal about me as a person. I'll do my best. My first conscious fear makes me think of my sister, Wendy, who knows me well. She has always been convinced that I'm a truly peculiar person—that I was born peculiar. Sisters, of course, always say things like that, but I always thought that she had a point. One of the many reasons for my peculiarity, from her point of view, was that I would run away when friends or relatives with itchy camera fingers came to the house. I was seriously afraid of having my picture taken. I don't know why, but my guess is that the word "taken" played a part. In some vague way, I felt that a vital part of myself would be stolen. Years later, I learned that some indigenous peoples, upon their first contact with invading Europeans, were terrified of being photographed for precisely the same reason: They believed that their souls would be stolen. Apparently, some of them were more afraid of having their picture taken than of being killed. That may seem foreign and "magical" to the Western mind, but I thought they had a point too.

I still don't like to be photographed, but I've learned to sit still and smile. I do my best to hide my feelings. My suspicion is that we, as a people, may be trading in our souls for all kinds of public images of ourselves, personas, and all that. I tell myself that I'm not going to be afraid of it. I'm going to live in this world, come hell or high water (given our refusal to take climate change seriously, high water is likely). I know that the soul is immortal, and nothing we believe, disbelieve, ignore, or forget can change that. I also know that the loss of soul in our lives every day could explain why we're anxious and afraid all the time without realizing it or understanding why.

In our day and age, and probably in any age, the peculiar nature of fear makes it not only personal, but also political and economic. For example, we tell ourselves that we're made in God's image (which is true), but we're filled with all kinds of fear that God never intended to be there. It gives the impression that we've made fear into a religion, if not our God, which is the most peculiar form of idolatry I can imagine. You would think that idol worship would be more fun. It turns out that it's not fun, and it's not funny. I'll give an example.

At a recent town meeting, I heard someone give an impassioned semi-patriotic, semi-religious speech about "the freedom to buy" as the American way of life and as the one true foundation for the kind of life that anyone would ever hope and pray to have. His fear was that local opposition would prevent Wal-Mart from building a megastore in town. The result: We would all become God-forsaken, back-to-nature socialists. I kid you not. He told the crowd, in effect, that our choice was either Wal-Mart or the devil. Sitting there in disbelief, I naturally assumed that he was either on drugs or on the payroll of Wal-Mart—or both.

It was a few moments later when the truth dawned upon me: He was stone-cold sober and utterly sincere. What struck me was that he seemed to be so "at one," not with himself but with his fear. I suppose that his fear was of whatever he considered social-ism and paganism to be, but the actual feeling that he expressed was of a free-floating threat to our survival, which he could read-ily attach to almost anything and anyone. In other words, the power of his fear had become who he was: a true believer in the very fear that possessed him. It pulled all his strings and gave him meaning and purpose in life. Otherwise, his speech would have passed for comic entertainment, rather than public service. Where fear is concerned, there's a fine but terribly significant line between the two. I've seen a lot of peculiar fear in my life—so have we all—but I had never seen anything quite like him, not firsthand. Of course, there is always tomorrow.

The Peculiarity of Fear As We Actually Experience It

I hope you can recall these beautiful words: *"For everything there is a season, and a time for every matter under heaven: a time to be born, and a time to die; a time to plant, and a time to pluck up what is planted . . . a time to weep, and a time to laugh . . ."* Read the whole piece in Ecclesiastes, chapter three, and notice that it does not include "a time to be afraid." My guess is that this was no omission on the writer's part. Rather, he was a person who respected the power and importance of fear as well as anyone, but he did not regard fear as a "season" or a part of his life, nor was his life ruled by it—which may account for his extraordinary wis-dom and explain why he has everything to say to us. He spoke a great deal about "vanity," or pride, and when he encouraged "the

fear of God," he meant primarily "awe." His beautiful words
lead us back to the possibility of wisdom found within ourselves
and to the courage that we need to move through our fear.

Keeping his wise and hopeful teaching in mind, I want
to sketch out the three major varieties of fear that people find
important enough to share with me, as their spiritual director and
friend: (l) *"My world is falling apart"*; (2) *"The world is pressing
upon me,"* the widely known "panic attack"; and (3) *"falling into
the abyss,"* the so-called bottomless pit, which is the worst of the
three. You'll notice that these fears are familiar and easy to recognize, and that the names of these fears are based on the feeling—
what the experience feels like—rather than the object of our fear
(e.g., the fear of dogs, lightning, public speaking, open spaces,
and so on). You'll also notice that they have little resemblance to
the "official" lists of fears used in clinical situations, which are
useful in their own way, but not relevant to our discussion here.

I should also add that these are the experiences of fear that
people describe because they're aware of them. Yet it is possible—
even likely—to have these fears without realizing it. For example,
let's say that I have a lot of money (I don't) and that I'm afraid
of losing it. I might not acknowledge this fear as "a fear." To go
to a counselor or priest would never occur to me, not until I lost
my money. Then, my experience would be of "my world falling
apart." I might also be surprised to discover how afraid I had
been, without realizing it, for a very long time.

A word of caution: Classifications of fear can be useful, but
they also have their limitations. What I've here done is to sketch
out a picture of these fears in order to produce a map of sorts. The
map has several purposes: to help us understand what the territory of fear is like, to appreciate more fully why we would want
to move through it, and to fix our minds on the importance of
cultivating our spiritual instincts in order to do so. The territory

itself, rather than the map, is quite a bit larger than the one I've sketched here, but that's okay. It doesn't take much sketching to make my point.

Writing about the varieties of fear is easy enough; actually experiencing them is an altogether different matter. There's no way around the fact that, in different degrees, they're all bad; and it would be irresponsible for me to sugarcoat any of these fears, making them seem less difficult than they really are. As the philosopher A. N. Whitehead and others have so perceptively said, the map—any map—is not the territory. Our goal is to move through the actual fears in our lives, rather than spending so much time reading the map (even a good map) that we never take a step in the direction we need to go. But it helps, now and again, to stand back and look at the big picture. It gives us the opportunity to remember where the path that we've chosen eventually leads (in the likely event that we've forgotten) and why we must keep our wits about us, and our eyes on the way ahead.

Reflecting on these experiences of fear has been useful to me for another reason too: It has helped me perceive fear's fatal flaw, the most peculiar of fear's many peculiarities, and the weakness hidden within its power. In a nutshell, fear has no power in itself; no power at all, except for the power we give to it, which relates to the five insights that we'll discuss in the next chapter and the spiritual instincts that follow.

I'll begin with the fear that people tell me about the most: *"My world is falling apart."* No reasonable person would deny that life can be scary: the loss of a job, a stack of unpaid bills on top of an empty bank account, the damage to a person's life that destructive coworkers or family members might cause, the breakup of a marriage, or discovering that you or a loved one have a life-threatening illness. I wouldn't minimize any of these fears, or pretend that they're anything but devastating. The world that we experience really can collapse. Yet I've seen a lot of fear, and in situations like these, we at least know what we're talking about and why. We know what the reasons are. It's the fear of the unknown, the unknown that lies ahead—*will my beloved live or die? Can I put my life back together again?*—that leaves us stunned and breathless; and that's the most dangerous part of this fear. If we get stuck in it, it can feed on the energy of our lives for a very long time.

Interestingly enough, we sometimes experience this same fear when circumstances are otherwise fun and celebratory; for example, as a wedding day approaches or the first day of a new job. A new life is unfolding before us at the very same time that an old one is fading away. Here, it's the betwixt and between that's scary, the passage between one world and the next: *Can I create a new life for myself? Can I actually do what I want to do?* Fear plays an important and necessary role in these passages. Moving through them deepens self-knowledge, which builds trust in ourselves and in others. But just as decisions must be made, responsibility for those decisions must be taken. On the one hand, it's possible that this fear (or parts of it) should be heeded. Perhaps we should back away from a decision that might be a mistake. On the other hand, the mistake might be to listen to our fear too much and get stuck in it. Then, we're unable to move through a transformative passage that the soul actually needs and our heart truly desires. In other words, fear is a part of life, and life is not always easy, which brings us to the second experience of fear.

Panic attacks can be deeply unsettling, especially when we don't know why they're happening. Usually, they set in motion a whole cascade of ideas and feelings that seriously undermine the confidence we have in ourselves and in life. I wouldn't say that panic attacks (or the fear of them) come up frequently in my work, but I'm not at all surprised when people tell me about them. The experience is not so much that the world out there is falling apart or collapsing around our feet, but that *the world is pressing upon us,* the result being that the once solid ground on which our lives were based now feels like quicksand. The feeling is akin to one's own personal earthquake: What was once familiar, secure, dependable, and, especially, taken for granted is no longer reliable. The experience quickly builds, seemingly out of nowhere, moments before the panic attack begins. After the fear has passed, we don't know exactly why it happened. Here again, it's the fear of the unknown that's so scary and disturbing.

Our immediate concern is to understand why the panic attacks are happening, although finding what we believe to be "a reason" or "the reason" is not usually enough to explain them completely. That's why the onset of panic attacks offers a good opportunity to have that medical exam that we've postponed far too long. Panic attacks may have an underlying physical cause, which could be a relief to discover. They can also signify the beginning of a "midlife crisis" (who knows what that really is?), which raises a different set of questions and some scary concerns: *What's happening to me? What does it mean? What will it mean?* Friends and loved ones may be a little worried too, given the stereotypic image (which is sometimes true) of spouses losing their good judgment during such crises.

Whatever the physical causes of panic may or may not be, it's the unpredictable nature of the "attack" that makes them scary. Often our response is to add one fear on top of another, the panic making us susceptible to additional fear. It's hard to keep our head when the world that was once so familiar seems to turn against us. Yet it's worth remembering that deep transformative processes initiated by the Spirit can have exactly the same initial symptoms, and we give nearly the same response—"*What is this and why is it happening to me?*" *Is it going to happen again? What can I do to stop it?* People who have no firsthand experience of panic may not realize that the words are both an utterly heartfelt cry of desperation, and a sincerely thoughtful question. People who have experienced it will understand why a cry for help may also be the beginning of the best thing that has ever happened to us—and within us.

The third experience of fear—the feeling of *falling into an abyss*—is considerably more intense and disturbing than the previous two. As a rule, we don't talk about this fear very much, even if we're aware of it. I'll admit to being hesitant about discussing it here. If it were not for the fact that a book about fear that omits this particular one would be incomplete or dishonest, I probably would overlook it. This fear goes well beyond the experience of panic. The feeling is of a "place" within us that might open to the so-called bottomless pit. It's not that the familiar world is no longer reliable or that we're losing confidence in ourselves. The sense here is that the world we know *within ourselves* and regard as structured, relatively secure, and meaningful seems to vanish. What we do know—as an urgent and immediate concern—is that events in our inner life are not separate from the world "out there," and that the lifeline that we're looking for requires reestablishing a spiritually grounded relationship between the two.

Given the sensitive and subtle nature of this fear, I want to explore it at some length, taking into account its religious, social, and political implications. I'll begin with four straightforward observations. First, I'm thinking of the abyss in two ways: as an actual experience that really can be hellish, and as the fear of a possible experience that usually lies well below the surface of normal, waking consciousness. Second, most people I know (on the religious and/or political right and left) regard talking about this fear as socially off-putting and politically incorrect, although their reasons for censoring the subject vary widely. Despite that, everyone has an intuitive feel for what "falling into the abyss" might mean, which is the important point.

Third, I'm not claiming that "the abyss" or "the pit" is a literally "real place," or that we "should" be afraid of it, in the sense that some religious believers emphasize. Yet solid spiritual traditions are right to suggest that the abyss is an experiential possibility in some sense. In other words, the abyss exists as a possibility—an "idea"—that can be expressed outwardly and materially in the here and now. Think, for example, of death marches, concentration camps, and genocide, which have become "familiar" facts of modern life. Where do we think they come from? The answer is definitely not "out of nowhere." They are part of "the world" that we create, but not "the real world" that God created for us. As mere mortals, we can, in fact, create hell or heaven on earth, and fear plays a large role in shaping the kind of world that we create for ourselves *and*—God help us—for others. We are all in this life together. To believe anything else is already a step in the direction of the abyss. My point is that we know, somewhere in our souls, that this is true; and, for whatever reason—probably fear—we push this knowledge outside of our conscious awareness.

Fourth, at one time or another we've all suspected that any of our ordinary fears, if they're given free rein, could spiral in the direction of the abyss, which is an especially scary thought. In effect, the fear of falling into the abyss is the fear that quietly lurks below all our other fears. We think of it as the fear of "going off the deep end." Yet, here again, life is peculiar. I've known people who have found themselves and God, after seeming to have lost their good sense; and a few who have been through worse. I'm thinking of soldiers who have been on the battlefield. They speak of the abyss more easily than most of us, but only long after the fact. They will tell you that anyone in a foxhole (a place of refuge within an abyss) either believes in God, or wants to believe in God. This kind of comment creates some ambiguity about whether they're talking about God, or using religious language to make their point—which is to describe what it's like to face the immediate possibility of losing your mind or your life. I suppose these distinctions don't matter very much, not in the moment that they're remembering. Either way, they're talking, directly or indirectly, about the abyss.

As everyone should know, it's also possible to find ourselves in the proverbial foxhole in places and circumstances other than an actual battlefield—for example, in the workplace. The same can be said for survival in any household filled with physical or emotional abuse. War can be fought in a variety of ways and with any number of weapons, which women and children know as well as soldiers. In fact, some women whom I know well tell me about the abyss all the time, sometimes using the traditional fiery image to drive their point home. It's not an easy conversation to have, but that is nothing compared with the daily experience of a real abyss in your own home.

People sometimes say that they really do find God in the abyss, and I have no doubt that this is true, having had the experience myself. Yet I have to believe that it's equally possible to lose your faith there too, as truly horrendous things can happen in all kinds of foxholes. Along the same lines, there are situations when the abyss opens up for no apparent reason, which is almost unthinkable. It would be unthinkable, except for the inescapable fact that it does happen, which usually leads us to grab any kind of explanation, including a convenient enemy or a scapegoat to blame. We might tell ourselves, desperately, that we need an explanation. Even an irrational or mean-spirited one *seems* to help. But it doesn't help. I can't emphasize this enough: The fact that it seems to help is an illusion.

Experiencing the abyss within ourselves is so scary that people are usually afraid to speak about it, except with someone they absolutely trust. They're afraid that everyone else will think they're "crazy," which is a legitimate concern. Mystics, healers, and spiritual seekers might put their experience into words, on occasion, using the language of "the dark night of the soul," which is the conventional, if not widely known, way to speak of these otherwise unexplainable happenings. When they talk about their experience, it's likely that they'll attribute it to the will of God and describe it as a test or ordeal that involves an inner cleansing. They're not looking for someone to blame, but trying to make sense of it. And it's entirely possible that the will of God really is behind their experience. Having experienced this myself, all I want to say here is that I would not wish it on anyone; yet the part about testing and cleansing is clearly true, especially as it relates to fear.

I can think of two other reasons why, under more "normal" circumstances, we don't speak of the abyss more often. The first is that we, as a people, do not know whether it's correct or appropriate to understand this fear as an essentially psychological phenomenon, which is our conventional, nonreligious, and contemporary way of putting experience into manageable boxes. In other words, this experience of fear may or may not arise from emotional complexes that the individual person may or may not have. Yet, when it happens to someone we know, any number of semirational, psychological explanations are given to explain it. Rarely are those explanations good enough to be totally convincing. The result is that we're disturbed, for a while, by what we've witnessed or heard about, but we do our best to push it out of our thoughts. What this really means is that we don't know what to think.

It's both interesting and strange that we would know so little about this fear, since we are probably the only creatures alive who either experience the abyss or imagine it as a possibility. The fact that we're also the only creatures whose survival depends on spiritual instincts that must be cultivated and used should give us a clue about the true nature of the abyss. Perhaps we secretly believe (or assume) that the abyss (or its possibility) goes deeper than anything the personality, the psyche, or the fields of psychology, biology, and theology can explain. At the same time, many people are repelled, as they should be, by the religious tendency to use "the bottomless pit" as a form of threat against ourselves and others; for example, *"If you do this, then you'll burn in hell."* Whatever we might think, and setting aside the use of this fear as a threat, the abyss is extremely difficult to identify, name, or discuss, even in a roundabout way.

This leads us to another, more down-to-earth reason for not talking about the abyss: The mere thought of it scares us to high heaven. This would be understandable and wise, if the consequences weren't so horrible and tragic. We routinely banish it from our normal, waking consciousness, which demonstrates how political the social and personal can be, and vice versa. An example: As a people, we consume massive amounts of legal drugs (including alcohol) to help us forget something about how we live (there may be one reason or many, but we often don't know what the reasons are), while we put millions of illegal drug users behind bars where they're *forced not* to forget how they're living. Crime and punishment, law and order notwithstanding, this is a peculiar thing to do. The lesser moral of the story: Stay out of prison, so you can freely forget. I know that seems ridiculous, but think about it. The greater moral: What we refuse to acknowledge or remember within ourselves, we will create in the world around us—for better or worse.

Hence, we witness the rise of prisons as a growth industry in a free country with next to no awareness of history. The outward signs of our fear (prisons) are staring us in the face everywhere we look. This is another way of saying that we give ourselves every opportunity in the world to see our fear and to move through it— if we would only look. Of course, we don't look. We're too afraid to look. The result: We're in the process of confining ourselves to a life ruled by fear. The solution: Cultivate the spiritual instincts that God has given us and we can be free. That's our purpose in life. It's what we're meant to do.

Another example: Political and religious demagogues (who tend to believe in heaven and hell in equal measure) tap into the fear of the abyss to generate mass movements. It's astonishing how skilled, consciously or unconsciously, these shapers of the public mind can be. Once we're caught up in their power (which is the cold power of fear magnified many times over), we tell ourselves that we're moving away from the abyss, when, in fact, we're marching into it like herded cattle. We confuse "the movement" energized by fear with actually moving through our fear. This is an exceedingly harmful fear cast in the guise of helpful fear, which, for me personally, is the most dangerous kind of fear imaginable.

The search for sacrificial victims by these perpetrators of fear should be familiar to anyone with a basic knowledge of human history. The fact that they truly believe that their victims have victimized them is a sure sign that the abyss is real. The lesson here is twofold: It requires real courage to perceive the possibility of the abyss, *and* it demonstrates the absence of courage among those who hold others accountable for the fear they do not want to acknowledge within themselves. The brutal fact is that whole cultures have gone completely off the deep end for this reason, and apparently no one is immune to the possibility.

I realize that the picture I've sketched is, in many ways, dreadful. We live in a world that can be scary, the reason being that we make it so. But keep in mind that we all have the spiritual instincts that will carry us through our fear, and we are not alone. No less a person than Jesus himself looked into the abyss, at least twice—as far as we know. On the first occasion, during his temptation by Satan, he must have been standing on its very edge. Satan offered Jesus the whole world in exchange for his soul. This happens to us too, the difference being that Jesus realized where he was standing and refused Satan's trap. The second occasion was of an entirely different sort. Hanging on the cross, even Jesus himself cried out for help, "My God, my God, why have you forsaken me?" He could have given in to the authorities and power brokers, succumbing to his fear, which is what we might do. But he refused to give in. For our sake and his, he chose to be who he really was and to do what needed to be done: to release those souls who have fallen into the abyss and the souls of those who have led others into it.

The story of his life tells us that the so-called bottomless pit is not so bottomless after all. Among other things, he was showing us that the purpose of religion is not to make us afraid, but to help us move through our fear, including the worst possible fear—the mere thought that something, anything, might forever separate us from the love of God. If you believe the story, as I do, then you know that there's absolutely nothing to be afraid of—nothing in heaven or on earth.

2.

FIVE INSIGHTS INTO THE
MOVEMENT THROUGH FEAR

No miracles, please.
Just let your laws
become clearer from
generation to generation.

—RAINER MARIA RILKE, *Book of Hours: Love Poems to God*

Nearly everything that I've written here is based on five key insights into the movement through fear. These insights are the cornerstones on which the entire book rests. Before discussing these insights in a more or less systematic way, I want to make some initial suggestions and offer some encouragement—not simply by saying that you can move through your fear, but by beginning to show you how.

I think we all understand that life really is the best of all teachers. Nothing compares with the lessons learned through firsthand experience. It's the details about how to apply those lessons to new and scary situations that trip us up—and that make us doubly afraid. For that reason, I want to repeat one crucial point and make it the foundation for the five insights that follow: *Most of the fear that we experience, especially the harmful fear, seems to have a life of its own, when, in fact, it has no life at all except for the illusion of life that we give to it.* We should know this: Where else could the power of fear come from, except from within us? Yet even in the best of times, we're not so sure; and when we consume a steady diet of fear (both large and small) for days, months, and years on end, it's quite likely that we'll gradually lose some of our otherwise good sense and forget the simple truths about life.

I'm emphasizing this for two reasons. The first is that we would all do ourselves a great favor by taking our experience more seriously. I realize that this is an odd and slightly judgmental thing to say, but I can assure you that it involves no trace of criticism on my part. The issue is that true self-knowledge is usually not what we believe it is. We mistakenly do a disservice to ourselves by assuming that knowledge of who we are is basically the same as how we routinely see ourselves and how others see us. Although those impressions might be important and occasionally true, they give only a small glimpse of the Mystery of who we really are.

None of this is helped by the nature of the times in which we live. For example, we've become highly trained consumers, listening to the relentless drumbeat of forces telling us what we want, what to be afraid of, what's good for us, and how to be happy. As far as that goes, which is not very far, we know something about our fears and joys, but this is not self-knowledge—not really. Rather, this is what "self-knowledge" has been reduced to, at a time when it is not valued very highly. I would be reluctant to say that any of us has a very good idea about who we are in the deepest part of our souls.

I'll give another brief example. If, upon deeper reflection, we discover that some of our fear offers us a degree of joy, then we need to give some serious thought to why this is the case. I know plenty of reasonable, well-adjusted people who are energized by disaster and the unfortunate things that happen to others. There's nothing wrong with finding joy in helping others. That's not what I mean. The problem comes when we seem to "need" unfortunate or fearful events to make us feel useful or fulfilled. When we realize that events that should make us afraid or sad actually give us meaning and purpose, then we know for sure that we're living in a world where fear pulls strings that we didn't even know we had.

The second reason is that in the movement through fear it's good to know what we're up against. Otherwise, we become dispirited and give up when our fear pushes back, which it will inevitably do. Let's imagine, as an experiment, that the illusion is real—that fear really does have a life of its own. This will give us an opportunity to perceive at least part of the illusion that we create for ourselves. First, our fear would be quite happy for us to remain stuck in the illusion. In other words, our fear does not want us to be free. That's why it's totally unreasonable to expect our fear to cooperate with our desire to move through it. It will not turn toward us and say, "Great, that's exactly what I want too . . . move through me . . . how can I help?" Fear will not let go of its control over our lives so easily. It's best to face this fact at the outset with a good sense of humor. Nothing disarms fear better than laughter.

Fear also has superb skills in the art of misdirection and distraction. It will do anything and everything to turn our attention toward itself (that is to say, toward its power), and with equal cunning, away from itself, when denial serves its purpose. In other words, fear wants us to believe that it is all-powerful *and* that it plays no significant role in our lives. If that seems to be a contradiction, it's because it is a contradiction. Last but not least, perhaps the worst characteristic of fear is that it can and will make us jaded and disillusioned about the possibilities in life. That's when we give up, believing, with utter conviction, that we have no choice. Fear is ruthlessly, deceptively irrational; and when I say "our fear," I'm thinking of the part of our lives that's been subjugated by fear—the part of ourselves that's slowly grown accustomed to being afraid without realizing what's happened and how it affects who we are.

But never mind what fear wants—that is the golden rule of moving through fear. Acknowledge the struggle for what it is, and then move ahead without brooding, worrying, or telling yourself that all is lost. All is not lost. *Above all, remember that the apparent power and strength of fear is really our power and our strength—misdirected, misguided, manipulated, and misunderstood, but ours, nonetheless—and we do not have to give it away.*

The question that matters more is, "What do we want?" What do we *really* want? There's nothing selfish about asking questions like that. It all comes down to a choice: Which side are you choosing—you or your fear? In other words, which part of your life has more life: the fear that you've given your life to, or you—the person? That's what I mean by "choosing sides."

Notice that I did not say, "Which side would you place your bets on?" A risk is involved, but it's not the same as gambling with your life. In fact, this is the very opposite of gambling. The movement through fear is the supreme act of taking responsibility for our lives. It is the risk we take for freedom.

First steps are hugely important. Without them, we never get anywhere. But to move ahead too quickly in matters like this can be a serious—but understandable—mistake to make. We want to give ourselves the best opportunity to go further—as far as we need to go to do what needs to be done. My experience is that the movement through fear is a gradual process. It almost certainly won't happen overnight. We mull it over, dream about it, read about it, talk with friends about it but for the most part keep it to ourselves—all this until a threshold is finally reached. Something within us shifts. This is the beginning of a decisive turn and a breakthrough, but it is subtle—we're very likely to feel it happening within us long before we realize what it means.

A first step often sounds like this, when it's put into words: *"I'm scared, and I don't know what to do,"* or *"I'm tired of being afraid,"* or *"I only want something to hold on to,"* or simply, *"never again."* Like saying "no" to fear, these words only seem to be weak and indecisive. In reality, they are powerful. They're spoken from the heart; they're truthful; they're clear-minded. These are our voices when we're beginning to take back the power that we've given away. Below the words and within ourselves, a fire is burning. This is the fire of desire, and it's not the kind of fire that should evoke fear. Rather, when we embrace the fire of desire, we're no longer denying that we're afraid. There's no rationalizing our fear or trying to explain it away. We know what we want—a lifeline, whatever it takes to keep our heads above water until the storm passes. And we know what we're doing—sending out an SOS. If you've ever been afraid of losing your life, of losing a person you love, a way of life you've worked hard for, or your last ounce of dignity and self-respect, if you know what any of these experiences are like, then you know what it means to take the first step through your fear.

Having heard words like these many times, I know them like the back of my hand; and I also know that we've just begun. Now, let's imagine that we—you and I—are talking about this privately. I listen, for the most part. Now and again, we share some give-and-take conversation. Eventually, I say something like, *"The most important thing you can do is to follow your instincts."* The key word here is "instincts." When someone tells us to "follow our instincts" or "trust our instincts," a light begins to brighten in our souls. It might be startling that someone else would imply or suggest that we have good instincts, much less that they might be trustworthy. Whatever our response is, whatever we might think, the words are encouraging.

Once the request is made—for example, *"I don't want to be afraid anymore"*—and the invitation given—*"the most important thing you can do is to trust your instincts"*—we're in the best possible position to do what needs to be done. It doesn't seem like much, but there are no gimmicks or tricks, not if we really want to move through our fear. The fact that we may not have a clue what our instincts are is one of the tragedies of contemporary life and probably the underlying reason that we're all so afraid. Nevertheless, the fire and the light are still there—within us. We could ignore them, acting like they aren't real. But then again, maybe we won't.

The Five Insights

Having said all this as background, the following five insights summarize what I have discovered about the movement through fear. These insights have stood the test of time in my life. They're based on nearly thirty years of work as a priest and cultural anthropologist in a variety of roles and settings: in the university, in seminaries, and in prisons; as a teacher and as an organizer; in pastoral counseling and in spiritual direction. One thing that I've learned in all these circumstances is that fear is always present, but it's rarely acknowledged as the tremendous obstacle that it really is. This is unfortunate, because once our fear is named, then any other problems or obstacles that we may face either fade or disappear rather quickly. But I must emphasize again that each of us must discover the truth about fear in our own lives. There is no substitute for the self-knowledge that firsthand experience gives.

The first insight: Fear can close our hearts, shape our emo-
tional life, and freeze our attention, but the only power that
fear has is the power that we give to it. We can take that
power back. What we need is to have some understanding
of what we really want in life and why we want it.

This insight recapitulates what I've said before; the discussion
below takes it a great deal further. By focusing almost entirely on
the power of fear, we habitually think of it from only one point of
view—from the standpoint of being afraid. This observation is so
obvious that it would be easy to dismiss altogether. It seems too
inconsequential and silly to take very seriously, which is exactly
what our fear would like us to believe. To look upon our lives
from the standpoint of being afraid can be valuable, especially
when we have legitimate reasons to be afraid, but the perspective
it offers is extremely limited. When it becomes our dominant or
preferred perspective, then it distorts our experience to the point
of being completely unreliable. To look upon our lives primarily
from the standpoint of being afraid only magnifies the problems
that fear creates and strengthens its grip on our attention.

I'll put it another way: There are some things that we can't
change. One of them is that life will always have its scary moments.
But we can choose to live our own lives, rather than letting fear
live our lives for us. People who simply want to live their own
lives are already on their way to seeing fear from a different point
of view. So let's not fall back upon the mistake of believing that
the words "I want" are inherently self-centered or self-serving.
I'm not thinking of the acquisitive form of "wanting" that trans-
lates into "taking," in the crude sense of the word, nor of "taking
charge of the situation," if that implies dominating or domineer-
ing behavior, or "getting what we want" by any means necessary.
The kind of "wanting" that I have in mind involves saying "yes"

and "no" to choices about the kind of people we want to be and to become. Think of "the narrow gate" described in the Christian tradition. Unless we want to pass through it, we never will.

To say "I want" in the deeper spiritual sense may be the most understated and subtle of all the capacities that we have as human beings. It involves a degree of self-direction that's an expression of "intent," one of the basic spiritual instincts discussed in chapter five. Perhaps this doesn't seem to be much of a gift. We may believe, for example, that merely wanting to be free from fear is a waste of time, unrealistic, and irrelevant in really frightening situations. "Wanting to be free" doesn't seem to be doing anything at all, at the very time when action is needed the most. But if we learn to use this gift well, it creates the space within ourselves that we need to breathe freely, to think through our fears, and to grow spiritually. Somewhere not very far down the road, our outlook on life will change, our relation to fear will change, and so will we.

The power of knowing what we really want and of pursuing it is one of the dimensions of self-knowledge that remain a secret until we no longer hide them from ourselves. Just how this happens depends upon the circumstances of our lives. In my case, it just so happened to involve the whole messy subject of sickness, "being sick," and how we talk about it. I'll explain that. In the South of my childhood, I learned that sickness was a very common topic of conversation, especially on the telephone. I don't know how widespread this was, although I do recall mentioning it, years later, to two friends of my age, one from Kentucky, the other from Mississippi. They knew exactly what I was talking about.

What I remember is that those conversations gave the impression that people were either sick all the time, or preparing to be sick. Feeling a little "puny" was how we often put it—a once distinctively southern way of saying, *"I'm not sick now, but I might be really soon.*" "Under the weather" would be a slightly less rural way of saying the same thing. In those days, polio vaccinations were new, as were bomb shelters in our basements, which might have created a general atmosphere of puniness. What I assumed was that people had an attraction, of sorts, to talking about sickness, broadly understood. As far as I knew, they might have been genuinely concerned about their friends and loved ones who were sick, could be sick, might have been sick, or would not have been sick if only they had taken better care of themselves. In other words, it's possible that they liked to talk about worrisome things, and the ready-made topic of "sickness" made it easy. Who knows? It's also possible that once the conversations were over, they forgot everything they had said and heard.

The truth is that I never really knew how people really felt about it, but I was absolutely sure that, for people who participated in such conversations (which meant almost everyone), it was an open-ended, never-ending, and, need I say, "peculiar" topic of discussion. What I knew, for a fact, was that most people weren't sick, and I had neither the desire nor the need to talk about sickness all the time—or to hear about it.

I mean no disrespect to southerners. Being a southerner myself, and having lived in New York City and then the Catskills for twenty years, not to mention lengthy stays in Latin America and Europe as an anthropologist, I know that every region has its peculiarities. The South is no different from anywhere else, at least in that regard. Yet all the talk about sickness made me laugh and feel claustrophobic at the same time. It was funny and really serious.

Today, when I look back on those conversations what comes to mind first is how fear distorts our experience of the world. For example, I think of the industrialized hog and chicken farms that have become big business in the South. That's a nasty way to make a living and to produce food, which is not very funny. People nowadays have good reasons to talk about feeling puny—really puny. Only large quantities of antibiotics and hormones make pork and chicken fit for human consumption; and that already sad state of affairs breeds antibiotic-resistant bacteria, which will eventually make us seriously puny, if not dead. The way I see it, this is a bona fide reason to get on the phone and talk about sickness. Phone trees and emergency hotlines would be good ideas too, but I would bet that people rarely discuss the subject. I bet they avoid it like the plague that happens to be brewing in their own backyard. It would make me feel puny and claustrophobic *not* to talk about it.

And I'll tell you something else that's peculiar: When I was a kid and people talked about sickness all the time, many local chicken farms were run by moonshiners, whose getaway driving skills might have made them NASCAR champions. I have to believe that they didn't give their chickens or themselves the quantity, much less the variety, of antibiotics that we receive today. The thought of routinely giving antibiotics to the animals that we eat would have seemed completely absurd. Any reasonable person would ask, "Why are those poor birds so puny?" Or, "How could anyone eat sick chickens?" The official answer would be that they're (the chickens) not sick, and never were sick. If that's so, then why give them antibiotics? The official answer to that question would be to protect the people who eat them from all kinds of things, including the deplorably unnatural conditions in which the chickens are raised. It's a vicious cycle, like all those conversations about sickness. It's enough to make you think that there really is something to be scared of.

But this is the thing: If we're always talking about what scares us—focusing, in effect, on the power of fear—and seeing the world from the standpoint of being afraid, then we never do anything about it. We lose sight of justice and love, and lose our way and ourselves in a shadowy cloud of fear. Along the same lines, I know a lot of people, some among my closest friends, who are scared to eat free-range chickens. Why? They believe that those chickens must be dirty and unfit for human consumption precisely because they haven't been fed antibiotics and despite the fact that those chickens are not raised in deplorably unsanitary conditions. It's hard to believe, but I hear it all the time—on both sides of the Mason-Dixon Line. The fact was that, in my childhood, no one I knew (human, chicken, or pig) took much over-the-counter or doctor-prescribed medicine at all. To do so was considered an unhealthy, bad habit that would eventually make us all addicts. Looking back now, it makes me think that talking about sickness might be an improvement over taking so many invisible antibiotics in our food without giving it much thought, if any.

In case you're wondering about my point, here it is: I didn't feel sick all the time, and I didn't want to spend my waking hours waiting to be sick or making myself afraid of being sick. What I really wanted was a way out of a life ruled by fear. The answer was easy: I made up my mind to avoid any and all conversations about being sick. It was one of my first nonfearful, nonviolent protests. Of course, there was a risk (there always is a risk), and it wasn't that I might get sick. The risk was the possibility of being shunned. People might have called me "peculiar," "sick in the head," or something along those lines. They might have refused to talk to me. I could have been afraid of that too, but I wasn't. From my point of view, it would have been an unpleasant but small price to pay. I generally was a kind and considerate kid (my parents gave me no choice about that); but on a deeper level, I didn't really care what people thought. It turned out that I wasn't shunned. In truth, I don't think people even noticed or paid much attention to me—they were too busy talking about being sick.

The story that I've just told is about a child who discovers the power and peculiarity of fear in the world around him. He learns that if we create a world governed by fear, then we can break free from it too. There was nothing unusual about anything that happened. It was all quite "ordinary"—in the "stifling" sense of the word. Children are sensitive to their surroundings, especially to the emotional life of adults. They have a lot to learn about surviving in this world, and they quickly pick up on everything else too. When I was a kid, wondering why people talked about sickness so much, it was the impact of fear on my inner life that concerned me the most—and not only its impact on me, but also on my family and friends. To see our experience from the standpoint of even "ordinary" fears makes us unnecessarily isolated within ourselves, trapped in a world of our own making, and frozen within it. Children probably perceive this much better than adults.

To talk about sickness too much gave me nearly the same feeling that I had when I actually was sick. In effect, it amounted to preparing to be confined to my room until my fever passed, and that was very much like being sent to my room when I was punished. I didn't like the feeling of being separated from others when that meant being cut off from the world. Why would we choose, as a way of life, anything that resembles isolation, punishment, or inward, solitary confinement? Why would we spend so much time talking about things that produce that inner feeling? Of course, nine times out of ten, a conscious choice is never made. We just learn to live in the world we were born into. All I knew was that I had a choice to make. We all have a choice.

Think about it. We take (and give) small doses of fear every day, and we pay for it with our state of mind, our bodily health, and quite possibly, our souls. The solution is almost too simple: Rather than letting fear live our lives for us, we can choose to live our lives ourselves.

*The second insight: The freedom we want the most is found
beyond the fear that we avoid the most; and when we move
through our very worst fear, we realize that, ultimately,
there's nothing to be afraid of.*

The most valuable truths about life are the ones that we
learn for the sake of love. Those are the truths that help us move
through our fear, so we can become who we are meant to be. I
know that this sounds a little corny, and it will sound corny until
we understand that where fear is concerned, the stakes are high—
but not in the way that we usually think. For example, our worst
fear often conceals a great love; and the greatest love of all—the
love and power of God—is found behind all our fears, including
our very worst fear. The result of all this fear is that we're afraid
not only of our fear, but also of God.

I learned the truth of this when I was a child. I'll tell the whole
story in the next chapter concerning awe and fear—the difference between the two and our confusion about them is crucial
to the movement through fear. If I had not experienced this truth
firsthand as a child, and if had I not experienced it more than
once in my life through the eyes of faith or met people who have
discovered the same truth in their lives, then I probably would not
realize that there is anything worth saying or writing about here.
Nevertheless, I still would suspect that we already know what
this means. We all suspect this. Maybe we haven't given it much
thought, not consciously; but in some deep place in our souls, we
know. We all know. Every one of us knows. The problem is that
we, as a people, have learned to tell a different kind story about
life's meaning. The story is misleading, and we're stuck in it; but
we can free ourselves from it.

Fear is powerful, but not so powerful that we can't become
free from it—and it's certainly less powerful than the Spirit that

lives within us. With the help of friends and loved ones, we can find it within ourselves to overcome our fear. Spiritual traditions tell us that dreams of freedom are more than just "dreams." They are the voice of the Spirit leading us where our souls want to go, yet we tell ourselves that they're too peculiar to believe and too out of reach to pursue. We could try; but for the most part, we don't. Instead, we hesitate. We stop, dead in our tracks. Why would we do this? How does the diabolic, inner logic of fear actually work within us?

Consider the following situation that took place in my life years ago. At the time, I was working in a warehouse, where, for no apparent reason, a fellow employee, a former soldier who suffered from post-traumatic shock, threatened me. As you'll see, the dynamics of fear played out in that particular workplace easily translate into countless other situations, including emotional and physical abuse at home and political persecution in any number of circumstances.

The story begins with the unmistakable threat of bodily harm. The exact words were, "Do you know what I could do to you?" That's all that he says. Not a word more; not a word less. It comes out of nowhere. My response is shock, disbelief—and fear. This is the second incident in as many days, but this time he shows a knife. I turn, walk out of the building and into the parking lot, where I get in my car and lock the door. He doesn't follow. I can't believe this is happening, not to me, and I have no idea what to do. I don't want to do anything. My instincts tell me that he's not a crazed killer but an abusive person who needs help. On the other hand, I realize that I could be wrong, and abusive people can kill, even if it's "accidental." What I want is for all this to be blotted out of my memory. If I had had a laptop in those days, I would have written his name and pushed the "delete" button, over and over and over.

Sitting alone in my car, I know that the situation will not simply disappear. My feeling is that I must handle it myself, which is a mistake. My thoughts are racing and chaotic. I want to confront him. I rehearse what it would be like to confront him. I tell myself that I could risk serious injury, if not my life, by showing any kind of resistance. To confront him could provoke an attack. Things like that happen. So I tell myself that it would be better to do nothing. As afraid as I am, at least I'm alive.

Later that afternoon, I return to the warehouse. I know that I must deal with the situation soon. Fear is setting down roots in my mind. I can feel it happening already. It's affecting my inner thoughts—how I "talk to myself"—and that shapes everything I do. Again I consider the possibility of talking to one of the supervisors in the factory, but I wonder whether he or anyone else would believe me. Why should they? My abuser will deny everything I say. I don't quite believe it myself. I don't even believe my strategy—avoidance—if you want to call it a "strategy." I believe it up to a point, and I know that I will believe it until I'm either worn down completely or my outrage builds to a point where I have to try something else.

A few days pass. Showing up for work is a struggle. I'm caught between two different unknowns: On the one hand, he could threaten me again at any moment; on the other hand, I wonder, hopefully, whether it's all show—more talk than anything else. I think about God too and whether I really believe in God. I pray for me, and I pray for him. I believe that God is with me; and yet praying neither removes the fear nor changes the situation. I remind myself that the light is not overcome by the darkness, and that I will not be overcome by it. I wish that I believe this more strongly, with real conviction, but I don't. In this situation, the light doesn't seem as real as the threat. I suspect that any serious belief in God may be pointless at the point of a knife.

The so-called "real world" plays by its own rules, and they're not God's rules. It occurs to me that he might want money. Maybe he wants me to pay him to leave me alone? Could that be what's driving all this? I've seen things like that on television but never in "real life." Perhaps money is all that he wants. All I know for sure is that I'm living in his world, rather than mine.

The weekend comes and goes. My thoughts become more desperate and self-defeating. To believe in God is one thing, but to act upon that belief is a different matter. "Who am I to believe that God would help me?" "How presumptuous!" That's how I feel. And why shouldn't I feel that way? Christian teachings plainly say it: "We have no power in ourselves to help ourselves." I've heard it countless times. To remember this teaching when I'm afraid, which is nearly all the time, only confirms my worst fear: that there's nothing I can do, and I shouldn't try. Not only that, it could be morally wrong to try, and spiritually dangerous. Only God can do what needs to be done, and I am not God. I half believe what I'm thinking.

But the inner logic of fear doesn't stop there. I work through two possible scenarios once again. I could tell my abuser to stop the harassment, or I could report the incidents to a supervisor. Either way, I would know that I'm in the right and that God is with me. Yet the possibility that God might be real suggests judgment—a spiritual test—which presents another kind of risk. I might succeed. I could move through my fear. But then again, I might fail. Failure is not just likely, but more than likely. That's when I rehearse the presumed judgment within myself: I look back on my life, finding reasons to believe that I'm a failure. Why else could I have let myself be manipulated and threatened like this? Perhaps God is on the side of my abuser. He probably believes that God is on his side, and now I wonder if he might be right. Yes, God is with me; but God is with him too. So who's to say who is right and who is wrong? No one but God knows such things, or so my fear would have me believe.

Now my inner thoughts take a very strange turn: Let's say that I actually confront my adversary and that I'm successful. Let's say that I overcome my fear and do what needs to be done. There's a risk with that too. I might gloat, claim the power of victory for myself, and become like him. It sounds far-fetched—that someone "like me" would actually do such a thing—but the thought crosses my mind. I smile at myself for entertaining such an absurd rationale for doing nothing. Yet, the result is that I'm defending my fear, rather than myself. By now, I no longer know the difference. This, in effect, is what I'm trying to believe: "My world and my fear are my own, and I won't let anyone take them away from me. I'll remain locked within my fear, because it seems safe enough, at least for now. And if I'm nice to my abuser and do nothing wrong, then he'll do nothing. I'm valuable to him! He needs someone to abuse, and that will keep me safe." I know it's absurd, but the power of my fear makes it seem sensible.

Finally, I realize that I'm selling my soul, and I can't let that happen. I have to do something. It's not that my life at work is unbearable (although it is), or that I can't coexist with my abuser (I have been doing exactly that). I've reached a point where I can no longer live with myself. On the spur of the moment, I confide in a friend and coworker. Everything that happened comes pouring out. I tell my friend that I've decided to confront my abuser, and I want him to be my witness. I'm going to tell him that if this ever happens again, I'll call the police. My friend does not want to join me, not really, but he agrees to do so. Finally, toward the end of our discussion, he tells me that he's not surprised by any of this—he once heard about a similar incident involving the very same person. He didn't say that the experience was his own, but from the look on his face, I knew he was talking about himself.

Immediately, the two of us walk to the back of the warehouse where my abuser often hangs out. With my friend standing beside me, I say what needs to be said. Unseen by the both of us, our supervisor is standing nearby, where he overhears everything. Later in the afternoon, he calls me into his office and explains that he has spoken to my abuser and put him on official notice. He tells me that he had been aware of the young man's emotional problems since he returned from Vietnam. He wanted to help him make a life for himself by giving him a job. He apologized and assured me that this would not happen again. He also made it clear that I should never keep situations like this bottled up within myself. A few hours later, my abuser apologizes too. I can't say that we became friends; but after that, we worked together well enough.

Not every frightening and abusive situation turns out so well. Yet we can always turn to friends, family members, and coworkers for the guidance and support we need. More often than not, they can and will do the right thing and help us move through our fear, and possibly their own fear. But it's the inner logic of fear that's my principal concern—how it digs into our psyche like a predatory beast feeding on the Spirit of our lives.

The most striking quality of the whole story is its familiarity. Most everyone has either heard about, or experienced, different versions of it, in different degrees, even if we haven't known outright threats, harassment, abuse, or persecution. Given half a chance (or less), our fear will make us afraid not only of the darkness, but also of the light. It will turn every good reason to be free and every good course of action on its head, giving us every excuse in the world to remain imprisoned in our fear.

What this story also suggests is that any effort to move through our fear can become a major spiritual issue in our lives— a spiritual test and an ordeal. When this happens, the integrity of our whole existence will be at stake. Faith is an integral part of the movement through fear, and faith is the leap we make into the unknown, even when we're not so sure about the light. This is a reality that we all eventually face, not just once, but many times in the course of a lifetime. And our question is always this: Which will we be afraid of more? Will it be the darkness that we know, or the light that we could know much better? Better yet, which will be the more trusted friend—our fear or our faith?

> The third insight: We don't need to become experts on fear to move through it. Rather, we must strengthen our Spirit, which means cultivating the very spiritual instincts that our fear would have us neglect or ignore.

If we're afraid of the world and of God too, then where can we possibly turn? Although there are no gimmicks, tricks, or easy "how to" steps to follow, there is an answer. It's not more knowledge of fear that will set us free. We're already highly skilled practitioners in the art of manufacturing, using, avoiding, and falling prey to fear. What we need is to cultivate the spiritual instincts that God has given us and put them to good use.

When I encourage people to trust and to follow their instincts, I have something very specific in mind. I'll spell this out as systematically as I can, drawing upon Yoga philosophy. First, human existence is grounded in four basic or *primal instincts—self-preservation/survival, food, sleep, and sex*—which we share with other animals. Fear is how the instinct for self-preservation and survival is most commonly experienced. It alerts us to the presence of danger and allows us to make the kind of response that maximizes our chance to survive. On this most basic level, fear is obviously good. All our primal instincts, including fear, are not enough to ensure our survival, but without them, we most surely would not survive.

In addition to these four primal instincts, we have what I call *spiritual instincts*—awe, love, intent, conscience, community, rest, and faith. These seven basic spiritual instincts are not entirely separate from our primal instincts. Rather, they modify and expand how our primal instincts are understood and acted upon. For example, the meaning of survival might be revealed through the pursuit of justice (conscience); the meaning of sex, through love; of sleep, under some circumstances, through a form of prayer called "resting in God"; and food, by living in communities that nurture the body and the soul in communion with others.

Primal instincts help us meet the prerequisite, survival needs that we all have as individuals, while our spiritual instincts take into account the survival and well-being of a much wider range of living creatures—not only ourselves, but also our neighbors, humankind as a whole, and the entire web of life, on which our survival depends. Acting alone, our primal instincts create harmful imbalances that feed upon our life-energy and unleash harmful forces into the world. Spiritual instincts, on the other hand, feed the body, mind, and soul, rather than feeding upon them, and create the inner balance that leads to a humane existence.

The degree to which we cultivate and use our spiritual instincts shapes the kind of people we become. We may not realize what these instincts are; we may not use them; and we may not use them very well—but we do have them. It is quite likely that we do not use them as much as we believe, perhaps because we're afraid to acknowledge them, or afraid to trust them, which amounts to losing contact with ourselves and with the Spirit. More often than not, we learn to cultivate our spiritual instincts to a limited degree. For example, when we're in the presence of someone who manifests the gift of love in an exceptional way, this should not suggest that we do not have the same gift, or the capacity for it. It only means that we have not cultivated that gift in the same way or as much as we could.

The fact that the word "instincts" is not commonly used in spiritual writing reflects the dualistic tendency in the Western worldview—for example, the separation of "nature" from "nurture." This kind of dualism may be giving way to a more holistic point of view; nevertheless, the habits of thought are still with us. Instincts such as fear are considered to be rooted in nature, genes, and biology, rather than in culture or Spirit. Taken to the extreme, the implication is that any kind of "instinct," by definition, should not be called "spiritual."

There are problems with a strictly dualistic point of view. To suggest or imply that we aren't born with spiritual instincts or the capacity to develop them—or that "some people" aren't born with them—not only denies a vision of life that spiritual traditions have worked for generations to preserve, but also undermines the development of the very instincts that give us our humanity. It is our birthright as creatures made in God's image to use our primal instincts wisely and to cultivate our spiritual instincts, just as it's the responsibility of families, communities, and institutions to make sure this happens. The most important point is this: If we ignore our spiritual instincts, then they diminish, much in the same way that muscles atrophy without exercise. If we don't use them, we lose them; and if we lose them, we become our own worst enemy.

When I encourage someone to follow his or her instincts, I watch closely to see how my words are interpreted, while doing my best to keep the conversation open and sensitive to deeper levels of meaning. Obviously, if the response is self-absorbed or without much reflective thought, then we have a lot of work to do. This is crucial because the word "instincts" can have many meanings, and some are far from spiritual. For example, we must be careful when political and religious demagogues or media stars draw out our "gut reactions." They may be speaking to our primal fear, while giving it a spiritual name; specifically, "faithfulness to

God," when they really mean "allegiance to country." I have no quarrel with healthy patriotism, but there is a significant difference between religious faith and anything resembling a loyalty oath.

That's why it's not enough to say to "Follow your instincts" or "Trust your instincts," or simply to make the claim that "spiritual instincts" exist. That would only be more talk. What we really need is a working, practical knowledge based on direct experience. We need to know what we're talking about firsthand and why, which brings us to the second suggestion that I routinely make.

I encourage people to "breathe through" their fear, much in the same way we deal with panic attacks and anxiety—by sitting quietly, gathering ourselves, and simply breathing easily. I'm drawing upon the well-known yogic practices of *pranayama*, which are also found in contemplative strands of the Christian spiritual tradition. By doing these practices in breathing, we soon realize that rather than inhaling and exhaling in a relaxed, continuous movement, which is the healthy thing to do, we habitually hold our breath. For all practical purposes, we've learned to adopt a primal fear response as a "normal" way of life. We do this even when we believe that fear doesn't play a significant part in our lives. Yet it's really *easy* to calm ourselves inwardly and establish a more balanced emotional life simply by changing how we breathe, without drugs or therapeutic intervention. By being mindful of a completely natural instinct—breathing—we can strengthen our Spirit and take a huge step toward moving through our fear.

The fourth insight: One fear contains the power of every fear within it. Burst the bubble of one fear, and all our other fears begin to lose their power over us too.

Now let's take the discussion several steps further, all the way through and beyond our fear. Let's imagine that we're looking back on what it *was* like to be afraid. In all likelihood, we don't have to imagine it. All we have to do is to recall just one occasion when fear released its grip on our lives and then remember what the feeling was like: complete exhilaration, an unexpected experience of freedom that we always wished for but never believed possible.

In that moment, we glimpse an important truth. We begin to realize that all our fears are connected and that our other fears might not be as difficult or dreadful as we once believed. Once we move through one fear, the power of all our fears diminishes. We discover the difference between looking upon fear from the standpoint of being afraid and seeing what it really looks like—from the standpoint of freedom and joy.

This is no illusion; it's not mere wishful thinking; and we've all experienced it in different ways. We've all tasted it, glimpsed it in fleeting moments, but then turned away from the larger implications. If you can't remember what this is like, keep trying. Your mind will eventually take you where your soul has already been—and wants to go again.

Once we perceive that the power of fear is, almost entirely, the power we give to it, we can understand that the whole edifice of fear can come down in the blink of an eye. That power exists in our hearts and minds, and it can be in our hands, which brings us back to the heart of the Christian faith and one of its most misunderstood teachings: *"We have no power in ourselves to help ourselves."* This actually means the very opposite of what it sounds like, the reason being that we hear it from the standpoint of being afraid. The teaching actually means that we are never powerless. Why? The reason is that the Spirit of God, the source of all true power, is with us always. The power we've been given is not ours to claim for ourselves, but to use wisely, respectfully, and mindfully of the Spirit from which it comes.

Because "power" is an ambiguous word, especially in relation to the spirituality of fear, I want to make a few additional comments about it here. Fear has no power in itself, but the power we give to it makes fear disempowering to us. Put another way, harmful fear has the power to take our lives away, only because we give the energy and Spirit of our lives to it. So when we say, for example, "I'm afraid, and I need something to hold on to," it's the power of God—the Spirit and love of God—that we really need. Or, in less religious terms, we need to take back the lives that we've given to fear. Actually, this way of describing it sounds deeply religious to me too. The words are not nearly as important as their practical meaning. Either way you want to think of it, this can be done. The Spirit is always present, always here, in the world around us and within ourselves. Nothing and no one can kill the Spirit.

The Spirit is the one power that fear would like us to believe that it has, when, truthfully, it has no such power at all. Primal fear is good, but it is not one of our spiritual instincts. In the same way, harmful fear would like us to believe that we literally *"have no power in ourselves to help ourselves."* Harmful fear would have us believe that its power is greater than the Spirit's power and that our spiritual instincts make no difference in "the real world." It would convince us that we should give up now, surrender to primal instincts, and accept the way things are—for our own good!

It's a hugely tragic fact that the word "Spirit" is often invoked by forms of religion that generate fear, rather than helping us to move through it. I don't believe that God wants us to be afraid to live our lives, or to make others afraid, or to pretend that we're other than who we are. Nor do I believe that it's okay, in the mind of God or anywhere else, to find scapegoats for our fear.

When I say "the Spirit," I mean the creative, sustaining, healing force that exists within the whole of God's creation. I would not say that "the Holy Spirit" is substantially different from "the Spirit" known to the all the world's religions and indigenous peoples. I'm well aware that this is a spiritually significant and politically charged subject; yet I've known the truth of this spiritual power in my own life and in the lives of friends in many cultures and religions. Ultimately, we're all talking about one God and one Spirit. To realize that this is true can wake us up, turn our lives around, move us through our fear, and transform how we live and who we think we are. If we're afraid of beliefs and experiences of that kind, then we should be asking ourselves where our fear comes from and whose interest it serves.

The fact that we can and do lose contact with the Spirit is one of the profound mysteries of human life and part of the larger Holy Mystery that all our lives are. That fear plays such a large part in this loss is the primary reason that harmful fear is truly *harmful.* I would not want to suggest that fear is a sin, or that it outranks any of the traditional seven deadly sins: pride, greed, lust, envy, gluttony, anger, and sloth. The ancient concept of *sin* has traditionally been understood as *anything* that would separate us from the love of God—as *anything* that makes us lose contact with the Spirit. In reality, nothing (including our fear) can separate us from the love of God. Nevertheless, fear can strengthen and rationalize our sins and shortcomings to the point where we believe they are good and morally right—the infamous modern phrasing "Greed is good" being one of the best examples I know. We have to ask ourselves what kind of fear lies behind this false belief. Sin or no sin, any way you look at it, fear is serious business, not to be taken lightly, taken for granted, or simply accepted as a necessary part of life.

> *The fifth insight: These two questions—"How can we move through our fear?" and "How can we become who we are meant to be?"—are, for all practical purposes, one and the same.*

The fifth and last insight is the culmination of all those preceding it, just as faith is the culmination of all our spiritual instincts (a point that will be made in chapter nine). This insight is so simple that it's easily overlooked and almost too simple to believe, but it's not too simple to be true: The movement through fear is not really about fear. The movement through fear is *not* primarily about what we're afraid of, although that obviously plays a part, nor does it depend on "defeating" our fear, as if the outcome can be determined by who "wins" and who "loses." Rather, the movement through fear is about us. It's about self-knowledge in the true spiritual sense.

Philosophers and psychologists are right to say that fear "contracts" the self into a shrunken, frozen version of who we really are. In the same way, spiritual traditions are right when they say that moving through our fear restores the self to the sacred ground of our existence—"perfect love casts out fear." This shift from the object to the subject—from our fear to us—puts the ball back in our court, as it were, where it has always belonged. It puts us in a much better position to move through our fear and become who we are meant to be as people.

I'm choosing my words carefully here. My purpose is not to make claims about human destiny or the will of God in an ultimate way, although this is exactly what the world religions, spiritual traditions, and some philosophical schools do—with good reason. There's no doubt that the way I put it—"to become who we are meant to be"—points in the direction of ultimate meaning. The same can be said for the central message of this book: that our spiritual instincts are the key to moving through our fear. But my interest is in pursuing what works in a genuinely spiritual sense; and I'm motivated by the fact that we all know, somewhere in our souls, that something profoundly significant is at stake when we struggle with our fear.

We live at a time when the coercive power of fear plays an

increasingly prominent role in the world we are creating. The world that exists "out there" reflects our fear on us, magnifying its power and increasing its influence on how we see ourselves *and* the world. We learn to see the world from the standpoint of fear, telling ourselves that it becomes all the more "real" with every new demonstration of fear's power. According to this view, any suspicion that the world we create is rooted in an illusion is seen as unrealistic, irresponsible, naive, and in the final analysis, an escape from what seems obvious and self-evident. This is the equivalent of believing that the teachings of spiritual traditions are an escape from "the real world."

But genuine spiritual traditions are not meant to be an escape, despite the fact that they're often put to that use. Simply by cultivating our spiritual instincts, we can learn to discern the difference between the helpful fear that alerts us to real threats and the coercive fear that makes us a danger to ourselves and to the real world. To discern the difference between harmful and helpful fear is to perceive the difference between reality and illusion. It should go without saying that the answer we give to the question, "What do we really want?" matters a great deal. It matters whether our answer is to trust our spiritual instincts, or to surrender our lives to whatever we mistakenly believe our primal instincts are telling us. The answer we give makes a difference not only for our lives as individuals, but also for our lives together.

I'll give a practical example. Let's imagine that I say something like this: *"I'm sick and tired of being afraid."* My words express obvious and understandable frustration. I'm not happy about the way my life is going, which is good, but that's as far as the meaning goes. I've told you something about my emotions and state of mind, but nothing about what I'm willing to do or how I might do it. It's possible that my frustration could lead me to blame other people, while believing that I'm no longer afraid. In effect, I would be choosing to make others afraid, rather than moving through my own fear. I would be using the power of fear for my own self-centered purposes, probably to get what I want from others, even if that only involves getting their attention. But nothing would have substantially changed because my life would still be ruled by fear. I would not have changed. I've only changed seats in a room filled with fear.

Our movement through fear goes beyond our frustration with and dislike of fear. It involves a radical change in how we relate to every part of life, including our own lives. A more empowering response might be, *"I don't want to be someone who's afraid; I want to become a truly loving person."* Then I would be in a position to put love—one of our spiritual instincts—at the center of my life, rather than fear. I can move through my fear by becoming a person with an entirely new perspective on life.

A well-known story about Saint Francis of Assisi describes the impact that this transformation had on him. The story, which I'll put in my own words, revolves around the relationship between this beloved saint and a ferocious wolf that took up residence in Gubbio, a nearby town. The wolf had been tormenting everyone who lived there. Having heard about the wolf, Francis decided to liberate the townsfolk by demonstrating the power of love over fear. This is what happened.

When Francis went to Gubbio and explained his intent, many of the townsfolk were angry. His suggestion called their good sense and frustration into question, as if their fear of the wolf's threatening behavior wasn't justified. Francis knew that he had to show some proof, so he went to the wolf's den. At first, he was struck by the ravaging look in the wolf's eyes, but he also realized that the wolf was just as tormented by the townsfolk as the townsfolk were by the wolf. Francis drew closer, addressed him as "Brother Wolf," and explained that the townsfolk would respect and protect him—if he would do the same for the townsfolk. The wolf drew closer to Saint Francis, extending his paw as a sign of friendship. The wolf never bothered the people of Gubbio again.

This is a simple story—a "just so" story, you might say. It's one of those stories that's too simple to believe, but not too simple to be true. It tells me that if we want to do anything truly worthwhile—such as moving through our fear—then we must keep our eye on the ball. Fear would like us *not* to keep our eye on the ball. Fear would like to keep our attention all for itself. I have to believe that Saint Francis was relentless in his pursuit of love, even to the point of showing respect for a creature that everyone else held in fearful contempt. He would let nothing stand in his way, especially fear, including fear of the wolf that terrorized everyone else and sent people running. His love for God and life moved him though his fear, just as it moved the people who knew him through theirs.

Having made my point—I hope not too many times—that fear will convince us of all kinds of nonsense, it's time to turn to the heart of the matter: moving through our fear. The way ahead is incredibly simple. It involves remembering what our spiritual instincts are, cultivating them, and putting them to good use. This may not be the easiest thing in the world to do, or so we believe. We've been mesmerized by the power of fear for a very long time, and it takes some time and effort to unlearn what we've learned so well. The following chapters and the stories in them describe how this can be done. What we need to remember is that no one can do what needs to be done except us, which is the whole point. The Spirit will take care of everything else.

3.

AWE: OUR HOMING SIGNAL

To see a World in a Grain of Sand
and a Heaven in a Wild Flower,
Hold Infinity in the palm of your hand
And Eternity in an hour.

—WILLIAM BLAKE (1757–1827), "Auguries of Innocence"

The Lord answered Job out of the whirlwind:
"Who is this that darkens counsel by words without knowledge? Gird up your loins like a man, I will
question you, and you shall declare to me. Where were
you when I laid the foundation of the earth? Tell me,
if you have understanding."

—Book of Job, 38:1–3

A we—our homing signal—is the instinct that turns our
awareness toward the sacred. We experience awe as profound wonder, beauty, reverence, and humility in the presence of
a power that is greater than we are, yet somehow within us too.

Awe helps us to create a genuine vision of life's meaning that leads us through our fear.

Our instinct for awe is basic, yet we, as a people, have come close to losing contact with it. We've grown so accustomed to thinking of awe from the standpoint of fear—and understanding it as fear—that we risk losing our sensitivity to God's presence everywhere around us, and with it, our capacity to discern. Our confusion about awe and fear makes us a threat to ourselves and to the whole creation. This is a risk that we should not want to take. Nevertheless, it is one that we have taken; and now we must work through the consequences of what we've done as prayerfully and thoughtfully as we can.

In our busy, media-driven lives, the great gift that awe offers has become anything but obvious: It creates a sense of inner silence and peacefulness that our souls long for. Awe is the very opposite of anything showy, loud, or fearful. The words we use to describe awe—"wonder," "reverence," "humility"—are all entirely right and appropriate, but it's important to remember that these are names for the indescribable feelings that arise from the silence within. To experience holy silence is to know that God is both near and far, within us and within the universe too, which makes awe the best and only true beacon of light when we're afraid. Awe reminds us that when we turn toward God, we will find our way.

None of our spiritual instincts work well in isolation from the others, and this is especially true with regard to awe. Awe releases the grip that fear has on our minds, and that energizes our imagination with new possibilities. Yet not every experience of awe is genuinely spiritual, nor is every power that seems to be greater than ourselves truly holy or loving. What passes for awe, love, or respect may not, upon closer reflection, turn out to be awesome, loving, or respectful. We know that awe is genuine when it dispels our fear, unveils the source of the spiritual instincts that we've been given, and nurtures the loving-kindness and humility on which spiritual freedom depends.

That's why I put two equally famous but seemingly contradictory quotations on the opening page of this chapter. Even if you don't consider yourself a particularly religious person, the issues these passages raise touch the hearts of us all. William Blake, the great visionary painter and poet who believed in the love of God considerably more than the fear of God, reminds us that we can experience spiritual awe in circumstances and places that we routinely overlook—in grains of sand and wildflowers that we hold in the palms of our hands. For Blake, the instinct for awe nurtures our creative imagination, and that helps us move though the same fear that robs us of our spiritual freedom.

Job sees awe in the same light, while understanding it from a different point of view. The mere idea of "holding infinity in the palm of your hand" might have made Job shudder with indignation. I don't know that for a fact, but I do know that Blake illustrated the Book of Job and held him in great respect. Notice the tone in the second quotation: "Where were you when I laid the foundation of the earth?" God asks from the whirlwind. God is not really looking for an answer. What God is looking for is a sign of genuine awe in us. And if "the question" sounds intimidating and judgmental, as if we're being cross-examined, then our ears are in good working order. Job is right about the source of our confusion: The awe that we usually experience is directed toward ourselves, rather than to God.

That's the moral of the story in Job, but there's another equally important lesson to learn: If we hear Job's sacred teaching from the standpoint of fear and intimidation, which we're likely to do, then we'll overlook the very spiritual instinct—awe—that the teaching could and should cultivate in our souls. This is why it's so important to cultivate awe, while remembering the difference between awe and fear. Otherwise, we remain stuck in our fear and lose sight of the spiritual instinct that points in the direction we need to go. The purpose of awe—our homing signal—is to help us find our way.

So, having done my best to describe the heart of this spiritual instinct, let's move ahead with some real-life stories and reflections. We'll explore several kinds of awesome experiences: encounters with honeybees and snakes, struggles with "the fear of God" and liberating moments of awe, some of the people that I would like to "put the fear of God into," and the confusion of awe and fear in politics and religion. But before that, I'll repeat the essential point: Awe, rather than fear, is our homing signal in the whirlwind of life. Awe gives us the capacity to experience, firsthand, the power that is greater than we are, and yet within us too. By cultivating this instinct, we loosen the grip that fear has on our lives and dispel the illusions that we create for ourselves—and confuse with the real world.

My friend Trish lives just down the road from my house. She says that my dog, Luke, is "a little goofy." She's right. When Trish first told me this, my thoughts turned not to Luke, but to some other friends who describe me in much the same way. The affection of my friends goes beyond the fact that dogs and their keepers take on similar characteristics. They're letting me know that they have some insight into me as a person. And I know that their perception is good because they're "a little goofy" too—a quality that I understand as a variation on "peculiar." The way I see it, my friends are reflective and honest enough to realize how surprising life is (all of life), and they're not so afraid of being who they are that they hide their own contribution.

Think about it: Who would have ever dreamed that the evolutionary process would produce goofy dogs and peculiar people? Not in four million years has anyone been able to explain something like that, not really—yet we can't explain it away. Speaking for my friends and for myself, we wouldn't even try. Instead, we celebrate it, sometimes out loud, but usually in quiet, nearly unspoken ways (like "Your dog is a little goofy") that I regard as an understated expression of awe. This is how we acknowledge the Mystery of everything. We're being intimate, without being too intimate; and spiritual, but grounded in the world we regard as the most real. It's how we create the kind of sacred space that lets the soul breathe easy. It's also one of the ways that we recognize each other as "friends."

There's another reason that my friends say things like that about me, and it's not because of my fears, which I surely have. Rather, they're thinking of what I'm not afraid of; namely, my honeybees. For me, a walk into the meadow behind my house to visit some very small friends is pleasurable and relaxing. I could not say the same for most of my two-legged friends. They know that one of my favorite pastimes is to unfold a lawn chair close to the hives and to hear the "buzzing" sound as they careen back and forth. When my two-legged friends visit, a few politely decline my invitation to see these astonishing creatures up close. Others hesitate at first, and then politely accept. Often, as we walk the short distance to the hives, I smile again and think of some other friends who have fearful feelings about religion. Somewhere, sometime in the past, they were stung by the fear bug in church. Now they won't go near it.

Needless to say, to walk the short and otherwise pleasant distance between my living room and the beehives requires letting go of a lot of baggage, which amounts to a movement through fear in itself. So, before sharing a favorite story about honeybees and awe, I must take you on an extended detour into the more general subject of awe and fear. And I ask you to trust me again. What I have to say may not always be easy to hear. I make no apologies for this. We are, after all, talking about fear, and I can't change the fact that it's an emotionally charged and often unpleasant subject.

No reasonable person can deny that our world is in a precarious and fear-ridden state. Fear, for example, permeates our lives so much that we generally regard awe as a variety of fear—even worse, we've become manipulated and mesmerized by some kinds of harmful fear, as if they are worthy of awe. To be mesmerized is not the same as awestruck, but we, as a people, have learned to accept the cheap imitation as the real thing. This is a serious and tragic mistake. We don't have to make that mistake, certainly not again and again, and there's no justifiable reason to continue doing so. It's like forgetting the difference between apples and oranges, and then refusing to discover why we let ourselves forget or why it matters.

Why would we do this? Why would we follow the drumbeat of manipulation so readily? These are not easy questions, but we can be sure that some cherished ideas about spiritual and political freedom are part of the answer, the well-known religious phrasing "the fear of God" being the best example I know. We've become scared of our own shadow; and because of it, we cast our own scary shadow onto ideas about God and God's creation. We're talking about a lot of fear, and we may not have much time to move through it. My job is not to blame anyone for this, which would amount to pointing fingers and stirring up anger. Rather, my job is to help us find our first and best homing signal. We need one right now—a reliable lighthouse on the unknown shore of a stormy sea.

With that in mind, let's go back to the beginning, all the way back, as far as our sacred texts and imaginations can take us. I'm thinking of the first few words in the Bible: *In the beginning, when God created the heavens and the earth.* It's the idea of "the beginning"—*both* a time in the distant past, *and* a dimension of our lives now—that evokes awe in me. It illumines my soul, and that helps me perceive a creative power that's beyond my comprehension, yet present within everything that exists, has existed, and will exist. I accept this as a truth about life expressed in religious terms. I also accept the "Big Bang" as a scientific truth; but the meaning of both cannot be contained in the words themselves. The awe that I experience goes beyond anything that *scientific* facts or *religious* texts tell me about its meaning. It's the same when my friends speak from the depth of their hearts, and in a lesser way, when they smile and tell me about goofy dogs, and speak in a politely roundabout way about peculiar people.

The opening line from Genesis is just one example, but it's important in relation to fear. The almost *too obvious* fact is that the Bible—the great holy text of Judaism and Christianity—doesn't begin with fear. It begins with awe. I don't know precisely when we turned this around in our minds—dislodging awe from "the beginning," and putting fear in its place—but that is what we've done. The evidence has become all too clear. Just look at history. Millions of native Africans were once sold into slavery to save their souls and work the "new world." Centuries later, millions of Jews were murdered for the equally unimaginably criminal purpose of "cleansing" an old one. And at the very same time, whole cities were incinerated to "cleanse" the world of war; that is to say, to create "a new beginning." The mass killing of civilians in "total war" became not only thinkable, but also doable, and it was done with brutal efficiency. Destroying one world in order to create a new one took on the same face, or so it was said.

Robert Oppenheimer described the terror of it when the first atomic bomb was detonated in the Nevada desert. He quoted, famously, from the *Bhagavad Gita*: "*I am become Death, the destroyer of worlds.*" In the original text, these words were spoken by Vishnu, in the form of Kali, but, as I hear them, Oppenheimer was speaking for our collective soul. He was announcing "the beginning" of a new age, such as it was. The place where all this happened was called "Trinity." The bomb was dropped on Hiroshima on August 6. In the Christian calendar, this is "the Day of the Transfiguration," when Jesus took Peter, James, and John to the mountaintop. They saw a cloud; Jesus was filled with holy light. Need I say that an atomic blast is not what God meant by "let there be light"?

Given the circumstances, "what else could we have done?" That's what we say to justify the atomic blasts in Japan. Death unleashed by the forces of light cancels out death by the forces of darkness. Do we really believe that? Maybe we do. But I'm no Manichean, and I don't believe that "spiritual warfare," which definitely has its place, is either meant to work, or that it can work in that way. After the bombs were dropped, a well-known Scottish minister named George MacLeod put it better: *We've taken the Body of Christ, and used it for bloody hell.* It's true that "all becomes one" in mystical vision, and perhaps the same can be said in the theoretical realm of physics. However, there is, should be, and must be a difference between the beginning and the end, creation and destruction, and awe and fear in the lives we live every day. When we fail to honor the boundaries between them, then our lives inevitably dissolve into one fear response after another, rather than rising up in true spiritual awe. Our souls are not transfigured by the presence of God, but transmogrified into something, I suppose, frozen. The fact is that we've been living recklessly in the danger zone for some time, and the boundaries that are meant to separate the different sacred realms of our lives have, in fact, been collapsing.

We've learned to take such a world for granted, pushing the truth of it out of our everyday thoughts. But I remembered the deeper truth again during the second war with Iraq—when the United States chose "shock and awe" to describe its strategy for bombing Baghdad. Perhaps this seems like a trivial point, given the very real mortality of war, and far be it from me to pass judgment on the work of military strategists, on which the lives of our servicemen depend, and for whom I have great respect; but they should have called it "shock and fear" rather than "shock and awe."

Of course, the message was intended for a much broader target population—the millions of people, like me, who watched the war on CNN at home. Sitting in "the audience," I remembered Oppenheimer's quote from the East; and I was struck, not by the bombs, but by the fact that very few people who witnessed it on the screen seemed to realize what was really happening or to notice the purposefully confused words, or to care much about it. Perhaps it registered briefly as a passing thought, and then we ignored the implications. Or maybe we just consented to the treacherous belief that the worst experience of fear *should* evoke feelings of awe. Could we really have done that? Could we have gone that far? It's horrible even to contemplate the possibility. But if that's what we've done, then we've completed the worst kind of idolatrous reversal: We've put ourselves in a terrifying godlike role that's the exact opposite of anything spiritual traditions regard as holy and worthy of awe.

Obviously, we have a great deal of soul work to do and some neglected spiritual instincts to recover. So let's start with awe, rather than fear, which is as it should be: *Awe is the combination of profound wonder, joy, beauty, adoration, and deep humility that we experience in the presence of a power infinitely greater than ourselves.* It should go without saying that this power refers to the love of God, rather than to any power that we might claim for ourselves or pretend that we have.

Genuine spiritual awe is our first and most reliable homing signal. We quickly become lost without it; and when that happens, the world we make for ourselves gradually crumbles at our feet or explodes through our own actions. Awe is our homing signal because it gives us the larger, more beautiful, and wiser perspective on which our survival depends. It restores the sense of inner balance that we're so prone to losing for any number of reasons, one of the most pernicious reasons being fear.

Fear, on the other hand, is our biologically rooted response to dangerous threats, whether those threats are real or imagined. This is why I would never say that I'm "afraid of God," despite the exceedingly wise spiritual teaching that says, "the fear of God is the beginning of wisdom." I'm fully aware that such a statement, made by a priest, might be seen as irreverent, cheeky, and perhaps attention-getting, not to mention peculiar. Nevertheless, I've thought about this a long time, and I'm quite serious. This is a very real truth of my life, and I know for a fact that I'm not alone. Let me say more.

There's no doubt in my mind that "it's a terrible thing to fall into the hands of the living God," as the Bible also teaches. I know what that means in my own life. To experience the love of God is to face a terrible lack of love within ourselves. It feels terrible, because it is terrible; and we are afraid. But the terrible part relates to us—not to God—and it's the best and most truthful thing that can ever happen to us. To be so afraid of God that we turn away is to refuse to see the darkness and the fear within ourselves.

What I just described is a very old truth and a very modern one. People in every culture have always known it. "Fear" can mean many things in spiritual traditions; but, almost always, the "fear of God" means "awe." It's hugely misleading and thoroughly false to imply, insinuate, or in any way suggest that God is ever, even remotely, and under any circumstances a danger to us or a threat to our survival. The real threat is humankind—us—running amok on the face of the earth without a healthy, well-cultivated instinct for true spiritual awe. That's why this chapter must be a bit longer than the others. It's not that awe is more important than love, faith, or any other of our spiritual instincts. The problem is that when we confuse awe and fear, then everything else becomes muddled and we become a threat to ourselves—and every other living creature.

Fear, like awe, is more complicated than that, but not by much. Let me elaborate on what I've just said by drawing upon a previous example. I briefly mentioned that my mother experiences thunder and lightning as a threat to her survival. Like a lot of reasonable people, she's afraid of it. I'm not afraid, but I think of her when a storm comes, and I know better than to stand under a tree. To do so with thunderbolts flashing overhead would make me afraid, and it would be really stupid and reckless to stand there. I have no desire to make the inevitability of my eventual death occur any sooner than need be. In the same way, if I were in the actual, face-to-face presence of God, then hopefully, I would act in an appropriate way too. In spiritual circles, this might mean either falling to one's knees in devout humility, or standing with hands raised in prayerful adoration. Either way that we position ourselves (we're always "positioning" about one thing or another), we're in the presence of a power that is infinitely, unimaginably greater than we are. But God is not a threat. God is love.

Therein lies the problem: the obstacle, the stumbling block, the threat to our survival isn't God. It's not God that makes me afraid. My "fear of God" involves you and me. It centers on us: our reckless, thoughtless actions, and the consequences of our actions. We are peculiar creatures. We're capable of extraordinary actions that illuminate the human heart and glorify God, *and* we can destroy nearly everything that God has given us to care for. In both cases, we mean well. We always mean well. Yet, at this very moment, the condition of the world suggests that we've given ourselves plenty of reasons to be scared to high heaven. God didn't do this. We did it, all by ourselves. Just to make myself clear, it's not awe that I'm talking about now, but fear of what the consequences of our recklessness might be. Despite all this, there is forgiveness, which is the best reason for awe, rather than fear, that I could ever imagine or dream of imagining. Seen in that light, kneeling sounds good; standing sounds good too; but running away because we're afraid is not an option, not in the real world.

> *Here is my point: Awe—profound wonder, joy, beauty, reverence, and adoration, all infused with humility, in the presence of a power infinitely greater than ourselves—is one of our most basic and vital spiritual instincts. To cultivate awe, we must learn to move through our fear, even when that means moving through what we habitually regard as "the fear of God."*

As you must realize by now, this "detour" has not been a detour at all. It's the prelude to a story about awe, told in a world where the difference between fear and awe has been utterly confused. Somewhere in our souls, we all know better than this. We have spiritual instincts; we just haven't used them as well as we could. So let's resume the story, taking up where we left off—with my truly awesome honeybees.

I don't want to play down the fear that my friends have toward honeybees, as both fear and awe come in many kinds and degrees. Some expressions of awe, for example, are truly deserved; others less so; and still others completely misplaced. What I know is that my friends would be considerably less in awe of me and less afraid of my honeybees if they had more firsthand experience with them. Nevertheless, I can understand their feelings. Like many beekeepers, I don't wear protective covering (a netted hat or gloves) when I'm working at the hives, not unless I'm taking one apart for close inspection or maintenance. By hanging out with honeybees long

enough, anyone would realize that they respond to the possibility of danger much like you and I do. When they sense a threat
from us, they sting in order to protect themselves, which says
more about us than them. For example, if I'm irritated or in a
foul mood, my bees would sense a threat or the possibility of
danger—so I stay away from the hives when I'm out of sorts.
They would sting me, and I wouldn't hold it against them. How
could I? I would have provoked their defensive measure.

Along the same lines, I've been told that you should never go
near a hive when you're intoxicated. Not being a drinker myself,
I can't testify to the truth of it, but I believe the advice is sound.
I know it's true among people. It is precisely when we're in a
foul mood or intoxicated that we're either stung or we deliver the
sting ourselves, even among those we love. This tells me, when all
is said and done, that people are much more likely to sting than
honeybees.

What I really want to share with you is one peculiar experience that happened at the hives. It began about 5:00 a.m. I love
the first light of the day, so I always get up early. I love to see the
sunrise; but even more, I love to breathe it in. I'm serious. There's
something subtle and deeply spiritual about sunlight in the early
morning. There was a time in my life when I didn't notice it, but
I'll save that for a later chapter. I walked to the meadow in the
back of the house to check the hives, which is part of my morning
routine. The reason was to make sure that no hungry bears tried
to steal the honey during the night. It was a normal morning, and
all was well. A few bees were beginning to stir, as they usually do
at first light, so I walked back to the house and into the kitchen,
where I poured a second cup of coffee.

Through the kitchen window, I could see the hives in the distance. Only a few minutes had passed, but in that brief time something strange happened. What appeared to be a faint, brownish

cloud surrounded the hives. Immediately, I left the house and walked, quicker this time, to the meadow where I found myself standing, not within a cloud, but in the middle of a huge swarm. Thousands of honeybees were flying all around me. The sound of their "buzzing" was remarkably loud. At first, I was confused about what I was hearing and seeing, having never witnessed swarming honeybees firsthand. It was a strange feeling. It would be easy to assume that "more bees" flying around would be "more dangerous," and an obvious cause of concern, if not fear. For a few seconds, that very thought definitely crossed my mind.

Suddenly, the unexpected happened. I was astonished to discover that swarming honeybees are unusually docile. Who would have guessed? Fifty or more bees landed on my upper body, on my shoulders and arms. I moved a few of them away, gently, with my hand. I wasn't stung, not even once. When I realized how peaceful they were, I became peaceful myself. My guess is that they hadn't even considered stinging me. It's entirely possible that they were only checking me out. I say that because after a minute or so, the vast majority of bees that had landed on me resumed flying.

Gradually, I was overcome by the immensity of what I was experiencing. Standing within the swarm for ten minutes or more, motionless and speechless, I had strong emotions, but not any particular ones. As you might guess, I was exceptionally alert; but even then, my alertness had no trace of fear. Rather, the feeling was of being spiritually alive—intensely so. This was not "aliveness" as the result of something the Spirit had done to me or for me. I felt alive as Spirit—as a spiritual creature—just as I am, and as we all are. I shouldn't neglect to say that the sensation also had a distinctly sexual feel, in the sense of the beauty and creativity of life flowing through me. I wouldn't say that it was erotic, at least as "erotic" is usually understood in Western culture—although I would have told you if it was. Never would I have dreamed

that standing in the middle of twenty thousand or more swarming honeybees would be such "an experience," or that it would
be so holy.

A few more minutes passed, and my mind began to form words
again. My first thoughts involved me, but they weren't self-centered
or self-absorbed. Genuine awe does that: It throws us back on
ourselves, but in a clearer light. We see ourselves more objectively. This is how I understand it: When the soul is filled with
awe; that is, when we stand in the presence of a power greater
than ourselves, the experience transforms how we perceive God,
the world, *and* ourselves. To a small degree, we glimpse what it
means to be "transfigured." In other words, I understood that
my relationship with my honeybees has a quality that I can only
describe as love. When I say "my bees," I don't mean that they are
"mine," in the literal sense of the word. What I mean is that I care
for my bees and about them in a loving way. Maybe I've always
known that; but in those few minutes, I really knew it. And I'm
not saying that love is the reason they've never stung me, or that
my love for them is the same kind of love I have for people, and
I certainly wouldn't say that my bees have anything like love for
me. What I do know is that I'm not afraid of them, and they're
not afraid of me. They know me, and I know them.

My second thought amounted to a simple rule: "Do nothing
to disturb them." You might think this was a response to some
hidden fear on my part, but it wasn't. I wasn't afraid *for myself*,
for my survival, or anything like that; I was afraid that I might
disturb *them*. I knew, very clearly, that I was standing in sacred
space, and that it was theirs—not mine. They created it. There
are many kinds of spiritual awe, and I suspect they all create the
same instinctive response in our souls: *Be careful, be respectful,
because this is sacred ground*. To disturb them in any way would
have been morally and spiritually wrong. It would have been an

act of trespass. Read the sacred texts in any spiritual tradition, and you'll find the same meaning.

Later, I understood that the whole colony was reproducing. It was dividing into two, forming a second colony from the first, which is a sign of very healthy bees. In a matter of hours, the new colony would find its home in an old hollow tree somewhere nearby; and within a few weeks, the old colony would create a new queen. That's how I would describe it from the outside. But the awe I felt went much deeper. A power immensely greater than me rose up from within their sacred space *and* from within mine— that is, within my soul. They allowed me to enter into their soul; and by doing so, I felt more connected to my own. This was their gift. All our spiritual instincts are gifts of God, but we receive them from each other—even from some very small friends that we might consider to be enemies, at least until we get to know them enough to realize that they are "friends."

I wouldn't dream of saying that every worry about being stung by honeybees is entirely baseless, especially if you're allergic; but that's very different from letting fear gain the upper hand in life, which it will do given half a chance. Besides that, our lives ride on an upward curve of fear these days. It's worth remembering that not very long ago people experienced not fear, but spiritual awe in something as small and unassuming as a simple honeybee. I've seen Renaissance paintings that depict Jesus in the proximity of a beehive. The ancient Greek oracles at Delphi venerated the honeybee as a vehicle of prophecy. In some Himalayan monastic traditions, a less known mantra is described as a "buzzing" sound similar to the one that a honeybee makes. These are only a few examples from an amazingly long list of homing signals. They're all around us, every day, in every part of life. We know that we've found them when we feel humble, loving, and joyful all at the same time. We know them too in people who aren't afraid to be who they are. We hear their Spirit calling ours, because they call out love from within us. None of these homing signals have any relation to fear, except that they help us to move through it. They help us to find our true selves and our friends—and that, by the way, includes God.

Setting aside politics and religion for the moment, I'll ask a simple question: Have you ever witnessed someone trying to "put the fear of God" into someone else? And have you ever thought about what's really going on? For me personally, it's heart-wrenching, if not heartbreaking, to watch; and for those young and impressionable souls who are usually on the receiving end, it can be a delicate moment with serious consequences. I realize that they sometimes need it, and that on rare occasions it sometimes works, or seems to work—for a while. Whatever the case may be, we're entering into the soul space of another person, and walking on very sacred, if not shaky, ground where careful steps are absolutely required. Awe should take priority over fear. It's definitely not the time to substitute fear for awe, or to confuse the two.

The way I was raised, we didn't "put much trust" in people who "put the fear of God" in others, so I never have. I can't honestly recall that anyone ever explicitly told me, "Don't trust people who make you afraid," but that is the lesson I learned. What would have been said, out loud, was the positive side of the same teaching: "You can trust loving people." Or today, "She's awesome" or "He's awesome." Either way, the underlying assumption is that "fearful" usually means "fear-ridden," which often is, in practice, the exact opposite of loving. Lessons like that weren't given in the form of gossipy opinions about other people. Rather, I was being taught a basic survival skill: how to protect myself from fear and how to avoid instilling it in others.

None of this should suggest that I've never wanted to put the fear of God into someone else. I don't actually have a list— a "people who need the fear of God put into them list"—but, like many of my otherwise God-fearing friends, I keep one somewhere slightly below my conscious awareness. Based on what I've observed in others and in myself, young people, teenagers, often go at the very top. I hate to say that this is understandable, but it is; and that's one of the many reasons that relationships within the family are so sacred. Parents want to protect their children from the trouble, if not actual harm, that they're likely to find unintentionally, and to stir up all by themselves. That's the reasonable way to put it. In practice, the desire of parents to protect them is the primal instinct of fear combined with the spiritual instinct of love. Parents love their children, *and* they're afraid for them. In this day and age, with drug dealers on so many street corners and policemen on school grounds, who wouldn't be afraid?

Yet we have to be fair about this. I know, from my experience as a priest, that some parents need protecting just as much as their children, and the children are all too aware of it. Because children are unusually observant of and sensitive to the emotions of others, they readily take on a caregiving role to protect their own parents. Some become highly skilled caregivers. The implication is that the very people (adults) who are the most likely to mete out "the fear of God" to others (and who are convinced that they know what it means) are the ones who need it the most.

That's why it's rarely advisable to try to put the fear of God into children very often, despite its obvious appeal. More positive examples of one's own thoughtful, responsible, respectful behavior usually get the job done much more effectively. If we think of awe as the carrot and instilling "the fear of God" as the stick, then a measured combination of the two, heavily weighted on the carrot side, is the way to go. We can't forget that when children (and adults) are given a steady diet of fear, even when it's well-intended (following the assumption that more is better), then they learn to live under a constant state of threat, which is a tactic more common to bullying—and terrorism. Gradually they become bullies, and possibly worse, believing that they too can "put the fear of God" into anyone they see fit, anytime they wish. In other words, they transform into the very people we hoped they wouldn't become. That's why we all need to take children off the fear of God list, or to put them near the bottom. They don't deserve it, even when their behavior seems to justify it; it doesn't work very well; and it's way too hypocritical.

Having said that, I can't let go of my list, not completely. As much as I might try, I can't wish away the fact that "some people" really do need "the fear of God put into them," including me sometimes—a priest, of all people. Nor can I forget, or should I forget, the ugliness that we're capable of pouring on ourselves and each other in the name of God and righteousness—in the name of protecting loved ones and making the world a better place! I know this as well as anyone, if not better.

Yet I still know, clear as day, the people that I want to put on my list. Let's begin with an extreme situation that I hope against hope you've never known. Imagine that some murderous maniacs have killed people you know. You want the criminals behind bars and the world to know that some crimes are paid for with a dear price. You can't take the law into your own hands, but you can expect the law to do something to stop the horror. In situations like this, the stick will play a much larger role than the carrot, much larger than any reasonable person would like—at least until we take the high road by putting our spiritual instincts at the very top of our priority list.

Most everyone I know would like to believe that we've cultivated our spiritual instincts already, but it would be way too hypocritical to make such a claim. We haven't cultivated those instincts anywhere near enough. We would like to believe that anyway, because we know that Jesus was a carrot (awe), rather than stick (fear), kind of person. By telling us to love even our enemies, he's telling us what works in the real world and where our efforts should go. Sometimes, I still find his teaching hard to swallow, but I'm not so afraid that I would dismiss his teaching and then rationalize my fear as a moral virtue.

In actual practice, my list of "fear of God" recipients sounds much more familiar: drunk drivers, domestic abusers, and polluters. In all three cases, they give themselves the right to do exactly as they please, without having the slightest respect or regard for any part of God's creation—people and the environment. They feel entitled to strike fear (in some cases, they actually believe it's the "fear of God") into anyone they see fit, but *never themselves*. Therein lies the core of the problem. While I would not want to say that abusive people live in exactly the same "world" as the respectful majority, it's still true that most everyone believes that some category of *other people* needs the fear of God put into them. It's always "them," but never "us" or "me." That is the exact opposite of anything even remotely related to awe.

But even then, there are times when it would be completely irresponsible not to intervene with "the fear of God" in full force. To do nothing would amount to complicity, which makes some version of "the fear of God" a moral imperative. This is when "the fear of God problem" gets really peculiar, and sometimes mystical, in an uncanny way.

I'll give an example. Men who abuse their wives and children are terribly wrong in what they do; yet they feel justified and righteous in the moment of delivering their assaults. I may feel even more justified and righteous than they do when I tell them what I think. Maybe my actions help. I'm not sure, but I do it anyway.

I'm absolutely right to intervene, and I will again. Yet eventually I discover the truth of the old saying—"What goes around comes around." Seemingly out of the blue, another very different and totally unexpected situation arises in my own life. I find myself perhaps being right (and perhaps wrong) about one thing or another, but definitely wrong in the way I pursue it—wrong in my understanding of how to express my outrage at someone's outrageous behavior. The point: We all want to put the fear of God in someone else, but none of us really can. Not really. Why? The reason is this: That job belongs to God, and God works with awe and love, rather than fear and threats.

At the very same time, the psalmist who wrote the words *"The fear of the Lord is the beginning of wisdom"* is absolutely right. This is a deservedly famous teaching, but it requires careful thought. It does not suggest that we are wise to be afraid, or that any or every fear is good, or that God is a threat. It means that God—a power infinitely greater than ourselves—is real, and that we must face the consequences of our actions. Only by looking honestly at ourselves and letting the truth about our lives change our hearts, can we receive the forgiveness that we desperately need, but generally deny to ourselves and others. Apparently, we think it's better to hold everyone (ourselves and others) hostage emotionally, than it is to forgive—which is yet another strategy for "putting the fear of God" into someone else, but not in ourselves.

Let us not forget that miracles do happen. They happen when we let the Spirit break through our awareness enough that we can see the darkness within ourselves and move through it. As a rule we're afraid to see that darkness. It's no wonder that it makes us afraid: That's the part of our souls that's crying out for redemption. Yet read spiritual traditions closely and you'll see that perceiving the darkness within our own selves is an integral part of self-knowledge. A loving God will help us face this darkness, and then move closer to the light beyond it. This is why God—a loving, miraculous God—evokes awe, rather than fear. And that's why awe, rather than fear, is our homing signal.

Now that I've shared some quasi-confessional material on what I call "the fear of God," I'll bare my soul a bit more by putting religion and politics back on the table. To be blunt, I'm talking about snakes—all kinds of snakes, both real snakes and mythological snakes (which are also "real" in the spiritual sense of the word). Few creatures evoke more fear and fascination than snakes, and a book on fear would be incomplete without a respectable dose of snake lore. But the emphasis here, as you might expect, will be weighted toward the snaky side of human lore, where "snake oil" and "snakes in the grass" exist in great abundance and "the fear of God problem" gets really murky—and even more significant.

Snakes, both real and mythological, deserve a better hearing than they usually receive. Knowing what I know now, I have to believe that the attributes and feelings that we normally give to snakes would be more appropriately assigned to people. I'll do my best to rectify this injustice in due course by telling a story of where and how I encountered the sacred, mythological serpent, which should prove my point. I'm well aware that what I just said goes well beyond the usual meaning of "peculiar," so I have to ask for your trust again. This is not a bad thing to ask—after all, moving through fear requires trust. First, I'll explain what the "mythological serpent" means. If you don't know this already, sacred stories and myths, like "the Garden of Eden," relate to the real world much more than we might assume. After that, I'll share a real-life story that ties it all together.

There's one more thing that I should tell you about the story:

It happened in church—peculiar, yes; but not surprising. In point of fact, the church is the perfect place, as this particular kind of snake is truly sacred. Although I've experienced the "fear of God problem" in many circumstances, this one event from my childhood carried me into the depth of fear and awe—which is why I keep it close to my heart. I've told part of this story in another book, but here I spell out what happened more completely. Like I said and as you'll momentarily see, it turns out that snakes are seriously misunderstood through no real fault of their own; as for people, that's a more nuanced story.

The truth about actual snakes is that they have many redeeming qualities, even if you can't stand the sight of them. They're basically shy creatures; they don't want to be seen or bothered; and they rarely strike, unless they're provoked. In fact, they will do their best to avoid you, which means they have at least one more or less "ordinary" characteristic in common with people. No, I can think of another: The only reason that we catch even a glimpse of them is that, like us, they love to warm themselves in the sun.

Because I often walk along riverbeds and rocky mountain paths, I see more than my share of snakes. Now and again, I come close to stepping on one. I see them; I either freeze in my tracks or jump out of the way; and then I laugh. My reaction is essentially the same every time this happens. Instinctively, my primal fear response jumps into high gear, despite the fact that I'm not particularly afraid of snakes. I'm bringing up this otherwise small detail because nearly every spiritual tradition draws upon snake symbolism to explain any number of truths about life, including our primal fear and *why* we must cultivate all our spiritual instincts in order to move through it. I'll explain that.

Consider the serpent that appears in the opening chapters of the Book of Genesis with the Garden of Eden and its sacred tree.

This is a great example, despite its terribly misogynist implications with regard to Eve. Stories like this should be read carefully with an active imagination and an open heart. Otherwise, as has happened in the past and still happens today, we'll continue to cast blame for human sins, shortcomings, misfortunes, and fear onto women, Jews, people with dark complexions, and God knows who else. Or we'll act as if the serpent is, quite literally, "the devil" or Satan and leave it at that. As a rule, we read the story too literally, putting it in the service of prejudice and fear, which means that we don't take it seriously enough. The whole subject takes us into deep, unfamiliar realms of the human soul, where our fear is rooted, while revealing the extraordinarily peculiar nature of the "ordinary" in human life. The fact of the matter is that we experience the impact of the sacred serpent in our lives every day without realizing its significance. This, of course, is the reason why the story is so important.

Need I say that no one likes to think that the serpent actually lives within us—not in "my heart" and "my soul." Or, "maybe in my heart sometimes, but not in my soul." That's what we tell ourselves. But this is precisely the essential, never-to-be-forgotten message of the story, which should make the question of how to recognize it within ourselves a matter of utmost interest, to say the very least. It should go without saying that the mythological serpent is not a real snake. In fact, it's a sacred symbol that points to something hugely important and deeply personal. We know what this serpent is like, if only because we experience it in every moment of our lives, in our heartbeat and breath, and especially in our emotions. Think of the raw, primordial power of life present within us, as creatures of the earth, our primal drives and instincts being its most common and pervasive manifestations. Every one of us knows what this is; we just don't put two and two together.

I realize that this can be confusing to think about, but the reason is that we confuse ourselves with our own confusing thoughts. Here are some more examples: First, it's easier to be afraid of God than to face the truth about ourselves; second, we act as if the earth was our enemy, when, in fact, the earth is the home we've been given to care for; and third, we believe that the serpent exists "out there," in "other people," and in the world generally, but not within us. In every case, it is our own deep-seated fear that confuses us. And in every case, fear is the one obstacle that prevents us from knowing who we are and becoming who we are meant to be.

Let's take this a step further by reflecting on the mythological serpent in a broader way. This snake has one quality that we should always remember: It is thoroughly transformative. According to tradition, it confers wisdom once the power of our primal instincts has been confronted, understood, and integrated into our lives in a healthy way. This, of course, depends entirely on the cultivation of our spiritual instincts—and the grace of God. In effect, the serpent within must be brought out of its hole in the earth (within our hearts and souls), where it can be taught to live in the light of day (the light of God). Or put another way, the serpent within must be raised on the cross (the tree of life), which brings its power into conscious awareness where it can be redeemed. The ego experiences the process of "raising up" as crucifixion—an event in the life of the individual on which true self-knowledge depends.

The process of raising the serpent is delicate, difficult, unavoidable, and necessary, which is the reason every tradition has some version of being lifted up, raised up, and transformed. This is a scary prospect. By its very nature, this process involves learning difficult spiritual truths on which our survival depends. Our spiritual instincts must be cultivated, and our egos strengthened in an atmosphere of respectful, wholesome living. For example, if the instinct for self-preservation and survival becomes our overriding priority in life, without due regard to the common good and respect for the integrity of others, then we will become a danger to others and to ourselves—if not worse.

Looking back now, to nearly half a century ago, I understand that the meaning of the mythological serpent has a direct bearing on my earliest memory of experiencing true spiritual awe—which, as it turns out, was tied up with my first confrontation with "the fear of God problem." The year was 1962. I was nine years old, and attending my first and only summer revival in the small country town where I was raised. I wasn't looking for trouble, much less trouble with religion and the church. I went to the revival because my grandmother loved me. She wanted me to go; so I wanted to go. More than anything else, she wanted me to be saved. I had no idea what that meant. So I went, perhaps not innocent as a dove, but as a young, impressionable child who was completely unaware of the hidden dangers on the rocky path that I had taken.

I heard a lot of things in church that day, but I took home the two most emotionally charged parts of the sermon. The first was that the world can be a dangerous, sometimes evil place; the second was that I would lose my soul in hell unless I gave my self to Jesus. I can hear some of you saying, "What's wrong with that?" That's a good question. From a certain point of view, there's nothing wrong with it, nothing whatsoever. The sermon was blunt, to be sure, and in my opinion, harsh and pessimistic about the world—not to mention the image of a punishing God that it planted in my mind. Nevertheless, it wasn't all that unusual, not as far as "fear of God" sermons go.

But what his sermon meant to me—and what it would mean to any child—was as plain as day: The words that I heard were a threat to my survival, pure and simple, and I'll tell you why. At that point in my life, I had no experience of evil or danger in the world. By any normal standard, I was an innocent and inexperienced child. I had no choice but to wonder whether the minister was talking about my friends and me. Was I one of "those people"? I wondered if I should be afraid of myself and of my friends. I wondered whether I would be counted, someday, among the damned, unless, of course, I did what I was supposed to do. This is no small matter in the mind of a small child or a grown-up: What are we, in fact, supposed to do? Who are we supposed to be? We don't always know; but often, we simply do as we're told, for better or worse. Not only that, the minister was speaking with all the trappings of authority. He was telling me that his words were God's Word, that he held the key to the prison that he had put me into, and that he was doing this for my own good.

In point of fact, the fearful tone of the sermon—which was meant to instill "the fear of God," while enticing me with "the love of God"—created a real spiritual darkness in my soul. Because of it, I lost touch, for several days, with the joy of life that every normal and happy child knows. I was truly afraid and troubled by the fear. But I did think about it—deeply. I turned it over in my mind in every conceivable way. The very idea that my friends at school may or may not be damned or saved created the dilemma in my mind that I found the hardest to swallow; and the idea of accepting that as a true picture of the world in order to save myself was something that I experienced as revolting, verging on nauseating. I really did feel sick. Were they no longer my friends? How was I supposed to relate to them—if I was saved and they were damned? In a very real and immediate way, my conscience came into conflict with my instinct for survival.

Before I finish this story, I simply want you to understand the significance of what I've described so far—my first experience of "raising the serpent." Today, long after the fact, I can tell you about it objectively; but in that moment, years ago, the situation that I faced would be either a turning point in my life or a breaking point. Quite honestly, it could have gone either way. The feeling was that my life was hanging by a thread, and that my fate would be determined by a choice between fear on the one hand, and love on the other. There was something about the situation that I instinctively regarded as spiritually real, and another part that I absolutely did not trust and couldn't trust. Now, I realize that I was following my instincts the best that I could. It turned out that my spiritual instincts were enough; yet, I couldn't have done it alone. Fortunately, I found my way through the fear, thanks to two thoughtful parents, a wise and exceedingly compassionate minister who lived nearby, the Holy Spirit, and, last but not least, the fear-ridden minister, my antagonist from the pulpit. Despite himself, he played an important role that I only understood many years later. Even "snakes in the grass" have redeeming qualities.

In a nutshell, this is what actually happened. Immediately after the fear-ridden sermon, I withdrew into myself. I was thinking over a dreadful situation that, through no fault of my own, surrounded me on all sides. This lasted for several days. My mom and dad, who knew I was upset, but without knowing why, watched patiently and asked if I wanted to talk about it. I wasn't ready to come out of my shell at that point, but their genuine love for me, combined with their desire to listen and their nonjudgmental sensitivity, was profoundly helpful. Looking back, I thank God that they never once asked if I wanted "to be saved." That question—or encouraging innuendo—would have undermined my spiritual instincts by playing into the hands of fear. I say this carefully, as there are different kinds of salvation. Some are based on fear; others invite us to move through it.

A few days later, my parents suggested that I might talk with another minister for whom they had a great deal of respect. I agreed to do this. He was a good listener too. I told him what happened, but we really didn't talk very much about the sermon or my experience in the church. Rather, he gave me some truly helpful spiritual guidance that I'll never forget. He told me *"to pray about it, and make up your own mind."* He was encouraging me to trust and to follow my spiritual instincts, which is what I had been taught at home. This simple, no-nonsense teaching, together with his and my parents' willingness to listen when they were the most afraid, gave me the courage to move through my fear.

After speaking with him, I realized that I had no choice but to return to the revival. My parents did not encourage this, but they trusted me enough to give their consent. The heart of the issue for me came down to this: Say "yes" to my fear, and either lose or save my soul; or say "no" to my fear, and lose or save my soul. The stakes were obviously high, but the issue was, in fact, fear—especially the meaning of "the fear of God."

As difficult as it was to rebel against everything I heard from the pulpit, by the grace of God I faced my fear. I know that this seems too simple to believe, but it's really true: I went back to the church on Sunday evening, the last night of the revival. I sat there quietly in the pew. The emotional atmosphere intensified through the sermon and the hymns. I gradually realized that I had already made my decision. Nothing was said out loud, but within myself, I said "no" to my fear, "yes" to my friends and God, and stood my ground. In a way, it was an issue of personal integrity, but it was also more than that. I was carving out some sacred space in a world of fear, while telling myself that "this is how I'm going to live." The outcome was immediate. In a split second, the fear was gone. I moved through my fear, and in that very moment, I experienced the light and love of God firsthand—true spiritual awe. I was free, and I knew it.

A peculiar irony in this whole sequence of events should not go unnoticed. My journey through fear and experience of true spiritual awe illustrate the ancient process of initiation practiced widely among indigenous peoples and known to all religious traditions.

The purpose of these rituals is to help people experience the Spirit as an immediate presence by going beyond the boundaries of the world that we usually know. The process requires lengthy personal preparation (e.g., studying the sacred myths that act as a guide, proper moral conduct, fasting), followed by the difficult stage of moving through all kinds of fear, including the fears that hold those boundaries in place, e.g., the fear of thinking our own thoughts. The process is completed when those who make the passage are reincorporated into the community. The role of the initiator/healer/shaman is to help the younger or inexperienced members make this sacred journey successfully, while maintaining the social, spiritual, and ecological balance on which the survival of the group depends.

Obviously, there are huge differences between traditional cultures and the circumstances of my childhood, beginning with the glaring fact that I was neither raised by nor was I living in an indigenous community, and ending with the salvation that I found outside the expectations and boundaries of that particular church. Yet, similarities in the process that unfolded cannot be emphasized enough. First, the story that I've shared is not really about me. Rather, it's about fear, the role it plays in our lives, and the power found in our spiritual instincts to help us move through it. This is a crucial point: Anything truly helpful that we learn about fear involves not only our personalities, but also our spiritual lives. What I did, as a child, is something any child can do, with the assistance of parents and friends who cultivate her or his spiritual instincts. An indispensable part of that process is simply to discern the difference between spiritual awe and primal fear. Better yet, the goal is to resist any temptation to be awestruck by fear.

Another crucial ingredient in the movement through fear involves the role of spiritual leadership. In the process that I just described, the role of the leader was transferred from one person to another. The first was the fear-ridden minister, who played the role of the tempting serpent: the one who torments and makes us think that there's no hope, unless we give our allegiance to him (or her). For all practical purposes, he called out the serpent within me, and he did it well. He certainly would not have understood his role in this way, but that is what happened. The second leadership role was filled by the kind, compassionate minister who reinforced what I had been taught by my parents, strengthened my spiritual instincts, and encouraged me to call upon the Spirit's help. The difference between the two ministers is the difference between primal fear and spiritual awe.

It's interesting that no one, including my parents, actually said, "there's nothing to be afraid of," and in those days, it wouldn't have occurred to anyone to put me on anxiety-reducing medication. Even my private conversation with the second minister would not have been seen as "counseling." The point is that no one was trying to play down the nature of the fear that I was experiencing. This is important because sacred myths and rituals have their scary parts. They're supposed to have them. Life can be scary, and it would be wrong to write it out of tradition and our lives simply because we're afraid or we don't like the way it sounds. Fear is part of life, but that is not to say that our lives should be ruled by it. The irony is that I would not have moved through my fear unless the serpent had been raised.

These four simple words—"the fear of God"—have created such a wariness about God and religion that huge numbers of people have abandoned the church because of it. Who can blame them? It's not the words alone that create the problem. The machinery of fear in politics and religion—through outright coercion and more subtle forms of emotional manipulation—distorts the meaning of the spiritual path and lures us into a different kind

of mythology, one that confuses "fear" with "awe," while plant-
ing a dividing chasm in our minds between "us" and "them."

I don't want you to think that I'm talking *only* about fundamentalist Christianity or any other fundamentalist religion. To
make that assumption is to fall into another kind of trap based
on the stereotypes that we all carry in our heads. Our confusion
about fear and awe in religion is so interwoven with issues of fear
and freedom in economics and politics that they've become virtually indistinguishable. They blend together as one powerful force
of fear that we absorb in our nervous systems and then re-create in
our homes, business offices, places of worship, and playgrounds. It
feeds on our souls and dictates how we live. This fear is powerful,
but not as powerful as our spiritual instincts. Even the instincts
of a mere child are more powerful. What I learned, beginning in
my childhood, is that we all must work our way through that fear
before more damage is done.

The story that I just told did not end there, not by a long shot.
It set the stage for my eventual vocations in life, first in cultural anthropology, and then the Episcopal Church. The issue for
me was never God. I might not have trusted every church that I
entered in my younger days—I still don't—but that didn't matter very much. I didn't take it personally. I understood that God
is real when I moved through my fear of God. And it was from
that day forward that I became a spiritual seeker in a world that
looked more peculiar by the day. That's what I want to tell you
about now.

On my twelfth birthday, my grandmother gave me a bible.
Maybe it wasn't the kind of gift that a boy of that age would necessarily want, but I was thrilled. I loved the pictures: the images
of Moses and Jesus, the photographs and maps of the Holy Land.

I memorized the place names and imagined what it was like to live there. In those days, my world in the foothills of the Blue Ridge Mountains extended directly into Galilee. I knew something about Israel, Palestine, Egypt, Sinai, Jerusalem, Bethlehem, and Corinth years before I knew the states in the United States or the capital of my own state.

In my early teenage years, I did my best to figure out the world around me. My parents encouraged me to follow my instincts and to discover life in my own way, which I was quite happy to do. In practice, this meant finding out what was expected of me, and what I expected from the world. In other words, I was testing the boundaries at the same time that I was testing myself and the world was testing me. One of those tests took place in the very last place that I would have expected in those days: a series of summer revivals on our high school football field. No one forced me to go. I did this entirely on my own. My friends thought it was a good place to meet girls. For me, this was only one part of the story. The revivals gave me the opportunity to explore "the fear of God problem" within myself and to better understand the nature of the community that I felt a part of and distanced from at the same time.

An overriding question in my life was whether I was the only one who experienced God in the way that I did. Later, I would discover that I wasn't alone; then, I wasn't so sure. I steadfastly refused to divide up the world into "us" versus "them," the sinners and the saved. For that reason, I sometimes considered the possibility that something might have been wrong with me—that my experience of God was weird, or wrong, or just too peculiar. What I really wanted was to understand who I was becoming as a person, and what it meant. The significance of this question had been looming large in my mind for several years, which made me afraid when I thought about it. Yet the same uneasy fear propelled me to pursue my questions with determination. I made a vow, within myself, to never give in to the power of fear, especially when and where God was concerned. What I needed was a place to test myself, and those summer revivals fit the bill perfectly. My desire to find some answers strengthened my spiritual instincts in ways that I couldn't have appreciated at the time—precisely because exploring their meaning was my way of cultivating them.

I wouldn't have put it that way back then, not in so many words. My thoughts were much more immediate. For example, I loved God and I loved sports. At Friday-night football games, people yelled and cheered. One team won; the other team lost. At the revivals, people sang, cried, and then walked to the front of the stadium to declare themselves in God's favor. God's team won. The devil's team lost. What bothered me the most, of course, was the fear, just as it had years before, plus the realization that what I experienced in church also seemed to happen on the football field—whether the event was "religious" or "sports." In other words, the "fear of God" wasn't only about religion and the church. It involved a whole way of life. The issue for me personally wasn't God, or whether God is real. I believed in God. I just didn't believe that God wanted me to be afraid. I already knew, firsthand, the answer to that question. What bothered me was this: Was I the only one who noticed the ambiguity?

It was during those years that the pieces began to fall into place—not all of them, but enough. I attribute this simply to being present at the revivals; to letting the fear I felt from so many people wash over me; and then trying to appreciate their point of view. Many of the people who attended the football field revivals were my friends and neighbors—which made me feel peculiar. I wondered what my motives really were—what was I *really* doing? Yet the process of working through my own feelings and reactions was very instructive. Instinctively, I believed that it would be disingenuous and morally wrong to attend the revivals in order to form judgments about others.

I was also well aware of the deep need that we all have for healing, individually and socially. I wasn't there to form opinions about them or to make judgments. To make other people "objects" in our minds is not only unfair to them, but it's also unfair to us. It creates a distorted, condescending version of the world that we constantly project onto others, and that creates the very conditions that cultivate a subtle form of fear within us, rather than awe. People are not objects. We are people, living souls—every one of us. To make people, ourselves included, into objects in our minds is to become a threatening presence in the world. That's how we generate fear and use it to manipulate others for our own selfish purposes. We may deny it, or fail to recognize it, but we're still doing it.

I make no claim to having the last word on any particular form of worship or any form of religion; but gradually, that summer, I began to understand at least something about my experience. I learned that we're not meant to know or understand all the ways that God works in our lives. God really does work in mysterious ways. By drawing out the fear that plagues us, naming it, and giving us a way to make sense of it, revivals provide real healing, inner peace, a sense of security, and direction in life—all of which are very easy to lose, especially in stressful times. They allow us to move through some of our fear, to find a renewed sense of belonging with others, and to carve out a space in our lives for God. We discover that we're not alone. This is no small matter, and its value cannot be underestimated. The lives of individuals and of whole families are preserved because of it.

Yet the problem of fear remains as a question and as an obstacle that should not be ignored. In those revivals, our fear was not so much "moved through," but "shifted" from one part of our personal lives onto the backs of others who aren't "like us," whatever that might mean. The serpent has been raised—which is good—but only partway. God "wins," but fear wins too. This creates a cycle of fear. Freedom and fear reach a temporary standoff that's repeated again and again—whenever doubt, fear, a guilty conscience, or the realities of the world return, as they inevitably do. This standoff should not be seen as an impasse, an unsolvable problem, or a symbol of "the real world." Rather, it's a door to walk through. The spiritual journey has not been completed when we reach it. The journey has only begun.

That's when I began to appreciate the depth and subtlety of the seemingly ordinary fears that we all face and the huge obstacle that they can be. These are the hardly noticeable, partly manageable, but tenacious fears that pull nearly all our strings: the fear of thinking our own thoughts, the fear of being excluded, of rejection, of guilt and shame, and the fear of not having enough, or losing what we have. Because these are the fears that occupy most of our life energy, they're the ones we should be concerned about the most.

It was considerably later in life that I really heard the biblical passage "The love of God casts out fear." You would think that I would have noticed it sooner, given the circumstances, but I didn't. Maybe it was too simple, or simply too obvious. *The love of God casts out every fear, including our mistaken ideas about "the fear of God," but it doesn't cast out awe.* That's how we know that awe is not a variety of fear, and it's why we should never let ourselves be in awe of fear. Love casts out all fear, including the very bad habit of making others the object—that is to say, the target—of our fear.

To move through our fear, we have to ask whether our primal instinct (self-preservation and survival) has a stronger grip on our minds than the instinct for true spiritual awe. Our answer will almost certainly be yes, but this will be true only in the sense that *we believe* that its grip is stronger. We must be vigilant about what we really believe and which of these two instincts we're actually cultivating, especially through our religious beliefs. Once fear gains the upper hand, it always requires new objects of fear to feed upon, which creates a cycle of fear that can be very difficult to break. Rather than becoming free from the fear that rules our lives, we willingly participate in one kind of fear-ridden manipulation after another—while telling ourselves that we're paying the price of freedom. Or do we mean "salvation"? Or both? Or neither? Until we cultivate our spiritual instincts enough to discern the difference between awe and fear, we probably won't know what we mean.

So how can we break the cycle of fear? The ancient answer is the one that still makes all the difference: Our responsibility and our birthright is to *raise the serpent within us* on the tree of life. Yes, Jesus died on the cross for our sins, and he was raised up. He moved through his fear. It's our fear that remains. And let me repeat: God is not a threat. God is love. If the God you have in your heart and mind is a threat to your survival or to anyone else's survival, then it's not God, but something else—most likely, some confusion between awe and fear.

This is yet another reason why faith and allegiance blend together so seamlessly in our day and age, and why fear is conflated with awe. We cultivate our spiritual instincts partway, and then use them for reasons that are sometimes good and other times murky. For example, the United States is based constitutionally on the separation of Church and State, yet our major institutions—political, religious, and economic—form powerful interlocking relationships around which our nation is organized. This is not necessarily a bad thing, not in itself, not when the higher purpose we pursue serves the common good of all and the rights of every individual, including people of all faiths or of no religious faith. It can give religious institutions a high degree of secular influence that its membership may not only want, but also has the right to exercise.

But influence comes with a tremendous cost: Its spiritual purpose is overwhelmed and lost in conflicting loyalties and allegiances, too often rooted in fear, that have very little if any relation to the spiritual path that religion is meant to demonstrate. For example, one vital purpose of religion is to teach and to exemplify caring for the earth as our moral responsibility and birthright. The environmental crisis is real. We should know by now that taking this crisis seriously creates conflict with social, economic, and religious institutions that use the machinery of fear to keep things the way they are now. That kind of fear is harmful, and we must move through it if we have any real hope of surviving—or thriving.

Everything depends on the cultivation and careful use of all our spiritual instincts. Awe, rather than fear, is our homing signal. For now, rather than cultivate our instinct for awe, we continue to indulge our fear in the name of God, which feeds our frightened egos, empties our pocketbooks, and threatens our survival. If we continue along this path, it will be our freedom that we're most likely to lose, if not our lives.

That's only one of the reasons that I'm in awe of my honeybees. If they sting me now and again, then I still won't be afraid of them. It only means that I've done something wrong, and I have a lesson to learn. They remind me that it's God that matters most, and next to that, caring for what we've been given, nurturing what gives us life, and discovering what gives us purpose in life. That purpose—the knowledge of who we are meant to be—lies on the other side of fear.

A Spiritual Practice in Awe

Imagine your worst fear. It could be anything. Whatever comes to mind, know that this practice is not a test. I'm not asking you to deliberate or to make anything like a list of your worst fears, even in your mind. In fact, it would be best not to deliberate at all. Any fear that pops into your mind first will suit our purposes perfectly well.

Having done that, I actually do want you to reflect for a while. Reflect long enough to realize what your hidden feelings and assumptions about this fear actually are. For example, you might believe that there's nothing you can do about this fear, or that you don't expect it to go away anytime soon. You might tell yourself that your fear will be with you tomorrow, and the day after that, into infinity—that it will always be a part of your life. You don't like it—and you might not realize just how much you don't like it—but you gradually assume that this is the way things are and the way the world works. We all make those kinds of assumptions about our worst fear, without appreciating the impact that they have on our lives.

The fact is that nothing could be further from the truth. This example may seem much bigger than your life and mine, but the Berlin Wall, one of the great symbols of fear in our time, did, in fact, come down. At the time, everyone was surprised and joyful, even as they wondered how it could have happened. No one thought it was possible. Yet it did happen.

Our feelings and assumptions about our fears are usually exaggerated, distorted versions of the truth, or they're just plain wrong. Even our very worst fear can disappear entirely of its own accord, or shrivel into something so small that it no longer matters. This might happen slowly over a period of many years, rather than overnight, but we should expect it to happen. A time might come when even our very worst fear is a distant memory of the way things were, rather than the way things are. This is not a fantasy. This is a realistic view of fear.

It happens not because our fear has moved, but because we have moved. It happens because we change, and that changes our relationship to fear.

Now, my suggestion is to follow the example of some friends who know how to put their fear in perspective by cultivating the instinct for awe. One friend who lives not far down the road from me doesn't like fear any more than I do. She knows how easy it is to get trapped in it. By cultivating her instinct for awe, she's become very good at avoiding the trap. In the warm summer months, she walks into an open field near her house to watch the fireflies danc-ing in the sky. It's such a simple thing to do, but it works. She can't tell you precisely why it works, nor can she tell you why the fireflies impress her so deeply. But her soul knows why, and she knows that her soul knows. A little awe can go a long way in the movement through fear, and a little awe every day works wonders—literally.

She wouldn't describe what she does as a spiritual practice— much less a "discipline"—but that's exactly what it is. In fact, she wouldn't talk about it very much at all. She simply follows her instinct for awe and receives the joy that she knows how to find. By doing so, she gives herself the opportunity to live beyond the reach of any anxiety or fear that lurks in the background of her life. I have heard her say that she's afraid the fireflies might disappear someday. Yet this fear doesn't prevent her from walking under the open sky to watch the light show at dusk. Instead, it gives her all the more reason to be there.

I have other friends who make watching the sunrise or sun-set their spiritual practice. Here again, this is the simplest thing in the world to do, so simple that we wouldn't believe it would help with our "worst fears." Nevertheless, it helps more than we would believe. Why? It helps because they do their practice routinely, and they've learned to ignore what their fear would tell them. They've learned that the power of fear is not as great as it seems to be. They've learned that it is fear itself, rather than their spiritual instincts, that would look upon these seemingly small practices as silly and frivolous, that is to say, a waste of time.

The best way to cultivate your instinct for awe is simply to give yourself a few minutes every day in the great outdoors. That is what I encourage you to do. Take a walk through a park or down a winding road. Listen to the sounds. Get up early with the sunrise, or take some time after dinner to end the day at sunset. Let the larger Mystery that surrounds us on every side turn your attention from the worries and fears, whatever they are and however fearful they may be. Like my firefly watcher, don't try to explain what you're doing or why you're doing it. Don't even think about it very much. You will be following an ancient thread to the sacred that passes through your soul.

After some time has passed, notice what has happened to the fear that you've named—your worst fear. Soon you will very likely find—in its place—the presence of a creative, deeply spiritual power that's greater than you are, but within you too. When you take a step, it will still be there; and it will be in the next step and the one after that. Again, don't try to figure this out or to explain it away. Gradually, your spiritual instincts will help you understand what this spiritual power is. Just trust your instincts and do the practice. A little awe every day will gradually convince you that the power of your spiritual instincts is greater than the power of your fear—even your worst fear.

4.

LOVE: THE RIVER OF LIFE

> You have heard that it was said, "You shall love your
> neighbor and hate your enemy." But I say to you, Love
> your enemies and pray for those who persecute you.
>
> —The Gospel According to Matthew, 5:43

> God's love has been poured into our hearts through the
> Holy Spirit that has been given to us.
>
> —Saint Paul's Letter to the Romans, 5:5

Nothing makes the world unravel more quickly than unbridled fear, and nothing but love has the power to create a world that we would want to call our own. The goodness that we see in each other testifies to the triumph of love over the power of fear. Everything else is waiting to be liberated. Love is the greatest of all gifts; love lives at the very heart of God; but in our hearts, somewhere, love is also a question. Will it be fear and the temptations of fear that determine who we are, how we live, and what the fate of the world will be? Or will it be love?

You would think that jumping in the great river of life would be easy. It's not so easy. Most everyone believes in love, but not always enough to trust it or live by it. I can understand that. We all can. Our wariness about life can make love not an answer to our fear, but another reason to be afraid. "Be practical." "Take off those rose-colored glasses." That's what the cautious and sometimes cynical part of our mind says. "Love is an unreliable, starry-eyed delusion; it distorts the way things really are; and if we're crazy enough to believe what we think we see, then we deserve what's coming to us."

Alongside our lack of trust, the still small voice within has its own mind, and it cannot be silenced so easily. That voice reminds us that, despite all evidence to the contrary, love will have the last word. That voice tells us that the old saying is true: Love really does "make the world go round"—that is to say, "the real world."

Depending on the circumstances, warnings about "rose-colored glasses" and "starry-eyed delusions" should be heeded, but the lesson is not that love is unworthy of trust. Rather, the lesson is that the instinct for love must be cultivated. The same can be said for awe and all our spiritual instincts. Some of our fear is justified, and to ignore it would be reckless, morally irresponsible, and devoid of love. Yet acquiescence to a life ruled by fear will do everything to deny what matters the most. It will deny the very existence of the greatest power of all—which is love—just as we convince ourselves that the many opportunities we have to move through our fear are nothing but wishful thinking.

So what exactly is love? We can't pin it down any more than we can control it, nor should we want to. Unlike fear, love really does have a life of its own. Our spiritually attuned ancestors said that "God is love." This is the same all-knowing, all-powerful

God *who gave us the freedom to make our own choices and shape our own lives, and who sent emissaries, prophets, and Jesus himself to help us find our way. Love moves of its own accord, and it's powerful enough to cleanse our hearts of the fear that makes us a danger to ourselves.*

The river of life flows though all our "loves," however misunderstood and distorted they may sometimes be. It flows from a never-ending well, always cleansing and giving life. We know it primarily as feeling. Love is the deepest, most romantic, and sacred feeling that we have for each other, but it is more than that. We sense love, unexplainably, in the pain of our incompleteness and in our becoming, which makes us loving and afraid at the same time. We know it in helping others with no expectation of reward or return. We begin to understand it, even a little, when we begin to realize that the world needs not love in the abstract, but real love—your love and mine. Love wakes us up, calls us out, and carries us forward in expectation of what might be. Love is the Holy Mystery that life is and that we are. "God" really is "love."

Look at the world through the eyes of love, and you'll see a place where love is tested. It is in the nature of love to be tested. This is the way things are, which makes it a waste of precious time to feel bitter about love's failures and faults or to believe that we've been singled out unjustly. Perhaps the greatest of all tests is found in our willingness to express love through forgiveness. Forgiveness is how the river of life heals and transforms our lives when we're held hostage to fear. Love grows into forgiveness one person at a time. It can be painful to grow in this way, but that is how love is cultivated in our souls.

No one is exempt, and no one is excluded or left out from the gift of love, the tests of love, and the river that is love. That's why we must make every effort to cultivate love in every circumstance, even when we think that love is not an issue. One way or another, love is always the issue. And we should never take it upon ourselves to put our love or another person's love to the test, or to believe we can—as if we can orchestrate the mind of God or have the wisdom to judge another person's heart. Life itself provides all the testing that anyone will ever need. We're tested not just once, but more than once, often under the worst and most fearful circumstances. We're tested until it finally dawns upon us that love carries us through every fear.

In this chapter, I've included five stories that illustrate the many ways that love can be cultivated in our lives every day. The stories begin with my grandmother's lessons in thankfulness and forgiveness, followed by some reflections on the courageous love that propels us to move through the most "ordinary" and the worst kinds of fear. The third story involves a married couple who make the mistake of testing each other's love, not from a lack of love, but because of their fear of losing it. The fourth story describes how looking back on our lives can deepen our capacity for love, especially when we're older. And the last story brings all this full circle, showing how unexpected events, over the span of a lifetime, work together in inexplicable ways to help us move through our fear.

I want to pick up that part of the story—concerning my grandmother—where I left off in the last chapter. She and I didn't live in exactly the same world through the 1960s and 1970s. We certainly didn't agree about everything in matters of religion and even less in politics; but we did agree on something basic about love. When the sun rose in the sky, we would both look up and see the light and love of God. About that, we were of one mind. After that, if we discussed it, we probably would part ways. We would debate how that one light should be understood and whether it can be found in everyone. She believed that Christians have more light than anyone else. I would not have said that.

Love was the reason that I found it so easy to forgive her. I'd better explain that. You see, I carried the memory of the revival and, of course, the fear-ridden preacher for several years. He was easy to forgive. He was consumed by his fear, and he didn't know any better. My grandmother was a different matter. She loved me, and she was family, which meant that I had to reconcile the fact that she had led me into the belly of fear. For a long time, I couldn't understand why she had let that happen or why she had encouraged it.

She wouldn't have understood why I had to forgive her, or that there was anything to forgive. We didn't discuss it, not in those terms. But I knew she was troubled, and the reason was that I had been troubled, despite the fact that it all happened a few years before. She did her best to let go of her worry, and I did my best to make sure that she didn't worry too much. Where love is concerned, people are always more important than our ideas about them.

I'm not saying that she had done anything wrong or that she was to blame. In point of fact, I wouldn't say that anyone did anything wrong or that anyone was to blame. Life is more complicated than anything that simple blaming can account for or explain—and there's nothing simple about blame. What I knew was that I had to forgive her in order to leave behind my mistrust of everything religious. Mistrust is rooted in fear, and fear is pernicious. One way or another, fear will find a way to divide both loved ones and strangers. You can count on it. Love, on the other hand, will find a way to unite—if our instinct for love has been cultivated enough. I loved my grandmother; she loved me;

God loved the both of us; and I knew that unless I forgave her, fear would gain power over the direction of my life. It would control my life and shape my relationship with someone I loved very much. I couldn't let that happen.

It's strange how those people who we hold accountable for our fear (even though we know better) can be the very same people who cultivate the spiritual instincts that help us move through it. This is one of those peculiar and sometimes troubling facts of life that's better not forgotten, and it's why I remember three well-chosen words that she frequently said: "Count your blessings." She never said "Count your blessings" with the harsh tone of discipline, reprimand, or punishment. Her faith was filled with the fear of God, but her voice was always gentle and meek. Yet I always knew that her words were a warning when she spoke them, which was exactly what she intended.

My recollection is that she told me to count my blessings whenever I complained about one thing or another—usually about other people. I wasn't forced to sit down and hear what she had to say. She didn't say, or have to say, "Jeff, because I love you, I have to tell you this." Love wasn't the carrot before the stick, small as the stick was. I listened because the one taken-for-granted assumption that my family shared was that love was the very nature of the world we lived in. For us, love was the real world. Different people might express it or share it in very different ways, but love was the essential ingredient. Anything else was a lesser, distorted version of "the real." There were no hidden agendas, no waiting for the other shoe to drop. Life was pretty much just as it seemed to be.

That's another reason why I was so deeply affected and confused by that first revival. There, I heard an entirely foreign story about God and the real world. I heard that God was a threatening figure waiting, for a good reason, to strike me down. If my grandmother really believed that, in her soul, which I doubt, then she would have been wrong. She knew, better than most, that God is love, and that was precisely the reason that I can remember "count your blessings" to this very day. Of course, she said that at the drop of a hat. It was her favorite expression. She probably said it to herself when there was no one around to hear. If that was true—and I would bet that it was—then she would have been cultivating the instinct for love within herself.

It was much later in life that I realized how deeply rooted this simple and easily dismissed saying is in the world's great spiritual teachings. I'm thinking of "thankfulness." But that's not how we usually interpret the saying these days. We take it too literally. "Count" means something like "counting up the things" we have, as if we had a ledger sheet in hand, giving thanks to God for all the stuff. We're not thinking of the basic necessities of life. We're probably not giving thanks for "the food we are about to receive" at mealtime, good health, and the well-being of our families and friends. It's not that we're really ungrateful people. We're just overloaded with stuff, which is a sure sign of some deeply rooted fear—perhaps the fear of losing what we have, rather than being thankful for the opportunity to give and receive, or the fear that we won't know who we are or what to do without something or someone to be afraid of. That's putting it a little strongly, but there's more truth in it than we like to admit.

The spiritual meaning of thankfulness—and the importance of "counting our blessings"—goes far beyond than that. Thankfulness is a daily spiritual practice that involves keeping our minds filled with loving-kindness, rather than fear or greed. As I said, my grandmother told *me* to count *my* blessings when she heard me make uncharitable comments about other people. The principle behind it is very much like the modern saying "You are what you eat." In effect, we become what we consume, whether those "consumables" are actual food or the fear that feeds on our souls. Unhealthy food shapes who we become, and so do unhealthy thoughts like fear. That's why harmful fear really is harmful.

Thankfulness is a strong antidote to fear, but the power of fear is tenacious and the medicine must be taken every day—every day of our lives. Think of my grandmother who, in my mind, was the world's expert on counting your blessings. As she practiced it, thankfulness was the equivalent of a serious yogic practice in mindfulness meditation and compassionate living. Jesus described this practice all the time, even when he seemed to be talking about something else. For example: "Judge not, lest you be judged." What possible connection does being judgmental have with thankfulness and fear? The answer is really easy: We judge others because we're afraid that others will judge us—so we beat them to the punch. That's just one answer, but it makes the point.

And why would we, as God-fearing Christians, go out of our way to be judgmental about others, despite the fact that we know full well what Jesus taught? That's easy too: Our primal fear is stronger than our instinct for love. You know what? Being judgmental doesn't work. It's better to take Jesus' teaching to heart, and to remember what my grandmother—and, no doubt, yours—said about counting our blessings. They knew something. It's peculiar to think of my grandmother as a practicing yogi, but in her own God-fearing way that's exactly who she was.

If we're fortunate, we know people who have gone way out of their way to cultivate good spiritual instincts in us. Their love was expressed through words, but only in part. The truth behind their words went beyond anything they could have said—as important as the words actually were. This tells me that our primary reality, which is spiritual, cannot be created, defined, or controlled by the words we use. It's easy, especially now, to turn this truth on its head, believing the opposite: that if someone says "love," then it is love. Or if someone says "fear," then there must be a reason to be afraid.

In our turned-around world, it's entirely possible to hear the word "love" all the time, while not many people actually bother to cultivate the instinct. That's a world where our blessings are literally "counted" and where our primal instincts rule our minds in the name of faith. I don't want to live in "a world" that only bears a resemblance to the one God created. I want to meet my grandmother in the real world, whether in this life or the next. I want the both of us to look into each other's eyes and to recognize each other. Just considering the unlikely possibility that this might happen makes me feel a little jittery. I know it sounds peculiar to put things that way. But is it? I don't think so.

So should "Count your blessings" be so easily dismissed as a cliché from bygone days? As the kind of thing that only grand-mothers say? I don't think so. I remember a time when a borrowed cup of flour was returned with a little extra, and a handsaw was returned cleaned and oiled. Now, I think of the mountains and rivers too. It's our responsibility to pass them on to the next gen-eration in a better condition than we found them. I wonder what they will think—the next generation. I wonder whether "count your blessings" will come to mind when they think of us, and whether they'll say that "love" was only a word we used.

When I think of them—my grandmother and the generation to come—I realize that the future is no great mystery: it will be the outcome of the blessings that we learn to count now.

I know some really great people who show me the meaning of courage all the time; yet what they do is so simple and unassum-ing that we might not recognize it as courageous. Like everyone else, they have their personal fears. Sometimes, they're really big fears; and as you might expect, they're often reluctant to say very much about them—or so it seems. They're not concealing anything, and they're not afraid to talk. They just don't identify themselves on the basis of their fears. In fact, their personal fears are not their overriding concern. The reason they want to talk with me, their priest, is not exactly because of what they're *afraid of*. Rather, they come to see me because they're *afraid for* the people they love.

That's the breathtaking part. They understand that in order to move through their own fear, whatever it might be, they must help their loved ones move through their fear. What I'm saying is that their instinct for love is stronger than the power of their worst fear. And what is their worst fear? It's that their personal fear might gain the upper hand and prevent them from following their heart, which would result in harm done to someone they love.

I'm in awe of the fact that the possibility of bad things happening to other people can make us afraid enough to take action. That's the best definition of "courage" that I know, and it describes what the hearts of these people are like.

Talking with a priest is mere preparation, and I'm more than happy to help in any way I can. The fact that they come to me for this reason makes me smile—their love draws out my love. But I smile for another reason too. It makes me think of the human-interest stories occasionally written in magazines and newspapers about our worst fears. I'll explain the connection.

Those stories cite scientific studies suggesting that our worst fears are nuclear attack and public speaking. They're meant to be objective *and* funny; that is to say, comforting. I don't want to debate the studies, but I don't believe that most people think about nuclear attack very much. Perhaps they should, but that's another matter. My guess is that when a pollster asks what our fears are, we think of things that would be scary, hypothetically, in order to give a reasonably truthful answer. The first thing that comes to mind is an image of apocalyptic disaster. I suppose that's what we see in the movies. Then, when we try to think of other fears, our thoughts turn in a more personal direction, which, among the people I know, nearly always means the fear of speaking in public.

My experience is that public speaking is, by far, the worse of the two. In my church, this is definitely true. The majority of my congregation, all people very much like you and me, will absolutely not stand up before their friends and read the appointed Bible lessons on Sunday morning. I know these people well, and I love them. I've asked them once, and that's enough. It would be cruel to ask them again, so I don't. Yet I find it very peculiar that not once in the twenty or so years that I've been a priest has anyone come to me as a result of fears about nuclear attack or public speaking. Not once! There's no secret here, at least not in connection with public speaking. They're not going to do it; I know it, and they know it. Case closed.

However, what I've just said is both true and very misleading. I've often witnessed situations where they move through their fear of public speaking, and they do this as a direct result of their *fear for* the people they love. I've seen parents work through this fear within themselves because they don't want their children to have the same fear. For example, one of the parents will quietly volunteer to read something in public or say something before a group. Their children see this courageous scene unfolding before their eyes, and they know what's going on. They realize exactly what's happening, and they know that love—real love—is behind it. They see, firsthand, that people who love them are willing to risk embarrassment, the judgment of others, and ridicule for their sake (not that this would happen, but the fear of public speaking is powerful). It's a powerful thing to watch: the power of love carrying someone through their worst fear—a fear worse than fear of nuclear war. I can't think of anything that better cultivates the instinct for love in the hearts of children. They never forget that true love is courageous, and that true courage is loving.

Jack called me on the phone with some bad news. His marriage was in trouble. He told me that his wife, Deborah, needing time to think, went to her mother's house for the weekend. Only a few months ago, everything seemed to be fine; but now, nothing about their relationship was right. Their lives at work and at home had become so entangled that they no longer knew the difference between the two. Both of them lived under constant pressure. Because of cutbacks and rivalries at the office, Jack could foresee losing his job in a few weeks—and they were already struggling to pay the bills. Now they were struggling with each other too.

Jack also said that the love that had shone so brightly only a few months before had all but disappeared. Neither of them could find it within themselves to say "I love you." As he spoke, I noticed—anyone would have noticed—that his way of speaking about the relationship was peculiar. I asked him about that. Apparently, they had fallen into the bad habit of scrutinizing their marriage as if they were partners in a business. The question they were asking—out loud and within their private thoughts—was basically this: "Who is contributing to the success of this marriage more?" In effect, they were "counting up" their respective contributions to their relationship, using a dreadful ledger sheet in their heads to determine who the winner and the loser would be. The mere possibility of actually remembering, much less counting, their true blessings was no longer a viable option, so to speak—at the time, I wondered if he had "stock options" in mind.

When Jack finished relating the grim details of his story, I thought to myself that I'd heard exactly the same story—as if it were a script—probably twenty times in the last few years. It's a story of really good, very loyal, loving, capable, hardworking people all but forgetting what matters the most in their lives for one overriding reason: They're afraid of losing what they have. I didn't mince words with Jack. I asked him a straightforward question: "What do you really want?" There was a long silence, before he said, quite clearly, that he wanted his marriage back. When I asked what he was thinking during the silence, he said, "I haven't thought about what I want." Maybe this was true. Maybe they were both acting in self-absorbed ways without realizing it. Who knows? Either way, he and his wife had been too busy making ends meet and arguing about who made the greater contribution to think very much about the deeper truths. They believed that they had no time. At least that's what they told themselves.

I often ask people with whom I work the question "What do you really want?" and I always tell them that it is not selfish to say "I want" or to think it. Under certain circumstances, it can be selfish, but "wanting" is not a bad word. It is necessary to come to terms with what we want—and with *what really matters in life*. When we get too busy, we will forget. We forget that the people in our lives—especially in our marriages, loving partnerships, and friendships—are people in the world, rather than objects in our minds. We lose contact with them as whole people, with what they really want in life, and with what we really want. Of course, we still "want" who knows what, and that kind of wanting can attach itself to anything or anyone that comes along, which is very different from what we "really want."

It's unreasonable to expect to get everything we want, and it's impossible to have everything we want all at once. There's always something more and something else. But that's exactly what the contemporary mind-set leads us to believe. A steady diet of wanting will do nothing to cultivate our spiritual instincts, especially love. The result is that we forget what really matters; we become frozen within ourselves, unable to act in the world with much foresight and wisdom, and afraid that we'll lose what we have. This is the situation that my friend was in. He told me that he wanted his marriage back, which was no surprise to me. I already knew that. What he didn't say was that he loved her. He was afraid to say it, afraid of admitting that he might be wrong about some things, and too angry and defensive to face the truth about himself.

Situations like this can be unusually complicated and really simple at the same time. In this case, it turned out that both sides of the story, his and hers, were nearly identical: mirror images with "he said" on one side, and "she said" on the other, forming a perfect match. Their separate lives at work had so invaded their common life at home that the two—work and home—were nearly interchangeable. "A way of life" had replaced "their lives together." Does that sound familiar? It should. It's the soup that we swim in. Texting had become their habitual form of communication (with each other) throughout the day, gradually supplanting any form of truly heartfelt, honest conversation at home. During the few hours they spent together in the evenings, they were too tired to say very much. Of course, all this was unintentional. Jack and Deborah never wanted it to happen or dreamed that it could have happened to them; but once they realized that it had in fact happened, they became frightened.

This is a very good kind of fear. It happens in the moment when the ego confronts itself, sending a chill, an alarm signal, down the spine. It's the fear that we sometimes experience when a deeper self-awareness begins to emerge—the fear of facing one's own self, one's deepest fear, and the spiritual darkness that we can easily create by the way we live every day. The way they put it, their fear was of losing what they had, even their love for each other—but they were afraid to acknowledge the fear. And they had taken all this one fateful step further: They told themselves that they were prepared to lose it all. Why? Because moving through this kind of fear challenges the values of the workplace, and they weren't sure what that meant. The movement through this particular kind of fear was unexplored territory.

Later on, Jack and Deborah explained it this way: Within the few brief years since their wedding, they worked so frantically to keep what they had that they nearly lost everything—and their love. In effect, they created a way of life that amounted to a protective wall around their marriage, which was understandable. They were being protective. Yet they spent so much time and energy building that wall that they forgot its purpose. Their primal fear overshadowed their instinct for love. They were too busy doing "everything right"—everything that they believed loving couples were supposed to do—to actually take the time to love each other in "real life."

In situations like this, the best way I know to cultivate love (once it's been lost, or nearly so) is to listen without passing judgment, while learning to be still within the silence—in those moments when no one is saying anything. Words matter a great deal, but silence is infinitely more meaningful. Those uncomfortable times when Jack and Deborah were unable, unwilling, or too exhausted to talk (and listen) may have been difficult, but those were precisely the sacred moments that they needed the most. In the silence, facing each other, looking into each other's eyes, they had no choice but to remember the true foundation of their relationship. The key for them was to go there, without filling the void with accusations or counting coup, which is what Jack and Deborah had gotten into the bad habit of doing.

Once Jack and Deborah realized what had happened, and

accepted the fact that no one was to blame—and that they were both equally responsible—they remembered what they really wanted. That's when they said it: "I love you." They found their lives again, and they knew that nothing else mattered.

It's peculiar how this works, but fear is peculiar. Those miracle-making words—"I love you"—are another way of saying "no" to fear and "yes" to life. The river of life carries us through our fear because it has the power to bring the lesser world to an abrupt but glorious halt. This basic principle applies to every situation I know, especially when we're afraid of losing love, or afraid that it has ended, or that we'll never find it again. That's when we're beginning to pass through a threshold to a profoundly sacred place in our souls. It's not easy to make this passage. Conscious inner suffering is the price of admission, and the ego rebels because it does not want to pay. Blaming others and self-doubt come to the surface like we've never known before.

From time to time, we all face situations like that. When it happens—when it's time for love to be tested and the passage to be made—the best thing we can do is to listen with every bit of attention and love that we can muster, particularly when our fear would have us say "Why bother?" That's what "courage" means. Listen to your beloved, and listen to yourself. And when the silence comes, as it inevitably will, have even more courage. Remember that listening does not mean believing everything you hear. We all spout off nonsense now and again, so listen anyway. Unless we care about each other enough to hear what our loved ones are actually saying and mean to say, then we'll never hear anything except what we want or expect to hear. We might as well be talking to ourselves, and pretty soon, we will be. That's how we lose the people we love and the real world at the same time. In my opinion, the fear of losing that is an exceptionally good fear to have—and it helps to remember that there is a "real world."

. . .

It was a real eye-opener to realize that people tell me about their souls all the time. The key, at least for me, was to understand that when we use the word "love," we're often talking about the soul. In the same way, we don't usually say that "love casts out fear" or that "the fear of God is the beginning of wisdom," but the stories we tell about ourselves reveal what we've discovered about love, fear, and the struggle between them in the soul.

Honestly, I'm thinking about older people more than anyone else. Sometimes their stories are told with an uncommon sensitivity that's easy to miss. It's entirely possible that this sensitivity is not at all uncommon for them. I really don't know about that. What I do know is that they don't tell their stories often enough, not as far as I'm concerned. But then, stories of the soul aren't supposed to be told very often.

These are some of the things that older people tell me in those rare and beautiful moments of sacred storytelling: *"I used to be afraid and worried about everything, but not anymore. Now I'm finally letting go, and I understand what 'living' means."* Or, *"There's so much about life that we just don't pay attention to, the most important parts."* Or, *"I wish I had the chance to tell an old friend about my life back then. I didn't think he cared very much, but maybe I was wrong."*

Their words are like windows opening to the meaning of life as the soul perceives it. When my older friends talk in this way, my feeling is that I'm running to that soul window as quickly as I can, listening to every word, watching their eyes and the nuances of meaning in their faces. I do this for one simple reason: They know what they're talking about. It's not just their words that captivate me. Large parts of our conversations might be filled with reminiscing or comments about the inevitably frail condition of once youthful bodies, but that only seems to be what we're talking about. If you listen with your whole self, letting your mind be free of expectations about what you think you're hearing, then you'll understand that they're not really talking about the past. Rather, they're talking about what it means to live a life. They're speaking about life from the soul's point of view. In other words, they're talking about the real world. More often than not, it takes a lifetime to find the real world, but we can find it—if we move through our fear of living.

I can't explain this any better than they can. Tradition describes it as "grace." More often, we simply say that it's "the wisdom that comes with age." However you want to put it, they're telling me that grace enters their lives and ours with the passing of years—which is how the love of God casts out fear in the course of a lifetime. One thing that helps this process along is to stop living in the past, which means letting go of old patterns of control, of the desire to control, and of believing that we should be in control. This "letting go," almost by definition, involves moving through the fear of losing control. And that is how life itself bestows its blessing of grace through the Spirit.

The irony, of course, is that our capacity for love deepens when we let go of the desire to control it. Love really is a great river that's much bigger than we can possibly imagine. To let go in this way doesn't mean we care any less. In practice, "the real world" operates in precisely the opposite way. To let go of controlling love is to realize how deeply we actually do care. Love for our families and friends can be as strong as, if not stronger than, it ever was. It may actually grow in entirely unexpected ways, the difference between "now" and "then" being that our station in life has changed, and with it, our perspective on life and ourselves.

Another blessing of age is the realization that, for too many years, we had been way too concerned about what other people think. This fear exacts its greatest cost, which we may later regret, when we're convinced that we don't have other people's approval. The fear of the opinion of others can be the very epitome of control—in this case, the fear being completely in control of us. Fear wants to be a master of control, and it makes every effort to play that role well by concealing its own actions. Given half a chance, or less, fear will rule every part of our lives by making us so afraid of the opinion of others that we never think our own thoughts. The result is that we're afraid of becoming who God wants us to be and, almost certainly, afraid of God too.

A third blessing that comes with age is the understanding that helping others, or wanting to help others, only goes so far. This is the lesson of control learned the hard way. We all need friends, and friends know that we must learn our own lessons from our own mistakes. But older friends are especially clear about one thing: Our loved ones are not "ours." Everyone knows this, or should know it, but they will actually say it out loud and claim it as a truth about life. They've realized that if the older generation cannot let go, then the younger generation is denied the opportunity to step up to the plate and take the responsibility that is rightfully theirs. It can be as much of a struggle to let go of responsibility that is not ours as it is to assume it when it is ours. In reality, these are two sides to the same passage from one stage in life to the next. Some resist this passage (often because of their fear), while others eagerly welcome it (perhaps naively overlooking some good reasons to be afraid). Either way, it's a passage that can and should be made with gratitude. The point is that older people often tell me how much happier, relaxed, and less afraid they've become because of it.

One older friend, Agnes, once told me about the blessings of age in yet another, especially soulful way. She started the conversation with some reflections on truthfulness—a virtue she regarded as considerably more elusive than we usually think. I believe she's right. She wasn't talking about outright lying or the smaller "harmless" fibs that we sometimes tell. Rather, she was telling me that we're actually wrong about some of the most important truths about life, even when we're entirely sure that we're right. For example, in her younger days, she was very sure about life's meaning; and on that basis, she was quick to make judgments about herself and others. In her later years, all this changed. She realized that she simply didn't know a great deal that she was once very sure about. "Knowing less," in her opinion, made her wiser, more loving, less afraid, and less judgmental of people who lived in ways very different from her.

Don't underestimate Agnes. In the moment that she was speaking, she knew better than me that her story had just begun. She went on to describe how her previous comments on truthfulness related to a struggle she was having with Tony, her husband. She began by saying that he was "afraid to wash the dishes." A slight smile appeared on her face when she told me this, but the tone in her voice and look in her eyes betrayed a feeling of sadness and grief, which she would never have expressed in actual words. Tony was not literally "afraid" to wash the dishes or "to help around the house," as she put it; and yet, she was absolutely right. He was afraid, and the fact that he would never "wash the dishes" represented another, more significant fear on his part. Never would he stoop to admitting this fear, much less to giving it a name. To do so would be an unspeakable affront to his self-esteem.

Many people—most of the people I know—might respond to the situation she described with a laugh, or at least a smile, which is understandable. But as you will see, everything she had said so far only scratched the surface. It's well worth remembering that each generation has its own ways of expressing its fears, and struggles to overcome them. In the same way, people in the next generation (there is always a "next generation") struggle too, in ways that define who they are. Their fears may be very different from those of their parents and grandparents, but we all have "our fears," and we're just as likely to deny them as a matter of pride or strongly held principle, which is yet another layer of fear piled on top of the others.

Agnes had not wanted to talk with me in order to prepare herself for a difficult discussion with Tony, which was my first assumption. I assumed that, after all these years, any discussion with me would create more problems than it would solve. To talk with me about him might have been interpreted by him as a form of betrayal—but I was not in a position to know that for a fact. Any comment that I might have made along those lines could have been a form of judgment on my part, which would only reinforce the stereotypes that we all have, rather than revealing anything very helpful. Those stereotypes may have some basis in fact, at least on the surface of things, but their significance dissolves rather quickly when we have the opportunity to perceive the deeper truths of a person's life.

As we talked a bit more, the conversation developed a "feel" that faintly resembled a confession, but very few words had been spoken and there was nothing to confess. In other words, it wasn't a confession. Soon, I realized that something else, something very different, was unfolding before my eyes. In fact, I had failed to appreciate the uncommon sensitivity that she had for the depth of her soul. Agnes was in complete control (in the best sense of the word) of our conversation. She wanted to be in her priest's office—a holy place for her—to say or do something important. I just didn't know what it was.

That's when it hit me. Suddenly, I knew that she had already moved through her fear. It was only when I finally realized that

Agnes was not afraid—not afraid of anything, as far as I could tell—that we reached the heart of her story. She never actually said this outright, not in so many words. Yet she had already "told me," quite clearly, only a few minutes before, when she smiled while making the comment about her husband's "fear" of washing the dishes. She had no desire to talk about the dishes or his fear. That was of no concern whatsoever. In fact, there was no "problem" that she wanted me to help her solve, and she wasn't seeking my counsel, not really, or any kind of pastoral guidance.

Agnes was offering me a gift. The gift was a revelation that was neither about herself, nor about her life, although it encompassed both. Her gift, which was her story, concerned the spiritual depth of a person's life—every person's life. She wanted me to know that the truth about her goes far deeper than anything we normally talk about, or see, or do, including household duties, as important as they can be. And—this is the crucial point—she wanted to know whether I understood what the real world is like in the flesh, rather than as a mere idea.

Did I understand that the meaning of a person's life should not be judged? That there is a realm of being where the spirit of love lives, and that the depth of love within a person cannot be seen—not really? We can't hide it, nor can we display it—not really. Love has a life of its own, and the only question that really matters is whether we enter into it and claim it.

Her story ended with a question. Love stories—soul stories— always lead to a question. I told her that I knew what she meant, but in matters of the soul, words are never enough.

I thought about our conversation for several days. I was sure that I, the priest, needed it more than she did. I was still struggling to understand what she was telling me, which was a good sign. Agnes was cultivating my instinct for love. She was doing her best to teach her priest how to be one.

Most of our fears and the predisposition toward certain kinds of fear are learned at a young age. One significant exception may be the fear of snakes. I feel compelled to raise this subject one more time, but my reasons are good. First, the story that I want tell is about love; and second, by telling it, I can bring the grisly matter of snakes to a close.

Some knowledgeable people claim that this particular fear—the fear of snakes—may always be with us. I'm not so sure. They claim that it's the genetic legacy of our ancient African ancestors, several million years ago. The implication is that the fear of snakes may not be learned, which both magnifies and explains the mythic, primeval quality of snakes. Even if this were true, it would be difficult to prove. For example, I've known people who are deathly afraid of snakes, yet they've only seen pictures of them in books. Would you call their fear "genetic" or "learned"? Who knows? As for me, I had never seen a picture of one, nor did I even know that such creatures existed when I saw one for the first time. I was absolutely terrified. That was the beginning of a long story that ended not in fear, but in love. Today, I wouldn't say that I love snakes, but it's a love story nonetheless.

Imagine that you're four years old—maybe five. It's a hot summer day. You're pedaling your red tractor with the inexhaustible energy that kids of your age have. A tall oak tree, the kind with long, gorgeous branches, forms an umbrella overhead. You're pedaling way too fast, which is really the whole point when you're a kid; so inevitably, you wreck, turning the tractor on its side. You're sprawled on the ground, slightly stunned, when you hear a peculiar "thud." In the very instant that you open your eyes, a full grown, three-foot-long, bright green vine snake has fallen from the branches not more than a foot from your face. A vine snake, by the way, has a very long, elongated head, which makes it look eerie, even for a snake. Both of you are stunned by your respective falls, staring at each other, eyeball to eyeball.

That's exactly how I met my first snake, and, I repeat, this was the moment when I first realized that snakes existed. I screamed bloody murder. Because I wasn't bleeding and had no broken bones, it took my mother a few minutes to realize why I was crying so hysterically. She was focused on me. When she finally realized what was going on, she called my great-grandfather Joel, who lived not far down the road.

As I gently stood up, I could see him walking toward the huge oak, cane in hand, decked out in the bib overalls and white shirt that he always wore. At first, he was smiling. He poked at the snake with his cane, trying to nudge it in the direction of the woods. The snake had other ideas. A few seconds later, my great-grandfather was yelling too—in one incredibly swift move, the snake had begun to crawl up the inside of his pant leg. My mom and I stood there, speechless, in utter disbelief of what we were seeing. Somehow, he managed to pull it out. Then, while we were still taking in everything that had happened, the snake skirted into the nearby woods, as quickly as it had appeared.

Except for dead ones on the highway, I don't recall seeing another snake until my early teen years. In those days, I liked to sit on the bank of a small creek behind our house. I enjoyed the quiet sounds in the woods: an occasional rustle of leaves made by squirrels, the trickling sound of flowing water, branches rubbing against each other in the breeze. One afternoon, as I was sitting there, I saw a small water snake uncurl from the opposite bank. It swam slowly across the small pool that separated us. When it reached the middle of the pool, it gently raised its head a few inches above the surface of the water and looked at me. From a distance of about three feet, we watched each other for maybe a minute, again eyeball to eyeball. It seemed like a long time. Then the snake quietly lowered its head into the water, returned to its side of the pool, and disappeared into the grassy bank.

By then, my earlier bout with panic-stricken terror had transformed into fascination. Still sitting by the edge of the pool, I wondered whether my fear of the vine snake years before had been justified. Of course, it was frightening, but the circumstances then were really peculiar: I had fallen off my tractor; the snake had fallen out of the tree; and we both stared into each other's eyes. He (or she) must have been as afraid of me as I was of him (or her). It's also possible that the snake jumped from the tree, but there's no way to know. This time, though, I sat quietly. And this time, years later, a second snake had assumed essentially the same stance toward me; and again, we looked into each other's eyes. This time, I wasn't afraid—not so much.

After that, I sought out and captured all kinds of snakes— garter snakes, water snakes, king snakes, ring-necked snakes, black snakes—but I always let them go. No creatures like to be penned up, including people. I never wanted to handle snakes, not with my hands; but I liked them anyway. I felt drawn to snakes. There was something mysterious about them, something that seemed archetypal and mythic. At difficult times in my life, when I had to look deep into my soul, I sometimes would dream about snakes. These weren't dreams of actual snakes, but extremely powerful images from the unconscious—like the image of the snake I later projected onto the fear-ridden minister at the revival, or the ones I read about in psychological, anthropological, and theological texts. These dreams were spiritual in nature, and transformative. They always involved fear.

I remember one particular dream in which a giant dark serpent looked me in the eye, much like the experiences of my childhood. Years later, another dream involved a white serpent that again looked at me, but with an entirely different, utterly kind, loving, and compassionate gaze. In dreams like these, the "sacred snake" doesn't symbolize anything inherently "evil." Rather, it represents something mysterious, earthy, and powerfully spiritual within ourselves. Those dreams tell us that the Spirit's presence is rising up within us, as the serpent rose up on Moses' staff and as Jesus rose up on the cross. They raise serious questions that we're meant to explore: Does the Spirit really exist? What are we going to do with the spiritual instincts that we've been given? What kind of person are we going to become? From the dreamer's point of view, it seems that our very lives—and our souls—are at stake.

A story that began on my red tractor when I was five came to an unexpected completion forty years later, at a celebration of Saint Francis Day at the Cathedral of Saint John the Divine in Manhattan, where I worked. I was sitting in the garden outside the church. There, hundreds of people bring their pets to receive a blessing. The very last person who came to me that day was a young boy. He walked up with a small cage in his hands. Inside the cage was a snake. I looked closely and noticed that it was a garter snake. The boy watched me intently, wondering what I was going to do. Garter snakes are harmless, but I knew from my own childhood experiences that they, unlike the more exotic boa constrictors, can be feisty and difficult to tame.

As soon as I saw the boy and his snake, I smiled. I had a choice. I could bless the snake through the cage, that is, without actually holding him in my hands. It would be a blessing of sorts. Or I could give the *real blessing* that the boy wanted to see. I was being tested. When I asked if the snake was tame, he said nothing.

Within those few moments of silence, forty years of my life had collapsed into one fateful meeting among that small boy, a garter snake, and me.

This is what happened. The boy looked me in the eye, just as those two snakes had done in my childhood—the one that fell from the tree, and the other, in the pool—and as the sacred, mythological snakes had done in my dreams. As I watched the boy, I realized that he could have been me, many years ago, riding my red tractor. I wondered whether my great-grandfather would have been afraid now, just as the boy was wondering about me. Those thoughts crossed my mind quickly—the people, the snakes, the fear, the stillness by the pool, everything—which is how the Spirit works. I'm serious. The Spirit—our loving counselor and friend through every fear—somehow makes all the arrangements, creates just the right circumstances, and gives us every opportunity to move through our fear. But the choice is always ours.

Rather than thinking about it or deliberating, I reached into the cage, gently took the snake in my hand, held it in my lap, and blessed it. It was the simplest thing in the world. The young boy and I looked into each other's eyes and smiled. All three of us had been blessed. Given the time and opportunity, the Spirit always helps us move through our fear. If you don't know this already, then be patient. Keep your wits about you—that is to say, use your spiritual instincts with a good sense of humor. The day will come when you'll know what I'm talking about.

A Spiritual Practice in Love

The purpose of this spiritual practice is to help us become more aware of the love that is already present in our lives and of the generous people who have nurtured it. Because love is an exceedingly powerful, but also tender subject, let me make three suggestions before we actually begin.

First, let's remember that love is a great deal more than something "we have." Love is also something we do. For love to be a living, vibrant part of our lives, it must be cultivated with the spirit of joy, commitment, and humility.

Second, following in the Christian tradition of self-examination that reaches back to Saint Augustine, let's acknowledge that we all have many different kinds of love. For example, love encompasses our families and friends, and it also includes anything that truly inspires us: places, music, and mountains, to name just a few. We have many more "loves" than we realize. Our "loves" also involve "what" we love.

We can ask ourselves about this in any number of ways: What have been our heart's desires? What, through the years, have been the motivating forces in our lives? What has inspired us and called us to move through difficult times? What has captured the greater part of our attention? What part of our lives has given us the most meaning and fulfillment? All kinds of answers may come to mind. They might relate to career, political involvements, finance, leisure, and certain kinds of activities at home and at work or simply being in places that are dear to our hearts.

Third, keep in mind that we often resist reflecting on these loves because we're afraid of becoming aware of anything that might be too self-revealing. Self-examination can touch upon our deepest vulnerabilities and regrets, and that makes us back away from anything that feels like shame or judgment. We tell ourselves that we have to give the "right" answer. Our resistance, regrets, and uncomfortable memories shouldn't surprise us, nor should we assume that we're doing anything wrong—or that something is "wrong" with us. Instead, it's best to understand that we're on the right track. The benefits of self-examination far outweigh the difficulties, one of those benefits being that we have the opportunity to perceive how the power of love can carry us through our fear.

Having made those suggestions, let's begin by thinking about the people we love and who have loved us. Take a piece of paper and jot down the names of the people who have drawn out love from within you. This is an amazing, important, and very sacred thing that you'll be doing. Write their names in the spirit of humility and gratitude. Remember the significance of your past experiences with them, while also taking into account how they drew out your love in ways that you might not have appreciated back then.

Then let's ask ourselves the really interesting question: What qualities within you were nurtured and strengthened by their love for you? Write the names of the people and the qualities they cultivated on a piece of paper. Some possible answers, for example, might be "She helped me to understand myself in a larger way," "He took the time to show me the birds in the park next to my house . . . I became more curious about the world," "His experience helped me show greater respect toward my coworkers," or "I learned to be more understanding of my family."

The same practice can also be done with regard to people who have had a negative influence on your life. We should not ignore or deny truly negative, destructive influences that have led us to act in similarly destructive ways. However—this is crucial—keep in mind that there is a hugely important difference between, on the one hand, truly negative influences, and on the other hand, influences that only seemed to be negative or that transformed in a positive direction with the passage of time. Those seemingly negative influences are the ones I want you to remember now.

Before writing their names on a separate piece of paper, let me give some examples. Let's say that someone hurt your feelings, but the situation resulted in personal growth—and a greater capacity for love within you. Or, perhaps a harmful action done to you enhanced your awareness of shortcomings and problem areas within yourself. Let me be really specific. Your thoughts might be something like this: "He and his friends were bullying me on the playground . . . everyone seemed to like them . . . so I wanted to be like them too . . . I regret that now." Or, "My high school teacher seemed to ridicule everyone in the classroom . . . he made us afraid . . . that's when I decided that I would not be that kind of teacher." It's wise to take plenty of time when exploring this area of our lives and to resist making hasty judgments.

Close the spiritual practice by imagining that someone else, someone that you know or would like to know, will be doing the very same spiritual practice. Imagine that the person you have in mind has jotted down your name. What do you want their answers and comments to be? What do you want that person to be thinking? What qualities do you want to cultivate in them? In effect, you will be answering the following question: "What kind of loving influence do you want to have on others?"

This may not be very easy—in fact, none of this spiritual practice will be very easy. Set aside some time, an hour or so each day for a period of several days, to reflect on this. Or take much longer, if more time is required to take the question seriously. Talk it over with yourself like you're having a heart-to-heart conversation with the person that you've imagined, while remembering that you're asking—and answering—this question of yourself: What kind of person do I really want to become? The whole point of this practice is to realize that we have a tremendous capacity to be loving influences on the lives of others.

5.

INTENT: INNER
DIRECTEDNESS

Blessed are the pure in heart, for they will see God.

—The Gospel According to Matthew, 5:8

Purity of heart is to will one thing.

—Søren Kierkegaard (1813–1855)

*I*ntent—*our instinct for attention and inner direction—is no more and no less easy to explain than love. But unlike love, intent is, by far, the most overlooked and underrated of all our spiritual instincts. Think of all that we do in the course of a day: working, eating, sleeping, caring for people, struggling with them, worrying about one thing or another, laughing, crying, watching television, playing, talking on the phone, walking the dog, and so on. That's just off the top of my head, and every bit of it depends on intent. Even in our dreams, intent is there; and in equally mysterious ways, it guides the creative process of artists and mystics who tap in to realms of* consciousness that lie beyond waking and dreaming. Without intent, none of us would be able to think anything: Reflecting on intent requires intent. But by putting this instinct to good use, we can find the direction and purpose to accomplish any kind of goal, however everyday and mundane or grand and lofty they may be.

The fact that we use intent more or less constantly in our waking life without noticing the nature of the gift or the potential behind it should not suggest that the profound Mystery at work has gone unnoticed. Philosophers and mystics have learned of it firsthand by making the spiritual passage between two realms of existence: from our usual experience of the world through words and thought (talking to ourselves and to others, as we commonly do) to profound encounters with the sacred that arise from inner silence. By making this passage with the help of introspection, prayer, and meditation, they discover (and so can we) that the ordinary meaning of human "will" is much too willful to account for the meaning of intent. How we "attend to" the world and create it by the power of our "intending" is a better way to put it. This means that the Spirit—the power that's greater than we are, yet within us too—is involved and would like to be a partner.

The significance and power of intent is also realized in profoundly less fulfilling ways. I'm thinking of people who feel occasionally (or chronically) depressed or reluctant to face the world, which includes most everyone I know on occasion, as well as those who are afraid of falling into the proverbial abyss—the "bottomless pit." They become aware of how powerless we are when intent seems to fade into the distance. This can be a dark and scary experience that we should make every effort to avoid. Yet those who have known it learn a rare and valuable lesson: When our capacity for intent diminishes, for whatever reason, all our other spiritual instincts diminish with it. In other words, intent is far more crucial to our survival than we ever dreamed, or than we ever imagined dreaming.

The more common word "intention" only scratches the surface of "intent" as a spiritual instinct, but our familiarity with it points us in the right direction. Consider those moments when we reflect on our "good intentions"—usually after we've done something regrettable or morally wrong. We try to sort out the difference between what we believed or hoped we were doing, on the one hand, and what actually happened, on the other. To say "our intentions were good" is one step away from an apology. Nine times out of ten, it might be part of an apology, or an excuse for not making the apology that is actually deserved. The implication is that we "meant well."

Yet something else is happening within us too, or could happen, when we reflect on our intentions: We learn how important it is to be mindful of intent. To mean what we say, to say what we mean, and to act in ways that are consistent with a good conscience matter a great deal. Very often, our failings are the result not of dishonesty or outright lying, but of a lack of awareness and failure of attention. Our attention might be working quite well (our minds were focused on the business at hand); our intentions might be good (we meant well); but our actions still can have unintended and often harmful consequences.

Therein lies one of the key ingredients in the movement through fear. We need to have a grasp of who we are, what the world is like, and what we need to do—all of which enter into intent. That seems like a tall order; but more often than we might think, our intent is weakened by a steady accumulation of otherwise small and insignificant distractions in everyday life. In effect, we get caught up in the whirlwind that life can be. The result is that we lose sight of who we are and what we're doing, and that makes us prone to anxiety and fear. For example, we might take offense easily, defend ourselves readily, or pretend that we don't care, without quite knowing why. On top of that, advertising and political propaganda distract us in powerful ways. We perceive their impact on our lives, while having little control over it. Add these obstacles, vulnerabilities, and personal shortcomings to the traditional list of sins—greed, pride, envy, sloth, and so on—and we can understand why our instinct for intent needs some serious work.

To the extent that we allow these forces to control our intent, we lose touch with our true nature and higher purpose in life. That is a great deal to lose, and it sets up patterns of self-deception in our consciousness. In everyday life, for example, we may believe that we're thinking our own thoughts, that we're not afraid, that our will is strong, and that we are the masters of our own destiny, when, in fact, none of this is really true. Gradually, our intent can become so impaired that we simply give up, which amounts to giving in. We might resort to using subtle or gross manipulation and other forceful means to achieve what we believe we want—all the while telling ourselves that our will is strong. And when the real world pushes back, we believe it even more.

From a spiritual point of view, a diminished capacity for intent accounts for a great deal of our frustration, suffering, and fear. This is why some of the most time-honored spiritual practices encourage us to cultivate our intent in clear and direct ways; for example, the Eastern practice of training our minds to become "one-pointed" and the Christian practice of letting "our will become God's will." Both traditions are grounded in practices of daily prayer and meditation that anyone can do. Jesus proclaimed the ultimate goal of these practices in the Beatitudes—"Blessed are the pure in heart, for they shall see God." But that happens, or can happen, only when we've cultivated all our spiritual instincts enough to gain a measure of control over our divided and unruly thoughts.

It's easy to believe that Jesus' words and the spiritual traditions behind it are too lofty for mere mortals like us. Although we're mistaken to believe that, there is some wisdom in the hesitation we may feel. Any honest person knows that our hearts are far *from pure, and so does God. Not only that, the word "purity" can suggest an attitude of elitism that actually betrays the meaning of these spiritual teachings. If we lose or reject our common humanity, then we turn away from the possibility of realizing what "purity of heart" actually means within ourselves or anyone else.*

Jesus is not saying that we have to be perfect. Intent is strengthened by the desire to move through our fear, regardless of how confused, divided within ourselves, and frightened that we feel. Rather, he's encouraging us to never give up on our heart's deepest desire, while being honest about who we are. When we give up or when we're overcome by our fear, as will surely happen, the Spirit will carry us where our souls want to go.

The following three stories illustrate how we can draw upon and cultivate intent to move through our fear. The first story explores the interplay between intent and fear, particularly the fear of public speaking, in my own childhood. The second addresses some of the most sacred declarations of intent we ever make—the vows of baptism and marriage. It delves into the struggle of one young woman who wanted to discern the true intent of her heart and of the heart of her beloved. The third story describes how we can harness the power of intent during times of personal crisis. In this case, the crisis is triggered by the news of a life-threatening illness.

People never change." Years ago, I knew a man who always found a reason to say that. He liked to say it. He felt proud and somehow justified by saying it. But what I heard, coming from somewhere beneath his words, was something like "I'm afraid, I have good reason to be afraid, and no one is going to make me change." Of course, he would never admit to anything of the sort or use the word "fear" in relation to himself.

The way I see it, everyone is entitled to his or her point of view, but all points of view are not equal. His point of view was governed by the fact that he was stubborn, bitter about life, and just plain wrong about a lot of things. No one can reasonably argue that it's easy to move through our fear, but people make that movement all the time—and they're changed by it. Bitterness has a way of making us blind, spiritually, and oblivious to the truths before our very eyes.

Other people are more realistic and, perhaps, honest. They say that "most people could change, if only they would try." The implication is that change is possible, but that's as far as it goes. I think of this as "compassionate pessimism." In other words, we can change, at least hypothetically, but we probably won't—and it doesn't matter anyway. Here again, people who believe this are really talking about themselves. In a roundabout way, they're saying that they "mean well," while resigning themselves to the way things are. I suspect that this outlook on life usually represents the interests of political and economic forces that try to pull our strings—often, I might add, with considerable success. In other words, there's a hidden agenda lurking not very far behind this supposedly realistic point of view.

Still others, myself included, believe that everyone changes because life is change, which seems the most realistic and likely. This actually is an *outlook on life*, rather than a rationalization or veiled comment on ourselves and others. We struggle with change of certain kinds—either by fighting the current, or wishing it would flow even faster—but either way, life is a river, and the river is love. The crucial questions involve where our intent is directed and what our true intentions are.

I know that I've changed a great deal over the years, and I've done my share of resisting and pushing along the way. Looking back, I'm happy that I've changed—and relieved. Some of my friends are just as happy (and relieved) about that as I am. Most of the larger changes in my life have been the outcome of facing difficult, often unpleasant truths about myself. It wasn't easy then, and it's not easy now; but it's obvious that every one of those changes involved a movement through fear. At the time, the consequence of who I was as a person came into conflict with the spiritual needs that I either totally ignored or failed to perceive and misunderstood. The soul suffocates when fear governs our lives too much, and it will let you know when it needs fresh air. The difficulty is that we often don't realize what the soul is saying or why.

I can't recall that I ever worked out full-blown strategies for moving through my fear. I thought about being free, in effect, rehearsing what it would be like. It would be more accurate to say that when the "I need air" symptoms appeared, I sometimes decided to run away, and other times not to run. The decision "not to run," which is the equivalent of saying "no" to fear, is a huge step to take, even if we don't make that decision every time. By doing so, we're cultivating intent, which is always a good decision.

The decision "not to run" is based on the third outlook, which says, "To live is to change, so people can't help but change." For me personally, the practical implication is expressed by a simple saying: *Every day is a new beginning*. I know that sounds corny. I absolutely loathed sayings like that when I was a teenager. All I knew back then was that the first words I heard in the morning, promptly at 6:00, were *"Rise and shine."* My dad was my disgustingly cheerful alarm clock. Every morning, I pulled the covers over my head and lay there in quiet disbelief, hoping that he would go away. I should say, on his behalf, that he was merciful. He knew that I disliked it, so he said it only once. He laughed about it. I didn't laugh, despite the fact that it was indeed funny. But that's not the reason he said it only once. The reason was that once was always enough. I got out of bed—or else.

The problem for me was that I felt conflicted about going to school. The teachers were great; I loved my friends and learning new things; I loved all kinds of sports; *and* I dreaded being there.

If my life back then was a painting, fear would have been one of the predominant colors in a scene that was otherwise pleasing to the eye. Today, I know exactly why this background of fear entered my life, and I know when it happened and what it meant.

I was in the first grade. It was recess. All the children were on the playground. The bell rang, which meant that it was time to return to the classroom. I was running, along with everyone else. Two older boys—fourth graders who were known bullies—ran close to me on their way inside. One of the boys knocked me down, and I hit my head on the blacktop. For a few minutes, I was stunned. I remained there in a dazed, dreamy state that could've given the impression that I was knocked out.

The next thing I remembered was the sound of my teacher calling to me from the classroom window. I slowly got up, went inside, and answered her questions about what happened. I didn't want to say anything, but I had to account for the knot emerging on my head. Later that day, the principal grilled the two boys about the incident. They said they had no recollection of knocking down anyone. Actually, I believed they were telling the truth. The two boys may have been bullies, but what happened really was an accident. They were several years older and bigger. I was little. They were running and they didn't notice me. It's true that they should have paid attention; and they didn't care very much about us—the small fry—which was part of the problem. In any event, that's when I first learned that the world can deliver a hard knock, sometimes by accident, and you never know when something bad will happen to you.

That's also when the fear of the unknown became a reality in my life. As bad and forbidding as that sounds, it was a very mundane fear. I wouldn't say that it completely ruled my life, but its impact was felt. I never talked about it. I put it in the background of my life, where it became an expectation of the bad things that might happen. Obviously, I continued going to school, as the courts and parents require, but after that incident I didn't really want to be there. From my point of view, it wasn't an especially safe place to be. By any objective standard, this wasn't true, but it is how I felt.

Gradually, the consequences of my new outlook could be seen in my resistance to doing certain things—especially speaking in front of the class. Years later, a counselor suggested that this was my way of expressing anger about being knocked down and out, which is possible. It sounds plausible, but somehow I didn't believe he was entirely right. Whatever the underlying logic might have been, what actually happened was that my fear of speaking in front of the class grew worse and worse. It's strange how our minds are affected by fear. The fear of one thing (big guys) gradually grows into the fear of something else (public speaking)—the initial fear transforming and magnifying many times over with the passage of time.

That's another reason that I laugh now about our supposedly two worst fears: nuclear attack and public speaking. My early school days were at the height of the Cold War. We had our nuclear alert drills at school—crawling under the school desks and so on. For me, those drills were just another form of play and a distraction from the classroom. They were not the reason I didn't want to get out of bed in the morning and face the world. I didn't want to go to school because I didn't want to talk before the class. I didn't want to be called on. The mere thought of giving an oral report filled me with horrible dread, but rehearsing nuclear war drills was a great thrill.

In those circumstances, the very last thing I wanted to do in the morning was to *rise and shine*. The best I could do was sort of half rise and half shine. I was awake, but seriously sleepwalking through life. Sometimes I feigned sickness so I could stay at home. That was the kind of strategy that I actually did spend some time thinking through—strategizing on how to run from my fear. But this worked so rarely that it would be best to say that it never worked. On the few occasions that it did work, I actually was sick.

I put it that way here, because the difference between real sickness and fake sickness wasn't all that important to me. That sounds peculiar, until you realize that the fact of really being sick was such a huge relief. Being really sick was far less significant than the hopeful possibility that I might not have to go to school. In those days, "rise and shine" seemed patronizing and obnoxious. Faking illness offered hope. On those rare occasions when my strategy worked—because I actually was sick—the weight of the world was lifted from my shoulders.

Well, almost. I always knew the truth. I was relieved and burdened at the same time. I knew that I was supposed to be at school. In my heart, I did want to be there. Gradually, I realized how painful it was to be tested spiritually each and every morning. Would my fear be so strong that I would run away from school? That's what the test amounted to. Every day became testing day. That's another way of saying that life is a river that never stops flowing. We so much want to be a part of it; but often, we're too afraid to jump in.

So much has changed now. Today, I love to speak in public— which, given my vocation as a priest, is obviously good. Like I said, for the most part I've never spent much time strategizing to overcome my fears. My strategies involved how to avoid them. But I have learned to cultivate my spiritual instincts and to say "no" to my fears when they rear their ugly head, which is the best strategy of all. In the case of this particular fear—speaking in public—the river of life brought together all the pieces that the Spirit needed to help me do what needed to be done. This is how it happened, nearly ten years later.

As it turned out, I wasn't standing before the class. Rather, I was standing near midcourt. I loved basketball. I was one of the co-captains of our team, and this was a really big game. Tensions were high on both sides. Of the hundreds of people who were there, some might have noticed that something peculiar was going on. It was a small thing really. There was nothing very big or obvious for them to see, nothing except one teenager standing alone, unexplainably, at midcourt, while everyone else had gone to their respective benches. A time out had been called. Our head coach, whom I liked, had a reputation for yelling quite a lot at the players and pinching our skin just enough to make it hurt, and sometimes, to leave a bruise. It was his way of getting our attention. Some coaches do things like that. Some parents expect coaches to be rough now and again. I suppose it reinforces the kind of treatment that the kids receive at home. In other words, it's "part of the game." But my parents didn't yell at me; I wasn't pinched at home; and I didn't like it when it happened on the court.

Over a period of a few weeks, my feelings about his behavior grew increasingly strong. I knew exactly what my feelings were, but I had some conflict about what to do. On the one hand, I told myself that because I was one of three co-captains, it was my responsibility to show leadership—I had to take a stand. On the other hand, I knew that not everyone would feel the same way, or feel it so strongly. After all, it was "part of the game." Plus, we won a lot of games. We were an exceptionally good team, and the reason for it, in large part, was the effectiveness of his talented coaching skills. He was an exceptionally good coach.

For a while, I considered enlisting the support of my teammates, but finally decided against it. I realized that I might be creating unnecessary division and conflict within the team, which would be irresponsible on my part. I also felt conflicted because I didn't know how effective any protest on my part would be. I would be taking a risk, and I had no idea what would happen. What I knew is that I could no longer live with a situation that I considered to be undignified on his part and humiliating for us.

That's about as far as my strategizing went. But like I said, life is a river; and during that big game, it flowed with an unexpectedly strong current. Time out had been called. When I heard the whistle, something came over me. I refused to go to the bench. Instead, I stood there, staring at my coach. And he stood there, staring at me. Our eyes locked. With his head, he motioned for me to join the huddle. I shook my head, saying "no." We both stood a while longer. He finally took one step in my direction. I thought about it for a second and took a step toward him. In that moment, I decided to tell him what I was thinking. No one would hear—no one except him; and yet, I would be saying it in full public view, while the team, the school, and much of the town watched. Then I stopped again, and said "no" out loud so he could hear me clearly. As soon as I said those words, he knew what I was talking about and why. I could see in his eyes that he was seeing me as a person. That brought an end to the yelling and pinching. It never happened again. He was a good man.

The astonishing thing is that, over the next few days and weeks, my fear of public speaking began to fade *and* I began to love hearing my dad say *"Rise and shine."* Today, I don't actually say those words when I wake up in the morning—not usually and not out loud; but when I think of them, I realize the spiritual truth that they express. *"Rise and shine"*—how annoying and how true. I don't want to be sleepwalking when I'm awake or running away from the real world because the world I believe I know seems like a bad dream.

Today, it seems peculiar to me that we don't think of our lifetimes as sacred time. The same can be said for the time that flows through each day, and especially those few precious moments between waking and sleeping. We wake up in the morning. We're groggy. Our eyes are a little puffy. Generally, we don't look very good in those moments before we wash our faces, and so on.

Maybe it takes all of us a little while to face the world, which we all learn to do, each in our own way.

But the Spirit within us sees things from a different point of view, and all points of view are not equal. What I know, for sure, is that the Spirit sees the world from a better perspective than I. The Spirit within us knows that our whole outlook on life begins to take shape at the moment we wake up in the morning. Right then and there, by the power of our intent, we set a whole world into motion, a world that we have more power to create than we would ever believe. So I thank God that life is a river. And I thank God that we can cultivate our intent, strengthening it enough to say "no" to our fear and "yes" to the simple joy of life. Otherwise, we'll never get up in the morning, not really. We'll never go to school, not really. And, most of all, we'll never go swimming. I think God wants us to go for a swim in the great river, loving every minute of it.

Alex and Chrisy walk into the church with two big smiles and the hint of nerves that I've learned to expect. It's November. Their wedding is scheduled for the second week in May. Several months before, they asked me to "marry them," much in the same way that people ask me to "baptize them." That's how people usually put it. It's a figure of speech more than anything else, but I always notice it.

Except in the most literal, physical sense, that's not what actually happens, not if God is real, if the soul is real, and if the Spirit searches our hearts and hears our very thoughts. It's the Spirit who really baptizes and marries; and in the case of marriage (and same-sex unions), the people in love are the ones who receive the Spirit's blessing by the power of their intent and the making of vows. Obviously, I preside over the event. I do "marry them" in the eyes of the Church, and I bless their marriage as a sacramental act. By mutual agreement of the Church and the State, I fulfill an important legal function. But having said that, my role is important, but also minimal in the grand scheme of things. As I see it, my primary purpose is to cultivate their intent and to help clarify what that means for those who make the vows. I believe this because I know that when their vows are made, the Spirit is with them, hearing every word they speak.

I prepare some hot tea for the three of us. We talk a while longer, until I give them *The Book of Common Prayer*. I ask them to open it to the wedding ceremony and to read through the marriage vows. Within thirty seconds or so, I can feel Chrisy becoming quiet, slightly withdrawn, and pensive. She's reading the Declaration of Intent, which is near the opening of the ceremony. Then I repeat the words out loud for each of them, as I will do when the wedding actually happens:

> *Chrisy (Alex), will you have this man (woman) to be your husband (wife), to live together in the covenant of marriage? Will you love him (her), comfort him (her), honor and keep him (her), in sickness and in health; and forsaking all others, be faithful to him (her) as long as you both shall live?*

I'm the one who will ask these questions when the big day comes; and I'm glad to report that, when that day actually came, they did say "I will" with joyful, self-confident smiles. It was a great wedding. But the story I'm telling now is about the conversation we had months earlier, in November. I wanted them to spend some time reflecting on the words that they would be saying in May. The words themselves are remarkably straightforward. There's no dilly-dallying around, no spin, no "buts," nor should there be. In effect, the Declaration of Intent is made on the assumption that the couple knows what they're saying and why they're saying it. Quite literally, they're revealing and declaring to each other, to everyone present, and to God what the "thoughts of their hearts" (as the Prayer Book eloquently puts it) actually are.

This is only the beginning. The Declaration of Intent lays the groundwork for the actual vows, which are yet to come:

> *In the Name of God, I ____, take you ____, to be my [husband/wife], to have and to hold from this day forward, for better or for worse, for richer or for poorer, in sickness and in health, to love and to cherish, until we are parted by death. This is my solemn vow.*

Chrisy remains quiet and pensive as we read, again out loud, the marriage vows. It's not uncommon for people to respond exactly like Chrisy has. I've seen this more often than I can remember, and I'm not at all surprised when it happens. Rather than indicate reluctance or a problem, it can be (and usually is) a very healthy sign. The "thoughts of our hearts" can be (and usually are) complicated. Chrisy's suddenly quiet disposition tells me, at the very least, that she's reflecting on the depth of meaning that the vows represent, which is what I hope to see. Vows are some of the most important words that ever pass a person's lips. The making of vows can be (and should be) a life-changing moment. Vows and the intent to keep them are serious business. We're talking about a great deal more than having "good intentions" or telling ourselves that we "mean well."

Wedding vows can also be a delicate subject for many reasons, and it just so happened that Chrisy's life experience was a case in point. She had made similar vows once before, in a previous marriage that had taken a wrong turn. She had been subjected to emotional and physical abuse that was devastating. Alcohol, and later drugs, had played a large part in her former husband's behavior, which he refused to confront or address in any responsible way.

According to Chrisy, he had many fears in his life, primarily the fear of being criticized or judged, for reasons that she traced to his abusive father. In any event, he had been both unwilling to move through his fear, and unable to enter into the relationship that the vows of marriage declare. Gradually, he turned his anger and fear against her. This had happened many years ago. The emotional scars had healed. Nevertheless, she was well aware of the meaning of these vows, and she did not take them lightly.

Alex and Chrisy were clearly in love. They knew it in November, they knew it in May, and they're still in love today. Love was never the issue in the months before their wedding. They were grown-up and practical people, who knew themselves well. Yet, Chrisy realized—at the time, better than Alex—that the inner reality of marriage is a movement within two souls that depends almost entirely on trust. Marriage is a journey made together into the unknown. Sometimes it can be rocky; other times, more than rocky; and still other times, smooth sailing on a calm sea. From Chrisy's point of view, the vows were not about having "good intentions." To say "I will" or "I do" is not, at its heart, an agreement made *only* by the rational part of one's mind—in effect, a contract, much less an act of consent, as if the vows represent an imposed structure that a person *only* decides to abide by. She understood what the vows meant to her, and she had every reason to believe that Alex could take those same vows very seriously indeed.

Although it would be wrong to say that Chrisy's life was ruled by fear in this regard, she was afraid, and she needed something from Alex that would help her to move through it. What she needed, but had not realized until we all read the vows out loud in my office, was for him to hear her story in a new way—which he did. There were no dark secrets. Even if there had been secrets, they wouldn't have made any difference. These two people really loved each other. She wanted him to understand how deeply into the soul marriage vows go, and that she fully intended to make those vows with him. She wanted to make those vows with the confidence that both of them could, if it became necessary, stare into the dreaded abyss without losing themselves, their common sense, or their marriage. From her point of view, a marriage really is the movement of two souls becoming one, through thick and thin, and she wanted the two of them to make that leap together.

All Chrisy needed was some time, but that didn't mean "doing nothing." She needed time to feel intuitively, more than to know rationally, what only she could perceive in her soul and his. Although the same could be said for Alex, Chrisy was the one who made it happen. She took the initiative to cultivate and nurture the instinct for intent in both of them. They were both wise enough, each in their own way, to let time—and the Spirit—work through them to strengthen their intent.

If love is the path that we want to follow (I hope that it is), then intent is the sacred power within us that turns our attention to it, even when our sense of purpose becomes weak. Chrisy had good instincts, and she followed them. She had learned, through difficult times in her life, that intent can and must be cultivated every bit as much as love. As strong as the bonds of love can be, without intent they can still become surprisingly fragile—so fragile that we risk losing it.

We do our best to describe the Mystery of intent with words like "commitment," "loyalty," and "will." Those are truly important words, yet they can't fully account for what actually happens in the depth of our hearts when the crises of life come. As strange as this may sound, we find the heart of intent most easily by listening to the silence within our hearts. This is where the Spirit lives, guides us silently, and hears every word. That's about all that anyone can really say about intent. Chrisy knew, better than most, that intent is a Holy Mystery.

Most people I know are loving souls who believe in love. The problem comes with following through when times get tough. This is another way of saying that vows are broken not so much because we lose sight of love, but because our capacity for intent becomes weak. The stresses, anxieties, and fears that everyone faces can make us lose our direction and true purpose in life. We lose sight of who we are and who we are meant to be. Love is the gift we have to give, but intent and attention is the way we give it. If we love, but fail to attend to it, then love suffers.

Having said that, we would not want to overlook the importance of support, especially the support of family and friends. More than two people make vows at weddings. Near the beginning of the ceremony, everyone is asked whether they will support the couple in keeping their vows, and to declare their intent by saying "we will." This collective declaration affirms the vows of the couple, but it's also meant to cultivate the instinct for intent in everyone present.

I don't want to be preachy about this—I really don't—but it's nearly impossible to move through our fear or to cultivate any of our spiritual instincts, unless we take the vows and promises we make seriously. We can't reasonably expect to be successful in anything that really matters without applying ourselves, without setting our hearts and minds on our goal, and saying "no" to some things—like fear—and a resounding "yes" to the truly important parts of life—like love. The leap into the unknown is made successfully when we fill our hearts with genuine intent, rather than good intentions. There's a risk involved (there's always a risk); but we take the risk and make the leap for one reason, and only one reason—for the sake of love. God is love.

Times of crisis have a way of focusing our minds in ways that we rarely experience. The church where I serve was built as a result of one of those times. The stained-glass window above the altar bears an inscription to a young boy who died accidentally in the mid-1870s. His father, a Wall Street broker, built the church in his memory and dedicated it to him. Above the boy's name, Cornelius Humbert, there's a large image of Jesus, and beside him, another inscription, this one from the Beatitudes: "Blessed are the pure in heart, for they will see God."

I don't know how people in the nineteenth century understood purity of heart. It's entirely possible, even likely, that the father saw it in the face of his lost son—and in his memory of him—which, one can only hope, brought a measure of consolation. I have to assume that people back then, like now, think of purity of heart as an ideal to be strived for, rather than a truth about the way things were, once upon a time. Because purity of heart seems so out of reach for ordinary people like you and me, we usually dismiss it out of hand, see it in the faces of young children, or remember it in our own childhood with a sense of nostalgia.

Another possibility is that we might reject it as a matter of principle. Women, in particular, often reject (with good reasons) some images of "purity" as a form of social control imposed on them by a world organized by and for men. It might then be reinterpreted to give us a better understanding of a virtuous life based on the lived experience of women. My point is that purity of heart can be seen from different points of view, and it is within all those many perspectives that we must search for the key to its meaning.

In our everyday lives, we don't usually think about purity of heart very much, in the same way that we don't think about intent; and we probably won't think about it until our lives are called into question. Personal loss and grief are good examples, especially when death or the possibility of death is involved. At first, we're understandably shocked. Then, a confusing bundle of feelings comes to the surface, including unexpected anger or rage, until they are eventually released. I have to believe that the young father passed through his grief and found purity of heart the best that he could.

The irony is that the very situations when we know, for sure, that our feelings are the most confused, complicated, ambiguous, and "impure" offer the very best opportunities to discover the spiritual power of intent. Until that point, "purity" may have been the very last word we would apply to ourselves; but then, something within us shifts and we know what we want, what we're doing, and why we're doing it. We might not even think of it in a particularly religious way; nevertheless, in moments like that we know what it's like to put ourselves in the hands of a power that's greater than ourselves, and that's when the meaning of "purity of heart" becomes clearer than it ever has. As you'll see in the story below, this shift within us seems to be passive, as if we have no say in the matter, but it only *seems* that way. In practice, to draw upon our instinct for intent is one of the most powerful, empowering, and faithful actions we may ever take.

A few years ago, Janet, a friend of mine, could have told you all about that; but now, I'll tell you about it myself. She's in an unfamiliar place—a hospital room. She's just heard some bad news from her doctor, and she's wondering why she, in the prime of her life, must face the worst situation she could possibly imagine. Why is this happening to me? Is it really happening? That's what she's thinking. For a few minutes, she wonders whether she might have misinterpreted what the doctor said, or whether she had just awakened from a bad dream. Yet there she is, wide awake; and the prognosis of cancer is quite real. She can't wish it away. She knows that she could die. She's despondent, she feels powerless; and she's terrified.

If you can, try to imagine yourself in her situation. Actually, I would highly recommend imagining it, as unpleasant as it might be. Death is one of the realities of life that we all eventually face.

The thought of it may be frightening, but it is unavoidable. The prospect of death can be a great teacher and the very best cultivator of our spiritual instincts. Think of it in the way that Janet lived it. Suddenly, in your hospital bed, everything familiar and normal about life has fallen away. The ego defenses you routinely use to get through an ordinary day no longer work. They're not even relevant. You realize that you're thinking about God in ways that you never have. You find yourself praying truly heartfelt prayers, talking to God like a friend sitting next to you. Your thoughts seem noticeably raw, uncensored, straightforward, and blunt. You remember some very faithful, devout people—friends—who have died of an illness just like yours.

But this is not about them. It's about *you* and *your life*. You want *your faith* to take away *your fear*. You want this more than anything in the world. You tell yourself, rightly, that the light is not overcome by the darkness, which you truly hope and want to believe. Yet, the darkness is still there. You say to yourself that God will not give you any obstacle that you cannot endure, including your fear. Still, you are afraid, and you are praying in the most faithful and honest way that you can.

Janet told me that her fear was terrible. She wanted her faith to make her fear go away, but it didn't work out like that. If that's not bad enough, the situation became unexpectedly worse as a result of some friends who loved her a great deal. Their intentions were good. They wanted to offer support and encouragement, which they did, except for one particularly troublesome piece of advice: They told her to "have faith." Most people would say that those are exactly the right words, and possibly the *only* right words. They weren't. Her friends meant well, but their "help" was anything but helpful. The issue was not whether Janet had faith. She did. The issue was that her prognosis completely undermined her sense of personal power, or nearly so; and the "encouraging" comments made by her friends took away what little personal power she had left.

Why did she respond in this way? How could it have been possible that her friends added insult to injury simply by encouraging a faithful person to have faith? Why was their advice *not* helpful or encouraging? Keep in mind that it might have been exactly the right thing to say in a different circumstance. But in this situation and with this particular person, the answer is so amazingly obvious that it nearly always goes unnoticed. In the midst of a terrifying crisis, Janet had no choice but to work through the practical meaning of her faith. In her vulnerable state of mind, she was considering the possibility that the cause of her illness was, in fact, a lack of faith, which would have made their "encouragement" seem to be an implicit reprimand. This, of course, was not their intention, but never mind—they "meant well."

Let me spell it out: To tell Janet to "have faith" could very easily suggest that she has little or none. To make matters worse, it could also suggest that an apparent lack of faith might not only have been the cause of the illness, but also the obstacle to her recovery. Even more, their well-intended advice would have the unintended consequence of making it more difficult for Janet to have faith at the very moment when she needed to know *how* to be faithful.

The good news is that their "advice" pulled the rug from under Janet's feet; and in doing so, it threw her back upon her spiritual instincts. The result was that she confronted her fear head-on by accepting the possibility of death and drawing upon her instinct for intent. Janet did something that was bold and courageous: She didn't deny the truth; she didn't run away; and she didn't ask God to take it away. Rather, by the power of her intent, she made a turn, within herself, and embraced the truth—and that carried her through her fear. Let me say that again: What Janet did was to embrace the truth of it. It was difficult, but it was also simple; and when she did it, Janet was free. The truth had set her free.

Janet would not have thought of what she did as an expression of faith. In fact, in that moment, and as result of her friends' comments, she believed that she had given up on faith and rejected it. I would not want to argue with her about that, but I would say that she had put her intent to a faithful use. I would also say that she wanted to know, above all else, "how" to be faithful, and that's exactly what she found. I have to believe—and I do believe—that God was with her every step of the way.

From a spiritual point of view, the power of Janet's intent matched the love of God, or as it's more traditionally put, "her will became God's will." She knew what she wanted and why she wanted it, and she found the courage to pursue it. She called upon her instinct for intent and trusted it. In that moment, Janet discovered what "purity of heart" means.

A Spiritual Practice in Intent

In all good conscience—and at the risk of making a nuisance of myself—I have no choice but to suggest a practice in intent that follows in the tradition of "rise and shine." Some of my dearest friends would regard this as the boot camp of all spiritual traditions, and they would be right. It's also the most clear-minded and effective practice in intent—and moving through fear—that I can imagine.

The first step is to get into the habit of marshaling your intent at the very beginning of the day, preferably at the moment when you wake from sleep. Think of an attitude toward life that you want to maintain throughout the day—an example might be "joy." Of course, there are many others that you can choose from, like "compassion" or "seriousness." I'm simply giving an example that I especially like.

Probably the most formidable obstacle in this practice is simply to remember it in the morning. If needed, write yourself a note, and keep it by your alarm clock or attached to the bathroom mirror where you'll see it. I'm not kidding. Do whatever it takes to get off on the right foot at the very beginning of the day— before your mind and the world have a chance to take you in a different direction. And do not, under any circumstances, turn on the television or check your cell phone and e-mail until you have done this part of the practice. It's easy enough to wake up in the morning; but it's quite another matter to take the next step toward "awakening" in the deeper, spiritual sense of the word.

The second step is to be mindful of your intent—let's say that you did choose joy—as you fulfill your responsibilities and duties through the course of the day. I'm not saying that joy, for example, must be your only thought, or that you shouldn't feel afraid when something fearful happens. I'm asking you to work on being open to life as it happens, while always being mindful of your intent. Again, the challenge is simply to remember what your intent is and to let it shape how you live. Put another way, the point is to maintain the strength of your intent so that negative influences, like fear, cannot gain control of your life.

Keep track of any distractions that you may have—I'm almost joking, as the number and frequency of distractions will very likely be mind-boggling. Don't feel disheartened by this. Rather, try to laugh. Our unruly minds are part of the astonishingly peculiar nature of human experience. Nevertheless, it's still a good idea, especially when you begin this practice, to make note of those numerous distractions, while turning your intent immediately back to joy whenever you're distracted. At first, if we can simply remember to do just this, then we are doing quite well.

I usually keep a slip of paper with me on which I write anything I want to remember in the course of the day—a "things to do" list—and on that list I include distractions of all kinds, including worries and fears. At the end of the day, you might enter them in a journal devoted to this purpose. Do you notice any recurrent patterns? Do they have their source in memories from the past? Or do they involve concerns relating to a specific situation now? The fact that you will begin to understand what these patterns are will build self-confidence and strengthen your capacity to choose your intent consciously.

Soon, we will realize that "rise and shine" is "the practice" of all spiritual practices. As simple and silly as it may sound, its ultimate purpose goes to the very heart of all spiritual traditions. From the point of view of the Christian tradition, the purpose of this practice is to make "our will, God's will"—which sounds anything but silly. Either way, be open about this. Observe your life with a good sense of humor, but without being judgmental. The practical benefits are immense: We gain greater control over our moods, feelings, and thoughts; we won't be thinking nearly as much about our fears and worries; and we'll be more likely to make sound decisions and to think for ourselves, rather than getting caught up in the hidden agendas of others.

One final comment: When we cultivate our intent around a higher purpose—for example, maintaining a joyful attitude toward life—then we realize that most of our fears really are nothing more than "distractions." By doing this spiritual practice every day, those fears won't seem nearly as powerful as they once did. The simple reason is that we're giving our minds something better to do. In a larger sense, we're also reclaiming the power that we've given to fear—and putting it to a much better use.

6.

CONSCIENCE:
OUR MORAL COMPASS

These then, are the two points I wanted to make. First,
that human beings, all over the earth, have this curious
idea that they ought to behave in a certain way, and
cannot really get rid of it. Secondly, that they do not in
fact behave in that way. They know the Law of Nature;
they break it. These two facts are the foundation of all
clear thinking about ourselves and the universe we live in.

—C. S. Lewis, *Mere Christianity* (1943)

I do not pretend to understand the moral universe;
the arc is a long one; my eye reaches but little ways;
I cannot calculate the curve and complete the figure
by the experience of sight; I can divine it by conscience.
And from what I see I am sure it bends towards justice.

—Theodore Parker,
"Of Justice and Conscience" (sermon 1853)

*I would be hard-pressed to say, and even more to prove, that one
spiritual instinct is more important than another. That each of
our spiritual instincts plays an essential part in the larger whole is*

the point that matters the most. Conscience—our inward feeling for the difference between right and wrong—is the moral compass that organizes our instincts and guides us through our fear. When conscience occupies its place at the center of our lives, the light of consciousness burns brightly within us. It points us in the direction that we need to go, while reminding us that doing the right thing is the right thing to do—and that knowing the right thing can take some careful thought. Sometimes, our conscience works the best when it tells us that we don't know the answers that we're looking for, that we can't know, or that we're not supposed to know.

Conscience is not infallible, but it is the moral compass that we've been given. With it, we have the capacity to foresee the consequences of our actions, at least within the narrow space that our light illuminates. It helps us to realize that what we want may not always be what we should have and that the way things are may not be the way they ought to be. It can save our lives by helping us to perceive the difference between the fearless courage that propels us into the worst kind of danger and the sheer recklessness that we often mistake for courage when we lose our good sense.

Without a lively conscience, we become subject to any number of harmful forces, including unacknowledged and unbridled fear. More often than not, it is fear that prevents us from acting in good conscience—we're simply afraid to do the right thing. And if we fail to cultivate and use our conscience, then fear either supplants it, putting itself in its place, or it hardens our hearts to the point where our conscience becomes frozen. The outcome is that we become self-centered and perhaps entrenched in the kind of selfishness that is difficult to see within ourselves. We no longer hear different points of view, believing that we already know everything that we need to know.

In his famous book Mere Christianity, *C. S. Lewis addressed this very dilemma. I'll summarize portions of it here: We may* differ on what "selfish" means in practice, but we all share in the belief that we cannot simply do anything that we please. In other words, the fact that we all have a moral compass makes us human. The instinct of conscience is found in everyone, with rare exceptions, which accounts for the remarkable similarity in the many and otherwise diverse moral teachings found among the world's cultures and religions. But the form that our conscience takes, its vitality, and its contents are learned. What we usually see are the differences, rather than our common humanity, and that limited perspective frequently hardens into prejudice and selfishness—especially when we're afraid.

What we also fail to notice is that moral teachings change and transform, but not completely or randomly. For the most part, our understanding of them changes; and over the long path of history, they change in a certain direction.

As Theodore Parker, the Transcendentalist philosopher, abolitionist, and Unitarian minister, said so famously over 150 years ago: The moral universe "bends towards justice." He was not equating justice with revenge, as we're prone to do, but perceiving a deeper truth that's perceived by conscience and that points to the presence of a power that's greater than we are, yet within us too.

This "bending toward justice" usually involves a struggle; and that struggle creates a tension between conscience, on the one hand, and code, tradition, and law, on the other. The relationship between them is subtle and complex, which should not be surprising. Conscience and tradition are intimately linked, and our very survival depends on both—the relationship and the tension.

This is how I understand it. All our spiritual instincts, including conscience, are spiritual gifts because we receive the light of truth through them. This light, working through our spiritual instincts, has gradually given rise to our many moral and spiritual *traditions. These traditions are tested through time in a process that never ends, nor should it end. They were tested in the past; they are tested today; and, if all goes well, they will be tested in the days and years to come. That's where tradition comes from and how it evolves. Tradition, in turn, shapes our conscience, as it must and should, but our conscience is not bound by it. The same light that has shone within us turns our conscience back to tradition when we forget its true source and purpose, and it propels us to change tradition when tradition no longer serves the deeper purpose for which it was intended.*

I'll give an example. Several generations of well-meaning, churchgoing people—people who lived not long ago—used their knowledge of the Bible with great skill and devotion to rationalize the institution of slavery. What they wanted to believe was interpreted as "God's truth." Gradually, their conscience helped them to see the difference between the world as it is and the world as it ought to be. The light of conscience became a cry for justice. They heard it within themselves, because they learned to hear it in those who had been enslaved. This was not easy. They had convinced themselves that letting go of their traditional beliefs would be a threat to their survival—which made them afraid. But they changed. Because they changed, tradition changed. They learned to move through their fear, and what they began to find, as a result of their movement, was the nature of the real world.

The fact that the struggle between conscience and tradition remains with us is a sign of a healthy moral compass. Today, this struggle takes place in any number of areas; for example, in relation to the Universal Declaration of Human Rights, sexual orientation, and the right of living creatures and whole ecosystems to exist—all bodies of life that are being destroyed at the hands of creatures who have neglected to cultivate their conscience enough to ensure our survival. If it is true that the moral universe "bends towards justice" (I believe that it is true), then the soul's thirst for justice will not only carry us through our fear, but also enliven our conscience to a point where, with God's help, we still might survive.

This chapter begins with a possibly hypothetical situation— the experience of waiting in line in heaven. The purgatory-like scenario, which illustrates the beliefs, desires, and prejudices that distort our moral compass, serves as a point of departure for the stories that follow. The second story involves my last conversation with a close friend as he approached the time of death. Together, we looked back on our lives and our fears. The third story, which has two parts, describes the loss of my fearless nature in childhood and its recovery with the help of my mother. It shows how learning the difference between fearlessness and recklessness shapes not only the course of our lives, but also the integrity of our very souls. The fourth story gives an account of two children who, in a span of only a few days, worked out the meaning of justice between the two of them. Their unexpected and difficult encounter ends with the giving of a simple gift—an empty birdcage—that would crystallize a friendship and stand for the meaning of freedom for years to come.

L et's imagine that we've moved beyond our fear of death, even beyond death itself. Now we're in heaven, standing in line, as it turns out, waiting to meet our Maker. The situation is, needless to say, peculiar. On the one hand, we're queued up before the pearly gates, having completed our course on earth.

On the other hand, in some part of our souls we still believe that we're living as we always have. Our experience is split between the two, which makes our minds divided and unsure about which part of our lives is real and which is a product of our imagination. Yet both are happening at the same time.

What would we be thinking, standing there, waiting in line? For starters, it's a very long line, and no one likes to wait. Many of us—those wanting to avoid the line altogether—are pleasantly surprised to learn that our cell phones actually work in heaven. We try to speak with God directly, and then through e-mail and texting. The fact that this is possible is a huge relief, as the line really is long; and, quite honestly, it makes us feel important.

However, we soon discover the real reason that our cell phones work, and it's not what we had assumed. What we should have known all along is that nothing can separate us from the love of God—not even our newest toys. They work, but they don't carry us any closer to God, or take us any farther up the heavenly ladder. We're a little perplexed and disappointed to learn this; yet we can't help but be glad about it. Like I said, our minds are divided: We're confused about where we are and why we're here.

It finally dawns upon us that God receives all our messages, with or without our cell phones. The reply that everyone receives, delivered through the Holy Spirit, is that we should simply relax. Each of us will have our appointment in due course. No one will be left out; everyone will have his or her turn; and this will happen in an appropriate, respectful, face-to-face manner, one person at a time—as always. The Holy Spirit assures us that God is all too aware of how busy we've all been (we're talking about millions of busy lifetimes), but there will be no exceptions. You would think that everyone would rejoice upon learning that justice in heaven is exceptionally just.

That's not how we respond. When we begin to realize that the universe really does bend toward justice, our outlook becomes even more divided. We're relieved to know that this is true, but in the familiar "I told you so" way that people in every culture and religious tradition seem to express. The result is that we become even more skillful in pursuing strategies for avoiding the long line. We apply those strategies with real diligence and commitment because we're convinced that our cause is good. Yet none of those strategies seems to work, which leads us to redouble our efforts even more.

Jesus sees what's going on. He has been working the line for a very long time, and he's seen this kind of fanaticism over and over again. He does his level best to give counsel and encouragement, while spelling out how things work as clearly as he can: "Just remember what I told you, *'Many that are first will be last, and the last first'*" (Mark 10:31). Upon hearing this, we all protest, loudly and angrily: "This is absurd." Some say it straight out: "Is there no justice? . . . I've been working my whole life, doing exactly what I'm supposed to do . . . Why am I back here? . . . I should be at the front . . . I deserve to be at the front." Some say, "But I'm a Christian . . . I should be ahead of the Muslims." Others say, "But I'm Muslim, I should be ahead of the Christians." Hindus and Buddhists have the same exchange. We all become instant experts on our chosen prophets, sages, and sons and daughters of God. We're convinced that we know exactly what they meant. We're quite certain about these things, quoting from them at great length.

You would think that Jesus would be exasperated or bored, but he's not. Having heard it all countless times before, he listens. We're the ones who are bored—with his constant listening. So we try another strategy: Each of us appeals to the Holy Spirit, adopting the most sincere, devout, and prayerful tone of voice that we can muster to make our case: "I really am a faithful person, and I'm quite sure God wants to talk with me as soon as possible. . . . There must be some misunderstanding. If you could only tell him that I'm here waiting." We haven't quite figured this out yet, but we're secretly afraid and asking for mercy, which we do not want to admit. In effect, we're saying that we've always had good intentions. At the same time, we're beginning to suspect that we've been wrong about something for a very long time.

At this point, Jesus is joined by Krishna, Moses, the Buddha, and Mohammed, who have been working the line too—for as long as anyone can remember. In a single chorus, they all explain that if we had, in fact, realized so much and done all the right things, then surely we not only would be content simply to be there, but also we would have gone willingly—even joyfully—to the very back of the line. Our responsibility is to help everyone else, down to the very last person. This, after all, is what "The first shall be last, and the last, first" means. Under no circumstances can anyone be forgotten, left out, much less sacrificed, so we can move up the line, getting ahead of everyone else. This is the way things are in the real world, whether in heaven or on earth. We can't change this; we shouldn't want to change it; and the sooner we realize this, the better off and happier we all will be.

We might have realized, looking back on our lives, that we could have made the earth that we once knew into the heaven that we know now. Instead, the protest grows wildly intense. When this happens, the leaders, founders, and prophets of the world's religious traditions are then surrounded by a cloud of witnesses from all the peoples of the earth: a multitude of healers, shamans, and sages who lived for generation upon generation, long before we created religion as an institution. They all explain the reason for our appointed meeting—that is to say, our meeting with God. What they tell us is that all the great moral and spiritual teachings are deeply sacred. This is not the issue. The issue is that God already knows what those traditions have proclaimed—he, after all, had a hand in writing them. We don't need to tell him what they mean. The reason for our meeting is to discuss the book that we've written ourselves—the one that we've written in our souls, the book that is our life. God wants to know how much (or how little) our spiritual instincts have played a part in what we wrote.

By then, it dawns upon us that our wait in line could be quite long. We've all written a lot, probably way too much, and it could take a while to sort things out. Jesus assures us that this may not be the case. God already knows what we've written in our souls too. He just wants to discuss it. And, best of all, there is forgiveness, very definitely, more forgiveness that we actually need. But we can't avoid the story of who we have become, as if that story doesn't matter.

Once the issue is put this way, the angry crowd begins to settle down, but that's about as far as it goes. No one has actually seen God, not yet. We're still waiting in line—every one of us. God knows that it may take a long time, but he also knows that time may run out. In some sense, it always does.

A close friend of mine loved that story. We told a version of it together, each contributing to the whole, only a few days before he died. More than anything else, he laughed. I've never known anyone who hated to wait in line more than him. I suppose that I rank a close second. A few days before, I had made the trip from New York City to Oxford, where he had been teaching, promptly rented a car, and drove to the local medical center that had become Darrell's home. Having made the trip several times, I knew the way quite well. Each trip gave me plenty of time to think about my friend's life and mine. Although Darrell had not been a beekeeper (not as far as I know), he had been trained in entomology and, like me, in cultural anthropology. He loved insects; and some of his closest friends, people and insects, lived in the world's most remote places, places like the Brazilian Amazon. That's another way of saying that he was one of the most peculiar people I've ever met, and he wasn't afraid of much.

If you look at life as a spiritual journey, which we did, then we were friends along the way. More than anything else, it was the pursuit of the sacred that wove our lives together. We wanted to discover as much about life and ourselves as we possibly could. At least that's what we said. Looking back now, I believe that's what we actually did. There were some rocky moments in our friendship, in addition to the usual personal disagreements, but none of that compared with the strength of the bond between us.

Darrell and I both understood that the end of his life was near. As much as I tried to deny it, the degenerative nature of his cancer was plain to see. I was grieving; and I expected that the visit would be difficult, which it was. Not every day was lucid, but this was a good day. For the most part, we sat on the edge of his hospital bed, remembering late-night shenanigans on more than one continent, some worthwhile trouble we stirred up now and again, an environmental book for the United Nations that we worked on together, and so on. Most of our memories actually involved hard work in the pursuit of human rights, justice, and ecology. From his point of view and from mine, there was little if any difference between the pursuit of justice and the joy of life; but in his hospital room, it was a tremendous joy of life that we remembered most. I wouldn't trade those few precious hours for anything.

There was a slight pause in the conversation, just before it took a more serious turn. I was facing Darrell from a nearby chair. He tilted his head toward mine. His eyes focused directly on mine, and he asked a question: "What is the most important spiritual lesson that you've learned so far?" My first reaction, as usual, was to smile. We both smiled. Then there was more silence. We knew each other well enough to let the silence be what it is, without feeling the need to fill it with words. That's when our conversation really began.

We talked for another hour or more, first about the environmental crisis. This was not an abstract for us, but a highly personal, soulful concern that had occupied our lives for many years. As long as I had known him, twenty years or more, Darrell also felt an inner call to work for the rights of First Peoples in the Amazon. He knew his life's purpose. He also knew that this purpose would eventually put his life in danger, which happened on more than one occasion. It was for that reason, among others, that he was honored with a prestigious international award for courage.

In his hospital room, our conversation went even deeper than that. It was one of those rare moments of truth that we spend most of our lives doing our very best to avoid—despite the fact that they offer the best opportunities for gaining the self-knowledge that we sorely need. We both suspected that this would be our last opportunity to talk; and Darrell, more than me, wanted our visit to be a moment of truth in the true spiritual sense. Because he was preparing himself (and me) to meet our Maker, he created the sacred space that was needed for some honest soul searching with a close friend. It was a no-frills, deeply personal examination of conscience, very much in the spirit of the Ten Commandments. We didn't actually count up all the things we had done, for better or worse, and "left undone," as *The Book of Common Prayer* aptly puts it—although it might have seemed that way to someone listening in.

Among all the times in our respective lives that we remembered, there was one that Darrell chose to describe in some detail. It involved something that happened to him that he wanted me to know and understand. This was the gist of it. Years before, he had been walking alone in the rain forest and lost his way. This is not very difficult to do, even for a seasoned explorer. After wandering frantically for hours, unable to find any familiar landmarks, much less a path, he sat down under the forest canopy and cried. I'll never forget his words: "I cried like a baby . . . I cried for my mother."

That's what Darrell wanted to impress upon me. In those moments when we confront the reality of death head-on, what we want, more than anything else, is the comforting presence of our mothers and God. As Darrell described it, I couldn't help but think of Jesus on the cross, crying out "Abba," which means "Daddy." The feeling must have combined faith and desperation with resignation: "Why aren't you here, when I need you?" The words themselves cannot do justice to the unspeakably devastating nature of the experience, and they should never be interpreted as a character flaw or a sign of personal weakness. Rather, this cry is exactly what it seems to be: a desperate plea for help in the face of the abyss—in this case, the fear of total abandonment in death.

Darrell wanted to impress upon me that we do not reach a point in our lives when we become completely free from fear, nor should we ever believe that we can. The issue is not whether we have fears, but whether we're willing to find it within ourselves to move through them, even if that sometimes means crying out for our mothers—and God. This cry for help lays bare our ultimate powerlessness (as Christian teachings put it, "We have no power in ourselves to help ourselves"); and yet, we are not completely powerless. From the Spirit's point of view, we are immensely powerful. When the power of our primal instincts runs dry, we will call out from the depth of our souls, and the Spirit will respond.

We reflected on this for a while, exploring its significance in different areas of our lives. I couldn't help but bring it closer to home. I remembered the advice that parents sometimes tell their soon-to-be-wed children: "You can't live off of love." It's an irritating cliché, but a wise one nonetheless. What they mean is that unless the bills are paid, households are managed, and the "realities" of life are met head-on, then marriages suffer. They might fail. Yet the meaning of one's life—and a marriage—cannot be summarized by the size of a bank account, whether it's large, small, or nonexistent. The fear of not having enough money can do as much damage to a marriage as a lack of it can, if not more. I suspect that "living off love" for a while might actually be a good way to learn about life—in the same way that being lost in the forest reveals the "true riches" of one's life in the Spirit. In the real world, there are times when families have no choice but to live off of love. My conscience tells me that it's better to be upfront about this than to deny it. We need all our spiritual instincts to survive in this world.

Gradually, our conversation circled back to his initial question: "What is the most important spiritual lesson that you've learned so far?" By then, the answer was obvious: The greatest obstacle that we had faced was fear. This was "the truth" that we had been looking for through the years of our friendship. It's the kind of truth that we usually ignore until it erupts with full force in extreme circumstances—like the possibility of losing a job, a career, even one's life, or the devastating loss of a loved one that feels like death.

This is when we reached the very heart of our conversation. Darrell said that he wasn't afraid to die, not now, not in the hospital room. He didn't want to die, but he was at peace with it. He went on to say that there was one special fear that he had felt acutely, almost painfully, years before, when he had accepted the fact that he might die in the forest. This was the fear of regret. He had not wanted to reach the end of his life having failed to do something he felt called to do—because he was afraid of doing it. There will always be some regrets in life; and about that, there is forgiveness when we meet our Maker. But he wanted to reach the end of his life knowing that he had done the best he could. I think Darrell realized that this was how his conscience, in the course of a lifetime, had guided him through his fear.

We were looking at the larger picture of our lives and saying that if we add up all our individual fears, whatever they may be, we find one big fear behind them all: the fear of becoming who we are meant to be. In practice, this amounts to a fear of living, which is the fear we both had in mind: the fear of being who we are, of standing up for what it is right, and of doing the right thing in the face of criticism, harsh treatment, abuse, or worse— which is the fear hidden behind our pretending to be someone else. It's very easy to pretend in this way: hiding, while pretending that we're not hiding; pretending to be ourselves, while hiding the truth about our complicity with the way things are.

This level of fear sometimes involves shame, which is a difficult issue to discuss. It is entirely possible to be opposed to shame, rightly and as matter of principle, without understanding that a deeply spiritual version of shame exists. This kind of shame doesn't involve stigmatizing. It's not a socially created category of people. Rather, it accumulates in the soul when, of our own free will, we hide from God and from ourselves, pretending to be someone other than who we are—which then raises the uncomfortable question of *who we really are*. Perhaps we think we don't really know; but somehow, somewhere within us, we know the truth. Our egos might resist this truth so skillfully that we create a whole world of illusions, while sincerely believing that it's real. We pretend so well that we rarely perceive what we've done, which gives our pretending a justifying, righteous, half-believable appearance.

I think this is where much of our fear of God really comes from: the illusions we create to hide the truth about life from ourselves. Perhaps the myth of "the fall" is meant to give an account of this one fear, where it came from and why. This is the pervasive, relentless, yet largely unacknowledged fear that takes so many forms, enters into nearly every part of life, and rules so much of our existence. It's too peculiar and too powerful to be ignored in spiritual traditions, so we have myths that account for it in some way—but that's only a guess, and guessing doesn't take us very far. I trust my instincts more, and they tell me that forgiveness removes this fear from the deepest part of our souls.

Darrell smiled again and said that he had no regrets. He had done his best with the little time that he had on God's green earth. But it was enough. It was important for Darrell to say that. Had my friend lived longer, he would have wanted to talk a great deal more. But I didn't see him again. I knew that he had no regrets, and all was well between God and him. I was the one who still had to sort through it all. I was frustrated and angered by the loss of my friend, and I wanted to be at peace with it. I wanted someone to blame, and I wanted to hold him accountable. I remembered times when I thought he had crossed the line between "fearless" and "reckless," and I wanted to believe that he had been reckless with his illness. I wanted to believe that he could have seen the doctors sooner, and I wanted to blame the doctors too.

On my way home, I remembered what he said about being lost in the rain forest and calling out for his mother. I wondered whether on that day he had been reckless, or whether it was just one of those things that happen. That's when I stopped blaming. I realized that I was the one who was lost, crying out for an answer. I wanted justice. I wanted a life with no regrets. I wanted to do my best by moving through my fear of living. That's what my friend had done. He told me so in a moment of truth, and I believed him.

· · ·

Like I've said before, it's not that we're bad people. That's not the reason that we fail to do the right thing, when we could. The reason is that we're afraid, and that explains why some of our most cherished memories come from childhood—from the time before we lost our fearless nature. Can you remember what you were like back then? Can you remember it now, like you're really there? If you can, then you're well on your way to remembering who you really are.

Why would we ever let ourselves become disconnected from such a vital, joyful part of ourselves? One answer—the most important answer—must be given in the negative. It's not exactly that we learn to be afraid (although we do). Rather, we learn *not to be reckless*. It goes without saying that this can be a very good thing to learn, but there is a problem: Fearless and reckless are not the same; and, as a rule, the price we pay for learning "not to be reckless" is the loss of our fearlessness. And the consequences are great: It turns out that fearlessness is the quality we need most to cultivate our conscience, especially in the pursuit of justice. For example, people who "thirst for justice" are more likely to say "Why not?" rather than "There's nothing I can do," or "There's no point in trying," or "It wouldn't make any difference." Like I said, it's not that we're bad people. We've just lost contact with something vital, fearless, and joyful on which our very survival depends.

All this happens gradually, imperceptibly, as we learn to become otherwise "normal" and "well-adjusted" people. At some point, our preoccupation with a specific order of fear begins to loom quite large: the fear of ridicule and shame, the fear of not being part of the "in group," the fear of speaking out, and the fear of being yourself. We learn what it means to feel safe and secure in a world shared by other people who are learning the very same thing. The fact that we learn this together makes it a hugely powerful force in our lives. The result is that the importance of moving through these unacknowledged but debilitating fears is overshadowed by our collective desire to keep things the way they are—and to rationalize them to ourselves and to others. To do anything else would be seen as reckless abandon, if not utter selfishness. It's a peculiar way to go about living—and to learn how to live—and it's how we fall away from the real world.

This is why remembering the fearlessness of our childhood can be a huge step toward recovering our fearless nature as adults—without falling into recklessness. I'll illustrate what I mean by sharing a story about two events in my life that are connected by a single thread. The first event is my earliest conscious memory of being fearless, which, peculiarly enough, took place at the precise moment when I lost it. The second event describes how, with my mother's help, I regained my fearless nature—which, for all practical purposes, amounted to the recovery of my soul.

If you were to ask my mom about the day at the bridge, she would tell you essentially the same story, except for one crucial difference: For her it was a moment of sheer terror, and one of the most obvious reasons to be afraid that she's ever known. She can laugh about it now, but now is now, and that was then. As for me, it was a great adventure that I had completely forgotten until I was grown-up. Just the memory of it, after all these years, helps me to remember who I am.

That fateful day began with one of those small happenings in a person's life that would never be recorded in a family album. For the very first time, I was allowed to go all by myself to play at a neighbor's house. My friend was about ten years old. I was about five. I can't recall exactly what we did at his house, apart from the customary showing of some prized toys and knocking around the backyard, but it was fun.

After a while, when we both got bored, he came up with a "great idea"—we would walk to the river about a half mile away. I thought it was a great idea too. Not just a great idea, but the best idea of all time. He was old enough to be out on his own without anyone noticing. I wasn't old enough; yet the fact that I was with him seemed to make it okay. I don't believe I had ever walked much of anywhere without my parents. All that I knew, for sure, was that I was on my own, and I was thrilled.

So we made our way to the river, with great enthusiasm and the illusion of innocence, which we more than half believed. The way there took us through the small town where we lived, beyond the gas station, the volunteer firehouse, the hardware store, and a small grocery store. Having made it that far, we continued even farther: beyond the railroad tracks, and another several hundred yards to our real destination—the river and the bridge that crossed it.

It had been a long but easy walk to the river—much too easy. This meant that it failed to qualify as "the test" that every true adventure must have. But it didn't take long to find another one. Our test would be a breathtaking act of daredevilry. We would walk on top of the small concrete walls that formed the boundaries of the bridge on both sides. The walls were meant to keep unruly people and their cars from falling over the edge. You don't see bridges like that anymore. Today, they're much more elaborate and considerably safer; but then, the walls were only a few feet high, low enough to make it easy for two kids to crawl on top. What I remember most was watching the water flowing below me, fifty feet or more. We knew it was dangerous—otherwise it would not have been a test—but we were careful, whatever "careful" means in a situation like that. Never mind that I didn't know how to swim. That small detail never occurred to me. Thankfully, neither of us fell.

While all this was taking place, the owner of the grocery store, who had noticed us walking through town, drove to my parents' house and reported what he had seen to my mother. He could have called, but he didn't. He could have followed us to the bridge in his car and told us to go home. He didn't do that either. To this day, my mother will tell you that he should have picked up the phone and called. In any event, within a few minutes, we had all gathered at the river: parents, kids, and concerned citizens alike. You would have thought it was a baptism—or that someone had drowned.

The exhilaration of looking down and seeing the water below was immediately replaced by the terror I could see in my mother's eyes as she approached. I could feel her fear within me, as if it were my own. Quite honestly, her feelings really did become mine, in a manner that only the close bond between a mother and child can explain. I was startled and considerably more disoriented by her than by watching the water below.

Be that as it may, in the moment that my awareness shifted, my fearlessness evaporated into thin air. I was learning one of the critical lessons that every child must eventually learn—the difference between being fearless and being reckless. I was also becoming aware of a great deal more: the power that a child has to evoke sheer terror in the soul of a parent, the power of a mother's love to transform her child, and the powerlessness that we feel in the face of death. In a flash, I understood that I might have died and that my friend's life might have ended too.

No one actually asked, "Whose idea was it to go to the bridge?" There was no finger-pointing, no overt blaming. Rather, there were only the lessons that had to be learned. In some deep, soulful way, I began to realize that we are all responsible for each other. We really are our brothers' and our sisters' keepers. This is the responsibility that is part of our spiritual nature. All these lessons were planted as seeds in my mind; and from that point forward, my world began to change—drastically.

Now, let's move ahead six or seven years. My previous lesson in not being reckless was played out, twice a week, during my beginner swimming lessons at the YMCA. I wasn't swimming yet, but my head certainly was. I absolutely did not want to swim, and I dreaded everything about going to the pool. My fearless nature of a few years before had been replaced by an uncontrollable fear of the water. I'm not entirely sure what to call it: the fear of water, of swimming, of falling into the water, of drowning, or all the above. That didn't really matter. What did matter was that my fear controlled me. It was a peculiar fear. I wasn't afraid of the bathtub, but I was totally petrified at the prospect of jumping into the pool. The mere thought of holding my head under water was too much to bear. In order to give a reasonable explanation even to myself, I let myself believe that the chlorine would burn my eyes. It seemed rational, generally plausible, and easy enough to accept—sort of. Sometimes, when the pool was overly treated, the chlorine actually did produce a mild burning sensation. Of course, it didn't seem to bother anyone else.

Lurking within me was yet another fear that I couldn't quite put my finger on. Only later did I realize what it was: the fear that no one would be there to come to my rescue and I would drown. That's precisely what I felt, despite the presence of numerous lifeguards, well-trained teachers by my side, and a loving mother looking on. As for her, more than anything in the world, she wanted me to jump in the pool; but that, of course, was my worst fear.

The irony, which I didn't appreciate at the time, lived as a dilemma within a wound that cut deep into my soul. Years before, the message was: "Don't fall or you'll die." Now it was: "Jump or you'll live a slow death, trapped in your fear." That's what I was telling myself. No one told me to believe it, especially my mom. I thought of it all by myself. I knew, better than I knew anything else, that I had to move through my fear. I had to learn the difference between recklessness and fearlessness all over again. This time, however, I had to cross a bridge of a different kind.

It often happens that we reach a point in our lives when it's not helpful to think much about our fears, the precise reasons for them, and so on. I tried to figure it out—to think myself out of the situation—but that only took me so far. Thinking my way through it was preparatory work, but it wasn't enough to help me understand the nature of my fear, much less to release me from it. And it certainly wasn't enough to help me make a simple jump from the edge of pool into the water, even at the shallow end.

My mother did her best to help me. She was encouraging and supportive in every way, which helped my self-esteem. Most important, the fact of knowing that she actually wanted me to jump was the catalyst I needed. That alone helped me to reflect on my fear in a larger way, which opened my mind to the real nature of my situation. I began to realize that I had become stuck in a world that I was creating for myself. In other words, I began to understand my feelings for what they were, rather than letting my fear do my thinking for me.

Gradually, over a period of several weeks, I foresaw what the consequences would be if I did not overcome my fear—this is the flip side of perceiving the consequences of being reckless. This realization—that "my test" was not one of recklessness, but of fearlessness—was my salvation. Without it, I would have set in motion any number of rationalizations that would allow me to keep the fear and defend my wounded ego. My situation had become crystal clear: I didn't like who I was becoming, and to conceal the shame—from others and from myself—I might be tempted to believe all kinds of half-truths and lies about myself.

What I knew was that if I didn't do something soon, fear would take hold of my life and it wouldn't let go. But by jumping into the pool, I could save my soul and restore the joy of living and the fearlessness that I had known years before.

Without being pushy, my mother tried her best to talk me through it. She knew that I was the one who had to jump, and she wanted me to understand that I had nothing to be afraid of, and that I could do it. I could also see in her eyes that there was something else she wasn't saying: that she was just as nervous as I was. Her fear was that I wouldn't find the courage within myself. Above all, she wanted me to know that she loved me, regardless of the fear that we shared. Looking back, I believe that was the one piece of "knowledge"—the fact that I knew what she was feeling—that gave me the courage to think through my situation in a more settled way. It gave me a point of view—a secure place on which to stand—that was separate from the fearful world I was creating within myself. I didn't like what I was seeing—the consequences of not moving through my fear—but I could see it.

Finally, the day came when I decided to confront my fear. It was, in fact, a decision. I was standing at the edge of the pool. I turned my head and saw my mother in the distance. She was sitting with the other parents, just outside the fence that surrounded the pool, watching. I looked again at the water, and I knew that it was only my fear that stood between the person I wanted to be and me. Suddenly, without thinking, as if something or someone pulled me into the water, I jumped. I was free, like the fearless child I had been years before.

It was many years later that I began to piece all this together. That last conversation with my friend in Oxford brought back many of the memories. I still don't know what name to give my fear at the edge of the pool. Was it a fear of the water, of jumping in, of falling in, of drowning, of not being rescued? But that doesn't matter nearly as much as the fear that actually helped me make that jump. I believe my friend put his finger on it when he talked about his fear of regret: that, someday, we will look back on our lives and realize that we created a world based on all kinds of excuses for not doing the right thing, because we were afraid. It's not that we're bad people, or irresponsible, or riddled with fear. It's not that at all. And I'm not talking only about swimming. The problem is that we confuse freedom with security, and this makes us afraid to make any kind of jump. It makes us unwilling or unable to help people who need it. It makes us unwilling or unable to help ourselves.

All that is true enough, but what we really need to know is this: Any particular fear that we might have contains the specter of all our other fears wrapped within it. Once we move through that one fear, whatever it might be, then all our other fears become much less powerful. We begin to recover that fearless part of ourselves that's been hidden, locked away, and forgotten for far too long. The movement through our fear is really not about fear. It's about us—about getting our lives back and recovering that part of our souls that we've lost.

A few more years have passed. Now, I'm in the seventh grade. Little did I know that I was about to learn my first grown-up lesson in social justice. Oliver was the teacher. I was the student. Although our ages were the same, we lived in the same small town, and we rode the same school bus, where I saw him every day, Oliver and I might as well have been strangers. We were riding home from school on that bus when I received yet another lesson in recklessness and fearlessness. Lessons like that are given all the time. We're fortunate to learn from them even once. In practice, once is rarely enough.

I should tell you now that the lesson began with a shiner; that is to say, a black eye. I was on the receiving end. Given that the circumstances involved fighting and a school bus, I feel compelled to make two comments on the story before it actually begins. First, I want you to know that my sharing of this regrettable incident in my life in no way condones or rationalizes fighting, especially among children, or any form of violence. In addition, a black eye should never be equated with the word "grown-up," regardless of who delivers the blow. I'm just telling you what happened and how the events that followed awakened my conscience and nurtured a larger sense of justice within me.

However, I believe that I deserved the black eye; and I confess to looking back on it with a smile. With no hesitation whatsoever, I am willing to call it "justice served" and a "lesson learned," although the story certainly did not end there. I realize that some people will not see it in the same way that I do, and I respect their point of view. Yet, I was there and I witnessed the truth of it. What I know, for a fact, is that on that one particular day in my childhood, on one particular school bus, what should have happened actually did happen.

Second, I think we all know that public buses, including school buses, are amazing places. Anyone familiar with the history of the United States knows this. Fifteen years before I reached the seventh grade, Rosa Parks refused to give up her seat on a bus in Montgomery, Alabama; and by doing so, she forever changed the nature of race relations and civil rights in this country. She stood up for herself, fearlessly, by refusing to get up from her seat. Children and adults of all complexions, nationalities, and religions meet the same challenges and face the same fears whenever injustice of any kind is involved. When they're given guidance and half a chance to develop their spiritual instincts, kids have the wisdom to do the right thing; and in the case of my friend and me, to sort out and settle disputes among themselves. The story that I'm about to tell began on a school bus; and as you will see, it did not end there, which was good. The result was that a raw lesson in justice was transformed into a door that opened into true friendship.

I suppose the story really begins with adolescent hormones. Kids—I should say boys—can act a little crazy when their hormones kick in. I certainly did, when mine did. I can still remember it, forty years later: I had more energy than I knew what to do with; I was curious about everything, but not focused enough to do much of anything, or to do anything right. I had very little understanding of or interest in the meaning of authority. From my point of view, authority figures were fair game. In my seventh-grade classroom, I wanted to give the impression of being "fearless," but "reckless" would have been the right word to describe me. What little self-awareness I had in those days was directed almost entirely into diverting the attention of others toward me. I had a bare minimum degree of respect for my teachers and classmates, which meant, in practical terms, that I planned my escapades carefully enough so no one would be physically harmed. Those were my rules, to the extent that I thought about it. In a nutshell, I was a holy terror.

I'm pretty sure that I was the reason that my homeroom and history teacher retired earlier than she had planned. This is not something that I'm proud of. When the principal of the school talked to me about this, I was more confused than repentant—although I faintly recall a trace of guilt cracking through my hard shell. It never occurred to me that anything I might have done would have had much of an impact on her. Well, that's not exactly true. I wanted to disrupt the classroom, and I wanted to have an impact on her. It was my teacher as a person that I hadn't taken into account, nor had I taken into account the fact that my classmates had feelings and concerns—and lives—of their own.

All this began to change on the school bus. It was Friday afternoon. I was sitting at the back of the bus, looking at the others in front of me. Everyone was quiet and well-behaved. I, on the other hand, wanted some excitement. It all happened very quickly. My options were limited, which was frustrating, so I did something that I had never done before: I started picking on one of the other students, mainly with words that, by the grace of God, I have forgotten. I knew Oliver's name, but I didn't know him. I knew it was wrong to torment him, but I did it anyway. I can't actually say that I made a "decision" to do this, although I was clearly doing it. I remember telling myself to stop, but I didn't listen to anyone, myself included.

Oliver looked at me in utter disbelief. Later, I understood what the look in his eye meant: "You idiot, what do you think you're doing?" In that moment, I was so wrapped up in my idiotic, reckless, out-of-control display (while believing that I was being fearless) that I wouldn't have recognized much of anything for what it really was. So, I continued. No, I took it a step further. Like in the script of a movie, I took his cap, forcing him to take it back. Suddenly, out of nowhere (or so it seemed), he socked me in the eye. I did recognize that—barely. Now, I was the one looking at him in utter disbelief. I was shocked, dumbfounded, and confused. I walked, sheepishly, back to my seat at the back of the bus.

By the time I got home, maybe thirty minutes later, my eye was beginning to swell. When I looked in the bathroom mirror, I could see the outline of a soon-to-be deep purple bruise, which I would have to explain to my parents. Things like that can't be hidden, as much as we might try. About an hour later, I gave my dreaded explanation. It wasn't easy, but I told them the basic facts of the story. They were concerned and perplexed. They asked whether I had hit Oliver. I said no. I don't believe my father regarded my black eye as the worst part of the problem that I brought home.

Rather, he wanted to know whether I had apologized. In all honesty, I couldn't remember. It all happened so fast on the bus. I tried my best to remember. I wanted to remember, but for the life of me, I couldn't. The fact that I couldn't remember meant that I would have to go to Oliver's house over the weekend and tell him that I was sorry. As you'll soon see, my lack of memory, in this case, was providential—and possibly the work of the Spirit.

The next day, Saturday afternoon, I walked the half-mile or so to Oliver's house. I knocked on the front door. His father greeted me with a stern but otherwise polite tone in his voice. He looked at my black eye, but made no comment, which reminded me of my dad's reaction. Then he called to Oliver. Without saying a word, Oliver and I walked together to his room and sat down. I told him that I didn't know what had come over me, and that I was truly sorry. But before I could completely finish my apology, he apologized for hitting me, which surprised me at first. It hadn't occurred to me that he might be feeling sorry too.

Then the conversation went in an unexpected direction. Oliver wanted to know whether my parents had punished me. I said yes. I had been grounded, the only exception being that I would visit him. In a sense, I had already received the greater part of my punishment, which I had no choice but to wear. Oliver said nothing about that. What he did say was that he had been punished for hitting me. He explained that his father was very disturbed by the whole incident and concerned that I might have been injured more than I actually was. Both Oliver and I knew that we had not been fighting, not really, and that neither of us wanted to fight. I had never hit anyone before; I believed that the same was true of Oliver; and on the school bus, I suspected that even he was surprised by what he did.

A few minutes later, Oliver's father entered the room. He asked how I was feeling. I told him that I was fine, and that I understood that what I had done was wrong. Again, I apologized. He made it clear that anything that remotely resembled bullying and fighting was a serious problem. I told him that I thought Oliver was completely justified in defending himself. His father emphasized again that any form of fighting was wrong: I instigated the incident, which was wrong; and yes, Oliver rose to the occasion (fearlessly, in my opinion); but we were both wrong.

After his father left the room, Oliver and I talked some more, but not about the incident on the school bus. We simply talked about our lives. For the first time, we actually got to know each other as people. We talked about our likes and dislikes, about sports, and about school. Then an amazing thing happened. Oliver must have been paying very close attention to me. While we were talking, an empty birdcage in the corner of the room had caught my eye. The door to the cage was open, which intrigued me. I said nothing about it to Oliver. It was one of those odd, seemingly coincidental things that we sometimes notice. Maybe an hour later, when I was preparing to leave, Oliver and I walked to the front door. As I turned toward him to say good-bye, Oliver handed me the empty cage and said, "I want you to have this." At first, I refused it. I suspected that he still felt bad about giving me the black eye, which I believed to be completely deserved. I should not have been the one to receive a gift, but he insisted.

Walking back home, I knew that something important had happened, something that I would always remember. I didn't understand all of it then, and I suppose I still don't. What I did know was that I had been set free. It wasn't the black eye that set me free. That only got my attention. It was Oliver. I've kept his empty cage to this very day. Someday, I hope to call it my own.

A Spiritual Practice in Conscience

Often, the reason that we fail to act in good conscience is that we're afraid. Put another way, we don't realize that the situation or circumstance that we're in needs the moral compass that we have, but are afraid to use. This is why strengthening our neglected, or forgotten, fearless nature is the best way to cultivate our instinct of conscience. It's also why it's so important to remember what the fearlessness in our childhood was like and to make it a part of our lives now.

If you think you have no memories of fearlessness, let me just say that I believe that you're mistaken. Keep in mind that an example of fearlessness might be something really simple: like keeping an uncensored journal or diary, walking barefoot outdoors, or making the biggest possible splash in a mud puddle. Give some thought to this over a period of days or more, even if some memories come to mind rather quickly. There will be more, memories that will only surface if you give them the opportunity. You can use your capacity for intent to help you do this (all our spiritual instincts are mutually reinforcing). For example, rather than wondering whether you can remember your fearlessness in childhood, tell yourself that you want to remember it. In a few days or weeks, your memories will probably surface at the most unexpected times. You may dream them, or they may come to you during a conversation with a friend.

Make a list; or better yet, write a paragraph or two that describes what the fearless child that you once knew was like. What were your feelings? Then, ask yourself what you would be doing—or what you are doing—when you experience those feelings now. What can you do—and what would you need to do—to regain them?

Obviously, the answers that we give will be highly personal. And keep in mind that the word "fearless" can mean very different things to different people. There is no "right answer." For me, fearless activities might be something as simple as playing outside during a winter snow, or walking barefoot outdoors in the summer or inside the house. That may not seem to be fearless to you, but I have this peculiar thing about keeping my feet protected, even when I'm resting at home. There's no need for it. Somehow, I know that it would be good for me to take off my shoes. My wife reminds me to do this now and again, and she's right. It's not that I'm afraid to take off my shoes; rather, I feel vulnerable without them. The point is that simply by taking them off, I'm opening the door to becoming fearless in other areas of my life—which is the principle that I'm getting at in this practice.

At the other extreme, I have a friend who likes to go skydiving when she feels stuck in her life and afraid that she'll remain stuck. I'm not recommending it, but it works for her. In whatever form your fearlessness may take, whether in seemingly small things or large, put it into practice now, even if that only means for a few minutes each day. Don't wait.

After reconnecting with your fearless side, the next step is to carry it with you into your public life. This can be a more difficult thing to do. The resistance that we face may be unexpectedly strong. Strangely—or not so strangely—the worst resistance often comes from friends and loved ones. I've known many people who are afraid of expressing themselves in public, and it's their friends who do everything possible to shut them up. Don't be surprised by this. Learn about the peculiar nature of fear from the many sources of resistance that we all have. However, my suggestion is to insist on being who you are, despite the resistance, but without being reckless. We all make mistakes in this regard. Apparently, the difference between reckless and fearless must be learned many times.

I would also suggest going to neighborhood or town meetings where issues of public policy are discussed and/or decided. Stand up for what you believe to be right. Your fearless nature will be known by your honesty in combination with a respectful attitude toward the opinions of others. Another possibility is to initiate discussions among your friends and/or with your children about what it means to be fearless (rather than reckless) in their lives and yours. Public discussions and more private conversations like these go a long way toward cultivating a vibrant, active conscience in everyone, simply because we learn not to be afraid to express ourselves.

We should never overlook the close relationship between our fear, on the one hand, and our reluctance or unwillingness to take the time to help others in need, on the other. The key words here are "take the time." Consider the inordinate amount of time that we give to protecting our self-interest, rather than helping others. "Self-interest" often involves the most ordinary preoccupations, worries, and fears—such as concerns about not having enough time. I know as well as anyone that it can be good, even virtuous, to lead a busy life; yet the degree to which our lives are "busy" suggests that we're afraid of something—or running away from something. By simply taking the time to help others, many of our ordinary but debilitating fears quickly diminish in strength, even to the point where we forget about them.

7

COMMUNITY: CONSCIOUS
RELATIONSHIPS

> There is neither Jew nor Greek; there is neither slave nor
> free; there is neither male nor female.
>
> —Saint Paul's Letter to the Galatians, 3:26–28

> But I say to you, love your enemies and pray for those
> who persecute you.
>
> —The Gospel According to Matthew, 5:44

L ove your enemies"—this is one of many Christian teachings that cover a lot of spiritual ground, but lands squarely on our instinct for community. There are times when I find this teaching hard to swallow, but to ignore it (and the instinct) is to let ourselves become a serious danger to ourselves and to everyone else. It's like waiting for a war to happen (whether across the street or across the ocean), rather than creating the conditions for peace. And if, by any chance, we've been led to believe that this teaching (or the instinct) amounts to a dysfunctional strategy for ignoring the truth about life or avoiding conflicts with mean-spirited people—something like "give gifts to a bully, so he won't hurt you"—then we should set that thought aside now. "Love your enemies" is in fact about survival, but on an entirely different order. Think of it as taking care of your survival needs by learning how to thrive—or as old-fashioned hospitality taken to the nth degree.

As Saint Paul put it, "We know that the whole creation has been groaning in labor pains until now, and not only the creation, but we ourselves" (Romans 8:22–23) for us to become who we are meant to be. From Mother Earth's point of view, this means realizing that our instinct for community involves everyone and every living creature. We all share a "life together" (here I'm borrowing two well-chosen words from Dietrich Bonhoeffer, the great Lutheran minister and theologian, killed by the Nazis), and that is the best definition of "community" that I know. We're all kin. We know this already; and unless we're taught or brainwashed into believing something else, we would remember it every minute of the day. The choice is always ours to make: We can love our enemies and become who we're meant to be, or hate our enemies and lose the lives that we're meant to have. You would think that we would take survival more seriously.

We would take survival and the teaching—"love your enemies"—more seriously, if it were not for our fear. Fear has always been the enemy of community—and of love. People often say the exact opposite. For example, I often hear that war creates community. Actually, it doesn't, at least not in the way we're taught to believe. It's true that the presence of a common enemy strengthens a sense of "us" among those whose lives are threatened by "them." But this does nothing to cultivate community as a spiritual instinct. This is primal fear, as the group experiences it, directed inwardly toward self-preservation and outwardly toward the destruction of the threat. With our right hand, we *create community among "us"; with our left hand, we destroy it among "them."*

I can understand why people, including myself, often look upon community with a confused mixture of feelings and memories; sometimes with nostalgia, other times with a wary if not fearful eye. It's not simply that we want to be individuals first or that we like our alone time. Consider religious, cultural, and political refugees. They have fled or been forced to leave the kind of community that offers a measure of goodwill and hospitality, but only to some—and certainly not them. Their lives testify to the worst failure of community and to the search for communities of a more benevolent kind—or else they give up on this human instinct altogether, which amounts to giving up a large measure of hope.

To make matters worse, communities everywhere are being ripped apart largely at the hands of economic forces that do little to cultivate spiritual instincts. This new experiment in living reaches into every continent, uprooting local communities in its wake, while destroying the web of life at a faster pace than anyone ever dreamed possible. This is another way of saying that the experiment isn't working, not for the vast majority of people. And what this means is that we're learning not to trust real, face-to-face communities as much as we could or should, not any more or less than we trust the half-nurtured instinct of community within ourselves—which is not very much. In other words, we're learning not to trust the very instincts on which our survival depends.

The fact that the ideal of "community" doesn't seem to be part of the post-postmodern equation could spell the end of what we once knew as a "life together." But Mother Earth plays by a different set of rules. While the communities that we've known become a thing of the past, the instinct for community remains, waiting as a mother in labor pangs. I've been fortunate to hear different perspectives on the absolute necessity of community

from a number of spiritual teachers in a variety of roles represent-
ing very different traditions. They have been healers, ritual sing-
ers, sages, shamans, and priests—all exceedingly generous people,
with a twinkle in their eyes, and they shared their wisdom freely.

Every one of them will tell you that life without some form of
community is no life at all. They will also tell you that their "knowledge of community" should never be considered the province of one
cultural tradition, one people, or one religion. True spiritual knowledge cannot possibly be owned, or claimed as one's own—in the
manner of "property." It "belongs" to everyone. In the same way,
our spiritual instincts are "ours," "yours," and "mine"—but only
because we are creatures made in God's image. It is our birthright to
cultivate our spiritual instincts and to use them, but that's as far as it
goes. To take even one step down the road of claiming this knowledge and these instincts as exclusively "ours," but not "theirs" is to
begin a destructive process that will end in our demise.

One of those same spiritual teachers from a tradition very
different from my own once looked me in the eye and put it
bluntly, "You can find everything in your Bible." Simple state-
ments like that say a lot. They express more meaning than the
words themselves can account for. He was talking about the self-
knowledge that goes beyond what we ordinarily consider the self
to be. True self-knowledge plants our feet in community; that is,
in "our lives together." It involves remembering the experiences
that have shaped who we are; our ideas about ourselves, especially
our emotions; the people who have been our adversaries and our
friends; the regrettable things that we have done to other people;
opportunities lost and the ones that lie ahead. To remember who
we are in this way is very nearly the same as remembering what
our relationships are meant to be—by bringing them into conscious
awareness. The implication is that the very people who can help
us to cultivate our spiritual instincts the most will be found in the

most unlikely places. As it turns out, this usually means very close to home. We would find them, if we bothered to look.

So why don't we look? The answer to that question is easy: We've learned to look everywhere else. This is understandable. Too often, we turn to religion for help, but then hear "love your enemy" in one breath and see a sword raised against an enemy in the next. The contradiction stretches credibility too far. What do we do? We tell ourselves that the truth must be found somewhere else—but not here. It seems reasonable enough. It's not much of a strategy for survival, but it's better than nothing. We might find what we believe we're looking for, but it's just as likely that we'll find more of the same. The really tragic outcome, however, is that we overlook the most important truth of all—that in one way or another, we must all find our answers in our lives together, in the here and now. And how do we do that? By cultivating the spiritual instincts that we've been given but overlook or ignore.

The following two stories exemplify the sensibility and spiritual insight of a few very close-to-home people who instilled a sense of community in me. As you will see, they followed their own spiritual instincts in very different ways. In the first story, an aunt and uncle cultivate my instinct for community by taking the time to explain their outlook on life through utterly heartfelt conversation. In the second story, a high school teacher doesn't explain anything about community with words; rather, she lets her actions speak for herself. The first story involves the instinct for community in religion and the church; the second, in education and school.

I wouldn't say that any of these people were "simple folk," although if you met them on the street you might believe they were. No one is simple—peculiar, yes; but never simple. They're very much like people we've all known and loved but often fail to appreciate. I've only recently understood that they cultivated a deep sense of community within me long before I realized that

*they had anything important to teach. With their hopes and fears
in mind, as well as my own, the last part of the chapter addresses
some specific issues around community that we must understand
better and pursue—that is, if we want to have a "life together."*

Walter and Deon took it upon themselves to teach me the
spiritual principles of community life, as they understood
them. To my knowledge, no one asked them to do this; but knowing them as I did (they passed away years ago), I have to believe
that they felt an inward call. If that was the case, and I believe it
was, then they would not have said as much. They weren't hiding
anything from me, or being in any way secretive or manipulative. They were the kind of people who believed in God, without
taking themselves too seriously. To be in the presence of Walter
and Deon was to be in a world where things were exactly as they
seemed. They gave to the community without expecting anything
in return, and they were generous in their giving. I'm not exaggerating. They really were like that.

The teachings that I received from them were simple, yet also
elusive and difficult to describe in a systematic way, as "simple"
spiritual truths often are. For them, community wasn't anything
like an object in the world that can be described or explained, but
an extension of the soul that must be lived. Their purpose was
to instill a feel for community within me, and it's why the telling
of this story must be based on a feel for what it was like to be in
their presence. Communities—"our lives together"—are always
like that too. Otherwise, it's not community.

I hope that you've known people like them: good-hearted,
always wanting to do the right thing, honest, hardworking, trustworthy, and loyal. Walter and Deon had good instincts. An example: They always let me know that they were glad to see me. I

remember that well. For my sake more than theirs, they wanted me to know that they felt happy when I was around. They smiled when they saw me, and laughed about everything, and I knew it was real. By establishing the fact clearly in my mind that they were glad to see me, I learned to be settled within myself and at ease—and that made it possible to trust and follow my spiritual instincts.

Without saying a word about it, they also taught me to be wary of people who made others feel afraid, stirred up, and agitated. I learned this primarily by the example of who they were, which was the very opposite of people who make us afraid. It's the same as being around people who never lie. You don't notice it until you're around someone who lies all the time. It's startling. You might not believe it, until you witness it firsthand. I'm not saying that Walter and Deon were never afraid or never worried or never told a fib, but I can't imagine that they used fear as a way of manipulating other people or to get what they wanted—and never in a million years would they have lied. If they did, it would have been hugely out of character; they, very definitely, would have been unhappy with themselves, and they would have asked for forgiveness.

Walter and Deon were patriotic Americans. Deon worked in Washington during World War II. She was a secretary in a department of naval intelligence (I've forgotten the official name). She never talked about that very much. Like Walter, she was proud to have served her country. He was such a quiet and peaceful man that I wonder how he survived in the army, much less the war. His three brothers served too. Ray was killed at Okinawa. My mom, the youngest and only girl among the siblings, was a child then. She heard the news of their whereabouts indirectly, like everyone else, on the radio. That was the kind of fear that people of their generation remember the most—wondering who would come back home and who would not. It's not the kind of fear that anyone would want to talk about very much.

After the war, they returned to their home in and around Elkin, North Carolina. Walter went to work in the local blanket factory, from which he eventually retired. Both Walter and Deon devoted much of their lives to the community, especially to the church. They taught Sunday school with great joy and devotion. They were loved in town for their kindness and for just being who they were. Walter was well-known as the slowest driver in the world. Riding, on occasion, in the backseat of their dark blue Pontiac, I often wondered if he was still driving his army tank, forty years later. It was a funny thought because General Patton's army, in which he served, must have traveled many times faster. Walter really was an amazingly slow driver. Everyone in town thought his driving habits were funny, except Deon, but she laughed about it anyway. His driving gave her no choice but to become the most patient person in the world. I believe she succeeded.

If my memories and overall impression of them seem too rose-colored to believe, I would suggest you call someone in Elkin who knew them. They'll tell you that what I'm saying is true. It's the kind of common knowledge that people in communities have. Sometimes their knowledge is wrong or a little wrong, but they have good instincts for people nonetheless.

What I really want you to understand about Walter and Deon is not common knowledge. I think of it whenever I see the letter that I keep in my desk at home. Deon wrote it for both of them when they learned of my decision to go to seminary. It's one of those beautiful handwritten letters that people sent years ago. She said that they always knew what my vocation in life would eventually be, and they were pleased that I finally realized it. I understood it as a straightforward, matter-of-fact comment that was both supportive and heartfelt. Throughout my teenage years, they never once suggested that I become "a pastor" (that's the word they used), or encouraged me along those lines. From their point of view, they would have been interfering in my life, which they never wanted to do.

Yet their foreknowledge of my eventual vocation was the reason behind the occasional talks that they made sure we had—that's what I meant earlier, when I said that they took it upon themselves to give me spiritual instruction. One conversation in particular comes to mind, although they touched upon this same subject on several other occasions. The subject was why they had left a particular congregation several years before. We were riding in their Pontiac. Walter was driving, so they had plenty of time to tell a long but important story. Looking back on it now, I realize that the breakdown in community life—which we're experiencing now at an accelerated pace and which they perceived long ago—was of utmost concern to them. In their own unassuming way, they could see it coming. This, in a nutshell, is the story that they told.

For Walter and Deon, community was the starting point and measure of the spiritual life. That's always where our conversations began, whether they were thinking of the church or any kind of community. "Our lives together" assumes and is based upon the bedrock principle of spiritual equality: We're all made in God's image, we're all children of God; and we're all worthy of the same respect as human beings. From Walter and Deon's point of view, this was not something any clear-minded person would debate. To do so might and probably would suggest an attempt to use one's own community for selfish purposes, in effect, elevating less than honorable motives above the well-being of others, which undermines the principle of spiritual equality.

Having discussed that for a while, they proceeded to describe how profoundly World War II had impressed the truth of this principle upon their lives. Like his fellow soldiers during the war, Walter witnessed not only the horrific impact of combat and death, but he also fought against the most profound evil imaginable: stigmatizing, excluding, persecuting, and killing people who were regarded as less than human. For that reason, Walter and Deon were exceptionally clear about where seemingly "harmless" divisions between "us" and "them" could lead: There's nothing "harmless" about it; the ultimate consequences can be terrible; and, as much as we resist the thought, it can happen in our own backyard.

They said very clearly—wanting there to be no misunderstanding—that a living, breathing sense of spiritual equality was the reason that they liked their current church so much. What they also wanted to impress upon me was that this was also the reason that they had left their former church. Over the years, some complicated changes had taken place there, which were a source of great joy as well as conflict and sadness. The joyful part was easy to explain. The push toward spiritual equality through the civil rights movement had a hugely positive impact on everyone in their former congregation. The transformation was gradual and, in many ways, too slow; nevertheless, the biblical ideal of genuine hospitality and respect was now being extended to everyone.

However, not long after the transformation toward political and spiritual equality began, another, entirely different form of division was setting down roots. Their experience was that a new kind of community was being formed, with divisions based not on race, sex, or gender, but on economic status and political power. The underlying principle (unacknowledged in those days, but openly proclaimed now) was that the reward of faith is affluence, and the reward of affluence is influence. Economic class quickly replaced race and sex as the new source of division (not that it was actually "new," and issues of same-sex unions were yet to come). Be that as it may, Walter and Deon were not at all happy about this new division, and they wanted me to understand why.

In their view, this new principle had the impact of transforming the poor into second-class citizens in "the kingdom of God," which flies in the face of Saint Paul's famous teaching: *"There is neither Jew nor Greek; there is neither slave nor free; there is neither male nor female"* (Galatians 3:26–28). A Franciscan friend commented, more recently, on this teaching by saying that these are the three divisions in life—race, class, and gender—that we're meant to overcome. His point, Walter and Deon's point, and Saint Paul's point was that these three "walls" that divide us don't come out of nowhere, and they're definitely not established by God. They're present in our lives together because we put them there. Our responsibility, as spiritually minded people, is to dismantle them. This—and precisely this—was the spiritual instinct of community that Walter and Deon wanted to cultivate in me.

It was obvious that this was not the easiest conversation for them, but only because issues of economic class in the United States are so rarely discussed. We're taught not to talk about it, so we're afraid to talk about it, which is why they made it clear that their comments were part of a private conversation. They were exceedingly quiet people who felt it was wrong to have uncharitable thoughts about others, and it was difficult for them to say anything that might be wrongly interpreted as critical of anyone. They were not wealthy themselves. In fact, no one in their former congregation would have been considered wealthy by any modern standard. Of course, some members had more money than others. As for Walter and Deon, by saving what money they had, and by rarely, if ever, spending it on things they didn't need, they were able to live a comfortable life. To my knowledge, they harbored no ill will toward anyone, including people who were wealthy or wanted to be wealthy. They admired and were inspired by people who worked hard, made money, and lived their lives as an integral part of the community.

Yet Walter and Deon were clearly disturbed. They were afraid for the future of the church, the community, and the country. Anything that resembled furthering our own interest at the expense of others, especially in the name of God and religion, was not, in their view, the Christian path. Within their former congregation, the influence of the "haves" was beginning to outweigh the well-being of the "have nots" (relative as these terms actually were in their town). The result was that "the community" that the congregation represented no longer belonged to everyone equally. Seeds had been planted that would make it an instrument of power in the hands of the few.

If all this sounds familiar, especially now, it's because it is familiar—and it's not "new" by any stretch of the imagination. Keep in mind that for Walter and Deon, and many others of their generation, the experience of World War II was a turning point that signified a new beginning for everyone. And what they witnessed, nearly thirty years later, was a decisive turning in the wrong direction—a turning back. The "new fear" was of losing those things that we feel entitled to have. It was not the relatively poor who felt entitled; rather, it was the relatively wealthy. Walter and Deon would have been too charitable and polite to say what Jesus had no qualms about: "*It will be hard for a rich man to enter the kingdom of heaven*" (Matthew 19:23).

Like many faithful, loyal, hardworking Americans, Walter and Deon felt reluctant to speak about this publicly. Yet their understanding of community from a Christian point of view was rock solid. My impression is that the whole subject of economic class seemed un-American to them, which put them in a position of conflict. It made them uncomfortable, and they were slightly afraid to talk about it with me. But they told me the truth anyway. Not only that, they overcame their fear enough to raise the issue openly in their congregational council. As it turned out, those economic forces were stronger than they were, but not more powerful than their spiritual instincts. In response and as an act of reluctant protest, they found a new congregation—a new community of the faithful. Not for one second did they stop cultivating the instinct for community in those they loved, and I'm thankful that their love included me.

Ms. Emma Cook was one of the most truly fearless people I've ever known. She was my indomitable Latin and geometry teacher in high school. Ms. Cook was a bundle of contradictions in the same way that awe-inspiring experiences involve a seemingly impossible conjunction of opposites. She didn't seem to notice this at all. My guess is that she would have laughed at the mere suggestion. For example, physically, she was a very small person, considerably smaller than I, and I was only five-five or five-six at the time. Yet she presided over the classroom with an air of unquestioned control, dignity, and good humor. She rarely, if ever, raised her voice, but when she spoke to you directly, she clearly had your attention.

In fact, she was in such control of our study habits that the lessons for the day began before she actually arrived. Hers was the only class where the students came early, sat quietly, and studied the lessons before the bell rang. There was no lingering in the hallway, no talking with friends, and forget the word "loiter." That would have been unthinkable. On top of that, the school bell was irrelevant. She arrived precisely one minute before the top of the hour—each and every day. It was the clippity-clop sound of her high heels coming down the hall, rather than the bell, that announced the beginning of class.

Although Ms. Cook was a religious person, she never mentioned it in class, at least not in a proselytizing way. Nevertheless, it was clear that everything she did was filled with Spirit. She was one of the most totally "alive" people that I've ever met. Just one hour a day in her classroom was all anyone needed. I, and many others, had two hours, which was a bit much. Her classes were all business, paying attention, thinking about life's meaning, and knowing that the experience of being in the presence of this exceedingly small spark plug of a teacher was something akin to the fear of God. The word for that, you might remember, is "awe."

One of Ms. Cook's most peculiar characteristics is that she seemed to have taught at Elkin High School forever. When I was in her classroom, she was clearly old on the outside, but young on the inside. She had also been teaching when my mom and dad were in high school, and they remember her in exactly the same way. She had a timeless quality that people acknowledged and quietly smiled about. It was part of her legend, and her retirement magnified the legend even more. What did she do? She became a missionary. Where did she go? Beirut. That's hardly retirement. She passed away long ago, which proves that she had a mortal side. It goes without saying that her presence still exists in me, and I'm sure many others would say the same about their experience.

Ms. Cook was a master of her craft. She wasn't just a teacher of Latin and geometry. She imparted something of the timeless quality that was who she was. She did this in part by insisting on sustained, disciplined, daily work. *The early bird catches the worm*—she said something along those lines nearly every day. It wasn't that she simply knew all the clichés, and recited them frequently. Our impression was that these old sayings might have been hers.

If all this sounds traditional, it's because it is traditional—thoroughly traditional. But that is the irony behind communities that thrive spiritually: They thrive because they change, and it's often the individuals who are the most deeply rooted in tradition who make the most important changes happen. Ms. Cook was one of those people. She had profoundly good spiritual instincts, and she followed them in every part of her life. In the classroom, her intent matched her work in a seamless way, which made her teaching into a true vocation. This was plain for all to see, which is one of the unspoken ways she cultivated spiritual instincts in all of us.

Apart from Latin and geometry (or I should say through them), she also taught us all about community—"our lives together." From her, we all learned not only that communities can and do change, but also that positive change often happens when the initiative of just one person multiplies into two or three working together, and then, quite a few more. How did she teach this? She did it very skillfully.

It was mid-July. Never mind that we were on summer vacation. Small details like that were never obstacles for Ms. Cook. Many of us worked at summer jobs, and we all savored the few remaining weeks of summer. That's what I was thinking when the bomb dropped. What I experienced was "shock and awe" of an entirely different kind. Ms. Cook sent every member of her class a letter in the mail, announcing that we would resume our studies three weeks before the usual opening of the school year. As she explained, we had a great deal of work to accomplish during the upcoming year, so we must begin early. Our studies would begin in her classroom each morning at 7:00, for an hour. My memory about the time is a little cloudy—it might have been 6:00. Whatever. She was also careful to say that any student who worked would have time to finish class and make it to work on time.

I was dumbfounded, speechless, and shocked. At first, I thought it might be a joke or a bad dream. This was the late 1960s, when students like me took great pride in holding liberal-minded ideals and opinions that were based on the belief in absolute necessity of change in every part of society. I still believe in those ideals. Yet, a few weeks after receiving her letter—as I was standing, at sunrise, at the entrance to the school, waiting with Ms. Cook and my classmates for someone to unlock the door so we could have class—I had a very different opinion. I was totally convinced that the school system and the whole way of life that it represented worked according to time-honored rules that should never be changed. How dare she do such a thing? Who did she think she was?

After a few days, and with considerable reluctance, I began to concede, within myself, that her actions had been brilliant. As you might imagine, I had given a lot of thought to what she had done, trying, for the most part, to figure out how to wiggle out of her well-laid trap. But the more I thought, the more I understood it from her point of view. It was such a small thing in one sense. All she did was to arrange for us to begin our schoolwork early. Yet that's not the real story. Ms. Cook had done her homework. I discovered that she had checked out all the practical details with the school administration and parents well ahead of time. Her primary concern was that everyone would be able to attend. If, for any reason, even one student could not participate, then the class would not have happened. In other words, she had made contact with everyone involved and enlisted the cooperation of all.

That was the secret, and the sheer brilliance, behind her plan. Family schedules might have to be rearranged to make it happen. No problem. The school would have to be opened and cleaned earlier than scheduled. No problem. She had to organize, in effect, a large segment of the entire community. This was no small task; but again—no problem. Who would possibly disagree with Ms. Cook? No one. She made no criticism of anyone. She held no grudge against the school system, which was, in fact, excellent. She had skillfully rearranged all our lives, forced us, without being "forceful," to look at our lives from a different, larger point of view, and challenged the assumptions of the entire faculty, administration, and parents about how education worked in our community.

I don't know how the teachers—Ms. Cook's colleagues—felt about all this. There was a substantial generational difference between a large portion of the faculty and her. I have to believe that some of the newer teachers weren't pleased. A few probably suspected that she was grandstanding or elevating herself and the importance of her courses too much. On the other hand, most of the teachers were in awe of her. I was aware that one or two of the newer faculty sought her out for friendship and unofficial mentoring. One noticeable difference between Ms. Cook and some of the new faculty was that they were inclined to relate to their students in a social way, sometimes as friends. Ms. Cook was friendly, but she was never "a friend," not in the personal sense. But I can't think of any teacher who made more of a personal impact on me. When all was said and done, anyone who knew her well would have known that her intent and her impact on the community that summer were right on target. She aimed her bow and hit the bull's-eye.

I wouldn't call her teaching that summer a lesson in "traditional values," or discipline, or hard work, although it clearly encompassed all those things. And, to my knowledge, there was no trace of school politics involved. If the words "conservative" and "liberal" mean, respectively, "to conserve" and "to liberate," then her actions exemplified both. She was the embodiment of "tradition," *and* she went well beyond our taken-for-granted ideas about what "tradition" might mean. She was teaching us how to be free spiritually, by taking us outside our normal assumptions about how "education" or "communities" should work. From my point of view, her most important teaching was demonstrated by the impact she made: She moved us through any fear we might have had of her, the fear we surely had of change, and the fear of whether or not we could change. Of course we can change. It's not easy to change anything; it may take some forethought and dedication; but in the end—no problem.

Ms. Cook believed in people, in herself, and in our God-given ability to sort out the difference between reality and illusions. The obstacle we faced was neither her, nor, as it turned out, our parents or the educational institution. When our communities are working well, we quickly realize that the only true obstacles that we face are our own selves—our preconceived ideas, our defensiveness, and our fear. She helped us to discover and claim our birthright as human beings: to cultivate our spiritual instincts and become who we are meant to be. This is how our communities *should* work. They're not meant to make us afraid, but to help us overcome our fear.

Would Ms. Cook's simple request be fulfilled today? Could that, or something like that, actually happen in our day and age? Of course it could. Insurance and security concerns in many schools might be greater now, but the truly important questions are more basic and essential: What kind of life do we really want? Are we willing to find a way to do what needs to be done?

If Ms. Cook were alive today, she would find a way to cultivate our spiritual instincts. Nothing, especially fear, would stop her from fulfilling her vocation in life. What we need—and should want—are communities that will seek out the new Ms. Cooks: people who will draw upon their spiritual instincts and put them into practice in a meaningful way. But the whole point is that we must create this kind of world together. Ms. Cook couldn't do it for us back then, but she could show us how it can be done. That, more than anything else, is what Ms. Cook taught. And she taught it well, not because of what she said, but because of what she did.

I would like to believe that we're standing at a crossroad. But we, as a people, made a decision long ago without really making it, without realizing what it is, and without trusting our spiritual instincts in any substantial way. The decision was to take our communities for granted: to assume that they would always be there and that it's not our responsibility to create them ourselves. The outcome of that tragic decision has been to head down the road that we've already taken for quite a long time.

The consequences are already affecting how we think about life, ourselves, and especially our communities—our "lives together."

We can see it happening—and what's not happening—in the way we use customary words that have lost their customary meaning. "The economy," for example, means "the financial system" today, which has no direct or obvious connection to the well-being of the overwhelming majority of communities. It has no direct or obvious connection to livelihood. Do we even remember the meaning of the word "livelihood"? Not very long ago, everyone understood that getting a job meant finding a livelihood. That was how we made the kind of living that contributed to families, households, and communities—even the nation. "Community" was the place where we struggled to create livelihoods, raise families, and cultivate respectful relationships. Would it be reasonable to say that any of these words describe our lives now? Perhaps yes, but probably no—not for the vast majority of people.

Another example involves the environment and the word "environment." Despite efforts to protect the environment through legal means, we still haven't realized that we're seriously mistaken to think of "the environment" as our "surroundings," a "landscape," or the place where we get "resources." We should be thinking of the largest of all our communities—the great web of life that gives us life—and all the "communities within communities" that make up the larger whole. Our lives are not separate from "the environment." The very ground on which we stand, the soil, is a community of life in itself. These ambiguities and omissions say a lot about where we've been headed for a long time. They give the strong impression that we've lost touch with the instinct for community within ourselves because we've lost our connection with actual communities outside of ourselves. In other words, they give the impression that we've decided not to live in the real world.

What's done is done. There's no turning back the clock, but

we still have a decision to make. We can draw upon our spiritual instincts, foresee the consequences of our actions the best that we can, and take a more sustainable road—one that will enhance our chance of survival by creating genuine communities rooted in the web of life. All we have to do is to recognize and respect the many communities of life that give us life, and then make the decision to live as part of those communities once again. This really is a decision.

We might say, or want to believe, that the situation is not so bad, that new kinds of human communities are emerging everywhere, especially those through social networking on the Internet. There is a great deal of truth in this. The benefits of these new communities are obvious, as I know in my own life. Because the international dimension of my environmental work requires the World Wide Web, I can't imagine doing work as well without it, and would not want to change that part of my life. Used in the right way, it can encourage democracy and cultivate our instinct for community. These new experiments in community demonstrate the resilience of the instinct itself, and they fill at least part of the void created by diminishing face-to-face, flesh-and-blood relationships.

Yet I constantly remind myself that virtual communities are a means to a larger end, rather than an end unto itself. Involvement, participation, and a sense of belonging through social networking transcend "ordinary" limitations of time and space, which has a definite appeal that people sometimes regard as fulfilling a spiritual need. But what we lose is the depth and richness that only the look in a person's eyes can express—that is to say, we lose a sense of the whole person, a feel for the nuances of community life, and worst of all, the capacity to discern in a deep and holistic way. None of this is helped by our apparently diminished attention spans, or by the all-too-common drugs that are meant to ease our long-standing, nationwide epidemic of depression. Although virtual communities might ease the depression and loneliness, they haven't taken us to the source of our lives or the ground of our being.

The mere mention of the ground of our being brings us back to the profoundly spiritual significance of our bodies. To cultivate our spiritual instincts, we need more than our eyes and intellect. We need the use of all our senses. We live our lives in and through our physical bodies. Every time I establish a new relationship on the Web, I think of the people in my own neighborhood whom I've never met. I would not like to think—or to tell myself—that I don't have the time for them, an interest in them, or any concern for the place where we live. Those people actually are my neighbors, and I need their thoughts and opinions, their feelings about life, and those difficult conversations and misunderstandings that we often have. I need them because their presence helps me to cultivate my spiritual instincts, just as my physical presence cultivates theirs. If I'm not actually at home or in my neighborhood or community, I have to ask myself whether I'm really creating any kind of viable community at all.

The crossroad has long passed, but the decision before us remains: Are we willing to believe, against all common sense that the instinct for community cultivated in conscious, face-to-face, on-the-ground, in-the-web-of-life relationships is a product of a bygone era? If so—if that's what we're really telling ourselves— then we've already reached the end of the road and we have every reason in the world to be more than afraid.

In times like these, it's important to know what we're feeling and why, and to reach out to others, especially to those who have different points of view, life experiences, and beliefs. The very last thing we should want now is to reclaim a sense of community based on uniformity rather than diversity, exclusion rather than inclusion, and consumerism rather than democracy. If or when we make choices along those lines, it is because we've let ourselves remain stuck in a world ruled by fear. It also suggests that we're preparing for war at home or escalating one abroad—which only creates the illusion of community among ourselves. War postpones the one inevitable choice that we have to make—either to survive by learning to create human communities that are rooted in the web of life, or else.

I know plenty of people, in my part of the world and the world over, who are well aware of what we're facing and why. They've seen communities ripped apart, and they respond by building and rebuilding genuine, respectful, sustainable communities where they live. They're doing this for a very simple reason: They know that our lives and the great community of life depend on whether we will trust our spiritual instincts enough to put them to good use. This is an old, very old, ancient truth—reaching all the way back to the very beginning of humankind. It's a responsibility that cannot be set aside, as if now we have better things to do.

A Spiritual Practice in Community

Times likes ours, difficult as they are, put a tremendous strain on every kind of community. It can sometimes stretch the imagination even to conceive of our "lives together," except on a small scale; and it can stretch the imagination even more to reflect on how we might actually cultivate the instinct of community. We might be tempted to believe that community is not an important part of our lives, that there's no real need for it anyway, that it's a waste of time, or that "communities" are just there and they don't need to be created. In my opinion, thoughts like those really are "temptation." Community is intrinsic to life itself, which means that our survival depends on how well we cultivate the instinct in each other.

So let's begin this practice simply by remembering that community is not an option—not in the real world. Here are some practical things we can do.

First, make an inventory, either in your head or on paper, of the people in your life who have cultivated the instinct for community in you. Here I'm following the pattern of the spiritual practice in the last chapter. Write down their names, and make a few notes about what they were like as people. What did they actually do in their communities? Did you hold them in high regard? How did they make you feel?

Keep in mind that we may not always like or agree with the people who have affected us the most. For example, we might have learned valuable lessons not only from those who were positive role models, but also from those who, unfortunately, set bad examples for us—yet we learned the right lessons anyway. Perhaps we will remember people who taught us (or tried to teach us) to be afraid of ourselves and of people around us. They may have had deep-seated racial prejudices that we found distasteful—and decided to reject. Finally, ask yourself whether their impact on you—positive or negative—was long-lasting. Was it something that you struggled with for a long time? Or do you still struggle with it?

Second, take some time to remember some situations when your instinct for community was called into question. This might have involved family crises—families are a very important kind of community—or a situation at work or school that had the potential to divide a community or to bring people together. How did people respond to these crises? Did they respond with their spiritual instincts, or with fear? In many cases, they might have responded initially with a combination of both; but ultimately, one or the other shaped the final outcome.

Then, ask yourself whether the crises that you have experienced firsthand made you afraid. Examples might involve financial difficulties at home or friends and loved ones with drug or alcohol problems. If they made you afraid in the past, do they still make you afraid today? Is this kind of fear helpful or harmful to you? Or is it a combination of both?

Third, we can go a long way to create community simply by engaging the interest of friends and neighbors we already have. Discussions about the communities in which we live may not happen nearly as often as we think. Specifically, I'm suggesting that you take the initiative in a deliberate way. For example, you might create occasions—perhaps at your home—when you bring together people from the different parts of your life; that is to say, from the many seemingly disparate communities that make up your life. My wife and I, for example, do this in a large way at least once a year. These gatherings do not need a spelled-out or elaborate agenda. You might do simple things, like sharing a meal or celebrating an event, while taking the opportunity to discuss your common "life together" in whatever way naturally occurs.

At the very least, gatherings like these cultivate a sense of community by helping people to become more familiar and to be at ease in the company of others. They build a degree of trust on which every genuine community depends, which also lays the groundwork to grapple with more difficult issues as they arise.

Fourth, consider the possibility of becoming involved (or more involved) in community events or community organizations that already exist, especially those that address issues of the environment and/or livelihood—"meaningful work." If occasions like these do not exist, then create them yourself with the assistance of friends and neighbors or through your church or local civic organizations.

Quite often, official or public community gatherings are very different from those that take place in our homes. You will experience the same, or nearly the same, differences of opinion and points of view; however, those views probably will be expressed more openly and sometimes more passionately at home. It's *especially important to monitor your feelings whenever anger and fear are voiced openly.*

Venting is not usually an effective way of creating community, depending on the sensitivity and respect with which the feelings are expressed. If you feel afraid as a result of the power of the emotions themselves, rather than because of the issue under discussion, then examine your feelings in some detail. Perhaps you feel threatened for a good reason. But it's also possible that the sense of threat has no real or immediate basis. Either way, you might step outside for a few minutes, reflect on the situation honestly, and breathe through your fear—taking slow, deep breaths, while exhaling slowly until your fear response subsides (see the spiritual practice in the following chapter on "rest").

The crucial point in this spiritual practice is to be with and to be part of the communities that are already present in our lives. Resist any temptation to give up on a community simply because it's sometimes difficult or unpleasant. The better course—the one that will cultivate your instinct for community—is to think through and understand what our different points of view really are, rather than assuming that one side is completely right or completely wrong. As a rule, everyone is right about some things and wrong about other things—and no one, ourselves included, is always right (or wrong) about everything.

8.

REST: THE STILL WATERS WITHIN

Even though I walk through the darkest valley, I fear no evil; for you are with me; your rod and your staff—they comfort me.

—Psalms, 23:4

Peace I leave with you, my peace I give to you. Do not let your hearts be troubled, and do not let them be afraid.

—The Gospel According to John, 14:25–27

Who would have guessed that of all our spiritual instincts, rest would be such a problem, so difficult to cultivate, and so hard to find? Do any of us really know how "to get some rest?" Do we even know what it is? I wonder about that sometimes. A cemetery, our "final resting place," doesn't count. We all know, or should know, that a life without enough rest will take us there much too soon. Sleep doesn't count either. It's almost cheating to say that sleep counts as rest. They're very nearly the same, but unless we're in real trouble, we don't have to learn how to sleep. We do have to learn how to rest. My point is that sleep is a primal instinct, while rest—a spiritual instinct—must be cultivated, and its spiritual significance goes far beyond what we normally consider rest to be.

So why is rest such a riddle? And why is it so important in the movement through fear? Rather than trying to explain this thorny subject here, in the introduction, it's better to show you what I mean. It will take an extra page or two and a few more minutes of our time, but surely we can agree to sit together just a bit longer than usual. Consider the example of my desk at home—where I'm sitting now. This is what you would see: a long table filled with all kinds of things scattered on the surface, a laptop, photographs, fly-fishing gear, fossils, feathers, religious objects from many spiritual traditions, several prints of William Blake's watercolors, and a wooden statue of Saint Francis of Assisi. It's an interesting desk, I suppose. I like my desk, but it is busy.

When I sit down to do some work, one particular object stands out from the others—a small picture depicting the miracle of Jesus called "stilling the storm." Nearly fifteen years ago, I photocopied it from a book of religious art. A few days later, Asha, my wife, put it in a frame. She knew exactly why the picture needed a frame: so it wouldn't get lost in the clutter, including mounds of accumulated papers that I won't bother to tell you about. She also knew, as I did, that the picture would play an important part in my life. It reminds me of the one spiritual instinct that I'm most likely to neglect or ignore.

Her good sense has paid off. I see the picture every day. When I'm really busy, I glance at it and carry the image in my mind while I work. Other times, I sit and reflect on Jesus and his disciples, who seem to be staring back at me. They're not really staring—not at me, not literally—but somehow it feels that way. When I see them, I can sense the Spirit drawing me to a place *within myself where I actually want to be, and would be, had I the good sense to listen.*

Today, I'm not so negligent about getting rest, but there was a time in my life when I was my own worst enemy. That's when the story of Jesus "stilling the storm" first grabbed my attention. I'll let the story speak for itself; then we can let the Spirit speak to us. This is how the Gospel of Mark (4:35–41) tells it:

. . . when evening had come, he said to them, "Let us go across to the other side." And leaving the crowd, they took him with them in the boat, just as he was. And other boats were with him. And a great storm of wind arose, and the waves beat into the boat, so that the boat was already filling. But he was in the stern, asleep on the cushion; and they woke him and said to him, "Teacher, do you not care if we perish?" and he awoke and rebuked the wind, and said to the sea, "Peace! Be still!" And the wind ceased, and there was a great calm. He said to them, "Why are you afraid? Have you no faith?" And they were filled with awe, and said to one another, "Who then is this, that even the wind and sea obey him?"

Whether this miracle happened in the literal sense is not some-thing I want to debate. Of course, "it happened." But if we insist on hearing the story as if it either is or is not an objective account, then we lose its deeper significance. As important as questions about "facts" truly are, it's easy to get stuck in what our minds believe they mean. Then we remain in a very peculiar place—frozen in our own thoughts—unwilling or afraid to move through our fear, while telling ourselves that we don't have any, not in any significant way.

That frozen "place" within that we've carved out by the power of our minds is really peculiar. Eric Voegelin, the philosopher, once described it as "the freedom not to be free." I believe he was right. We like to be busy and to think of ourselves as busy; we get in our cars and go places. We're always doing something. No one would seriously debate whether we're active people. This is a freedom of sorts, and a lot of people really do want this kind of life. But if you look closely, you could get the impression that we're being chased or that we're running from something—the proverbial "storm." Is it possible that we've confused freedom with fear—in the same way that we've confused awe with fear? Perhaps so; or maybe we just give that impression. Perhaps we're not so confused, but we've grown so accustomed to mixing freedom with fear that we no longer know the difference. Maybe the answer is all of the above. You decide.

Getting back to the Bible story, I have always been struck by Jesus' apparent "sleeping" during the storm. It's difficult to know what to make of it. He's very definitely not busy, and I have to believe that there's more going on with the words "sleeping" and "waking" than we might think. We're like the disciples: On the one hand, we seem to be awake, whether the circumstances are stormy or peaceful; on the other hand, we're also half asleep—sleepwalking through life—generally unaware or oblivious of what we're doing and why we're doing it.

Yet, the story clearly says that Jesus is "sleeping." The gospel writer even puts a pillow under Jesus' head, a small but otherwise significant detail that he (the gospel writer) must have gone out of his way to include. So I have to ask myself what kind of "sleep" this really is. The Jesus I know is more awake, spiritually, than we are, even when he's sleeping, which leads me to believe that whether he's awake or asleep, he's resting in a way we never dreamed possible. And then, after Jesus "wakes up," he asks his disciples (and us) this one penetrating question: "Why are you afraid?" If he had been anyone else, we would say in utter disbelief, "Are you kidding me? "Can you not see the storm?" "Are you living in the same world as me?" Take the incredulous cynicism out of our thoughts, and those would be very good questions to ask. In other words, what kind of "rest" is he getting? I want to

know what it's like. Whatever it might be, I want some of that rest
for myself. Why? I want it because my soul needs it. We all need it.

In the gospel story, the opposite of fear is rest. It's a special
kind of rest to be sure, but it's still rest. Spiritual traditions speak of
"resting in God," which would be the answer Jesus would give to
the question "What kind of rest are you getting?" That's where he
had been—while he was "sleeping." In this sense, I believe the story
is literally true. This is "the place," within ourselves, where we go
when we move beyond our fear. This is where we find our true
selves and the love of God at the same time. If we call it "home,"
in the deepest spiritual meaning of the word, then "resting in God"
is the ultimate homecoming in the here and now. The great irony
is that rest is the instinct that we neglect the most, while telling
ourselves that it has little or no spiritual significance whatsoever.

I've devoted a great deal of my adult life to finding this place
within myself and trying to describe how to get there to others. The
following stories give the essential elements of the answers that I've
discovered so far. The first describes how a Tantric master, with
great spiritual insight and skill, helped me discover the meaning of
"rest." The second story offers a glimpse of what "resting in God"
was like during a time, in Manhattan, when the world we knew
suddenly transformed into a stormy sea. The third recounts yet
another similar circumstance, in the same location, but with a dif-
ferent outcome. The chapter concludes with some personal reflec-
tions on "stilling the storm" and its meaning for our lives every day.

Have you ever been "on retreat"? Peculiarly enough, a retreat
has some similarities to two very different activities: the first
is a vacation; the second is the military maneuver that's called "a
retreat." I assume you know what a vacation is. Let's just say that
a "vacation" is not a time to get work done in a more relaxing and

fun place. What you may not know is that a "retreat," in the military sense, is one of the most wise and skillful strategies that can ever be employed on the battlefield. I'm bringing this up because the world can be like a battlefield (a scary place); and if our goal is to remain standing at the end of the day, then we need to strategize with all the skill of a military commander. My point is that going on retreat, in the spiritual sense, is far from "doing nothing." It involves remembering what really matters in life, while letting go of the fear that would make us forget. That's why learning to get some real rest is a survival skill that we all need to learn—and to practice.

The first "official retreat" that I ever made (having told myself that I was going on one) was another eye-opener in my life, and I'll tell you why. My motive was simple, or so I thought. I wanted to get away from it all; I wanted an escape; and I believed that all I needed to do to be free from my preoccupations and worries was to go to a new and different place—in effect, a vacation. What I discovered was that the world was not so easy to leave behind and considerably more skillful than I in the art of the chase.

In those days, I would have said "preoccupations and worries," rather than "fears." I didn't realize that I had fears, not really. It wouldn't have occurred to me that any kind of fear played a significant part in my life. I was wrong about that. And I'm not thinking of the big fears, but the smaller ones that accumulate over time and add up to a great deal of unacknowledged fear. It can take some time, more self-awareness than we normally have, plus some experience with actual "rest," to perceive the unacknowledged fear that we habitually carry around in our minds and to realize what a heavy burden it really is.

The world doesn't really "chase" us, but it seems that way when we sincerely try to escape from it. Maybe this goes without saying, but the reason we find it so difficult to get away is that we insist on carrying the world along with us. Think of it as wanting to go on a leisurely, restful stroll through a park on a sunny Sunday afternoon, and then deciding to carry along a very heavy backpack. We might not actually decide to carry it. We probably don't think about it, but we end up with it anyway. It's filled with all kinds of things that we don't want or need; and, very soon, we notice how heavy it is. Who in their right mind would do that? No one—not in his or her right mind. Yet who was it who "decided" to carry all that stuff along? We did. That's basically how "the world" chases us when we want to escape from it. It seems to be "attached," which makes "detachment"—letting go—the key for anyone who would unlock the secret of getting some rest.

It's hard to let go, especially when we don't realize that we're holding on, which is the experience I want to share with you. On retreat, the realization that those heavy burdens even exist can be the very first and most significant obstacle that we face. When those burdens are anxiety and fear, as they usually are, it's not uncommon to learn this quickly. Very often, one single day of real peace and quiet opens the door just enough for our anxiety (and fear) to pour out. This is an instinctive form of release, which, at first, *feels like* a panic attack. Then it dawns on us that it *actually is* a panic attack. *"I can't believe this is happening to me"* is the usual reaction. We might want to call the doctor. Perhaps we should. But in all likelihood the doctor will simply advise us to get some rest. It's not at all uncommon for things like this to happen. It can also be a humbling experience—and, for that very reason, instructive.

Whether we're alone or with a group, every retreat is a "fast." To be "on a fast" or to "make a fast" is to let go of some part of the world that we habitually carry around in our hearts, bodies, and minds. But "fasting" does not necessarily mean "giving up" anything we actually need. Rather, it involves bringing our way of life and ourselves back into a balance. Adequate sleep, physical exercise, a healthy diet, and good companionship (even when the retreat involves silence) can be just as important as regular prayer and meditation—not to mention a respectful, wholesome, and ethical manner of living. They all play integral and necessary parts in a fast, just as they do in the workaday world and on the spiritual path. Companionship, for example, may involve occasional guidance from a friend or spiritual director. Exercise might take the form of a daily walk. Our diet might be restricted to smaller, free-from-sugar portions that allow our internal organs to get some rest and rediscover their true purpose in life—the purpose that our "normal" way of life has probably helped us forget.

Early in the retreat, it's likely that we'll feel an overwhelming urge to sleep, perhaps a much stronger urge than we would have expected. We may feel ambivalent about this. Why? Because we want to do other things, believing that anyone on retreat "should" have more serious spiritual pursuits (anything but sleeping), which makes us feel a little guilty. Yet the need for sleep is clearly there, and it shouldn't be ignored. Our bodies have been trying to tell us to get some rest for a very long time, and we would be wise to listen to what this primal instinct is trying to tell us.

In moments like that, it might occur to us that sleep deprivation is one of the techniques that torturers use. In effect, we willingly inflict a mild form of this torture on ourselves, believing that it's our personal and moral responsibility to do so. Yet there may also be a justifying reason; for example, we don't get enough sleep because we have responsibilities that cannot be ignored. In other words, unless we do what needs to be done, no one will do it. We live in "the real world," after all. We might begin to wonder what this means. At a bare minimum, going on a retreat gives us the opportunity to get off the treadmill long enough to reflect on what the "reality" of our lives is really like.

After a few more days on retreat, our dreams may become unusually rich in content and vivid—or perhaps we're just paying more attention to our dreams and remembering what they are. Either way, they have our attention. We ask ourselves why this would happen. The basic answer is simple: The energy we usually give to our "normal" concerns in life has been redirected. If our conscious minds aren't working on the world "out there," then they find some other material to work with within ourselves. This can be a very helpful turn of events, depending, in part, on the nature of the dreams and our interest in them. But we can count on the fact that we're getting back in touch with our souls.

This is when we begin to realize that the kind of sleep that we're getting now, on retreat, while it's a considerable improvement, is still very busy. While we're sleeping, we work through desires of all kinds, struggles, frustrations, and fears in our dreams. When we're awake, our intellect is preoccupied with the content of our dreams, doing its best to figure out what's going on. It can be unsettling to be overwhelmed by a flood of unconscious material pouring into a waking life. We might wonder whether something is wrong—that is to say, *wrong with me*. That's what we tell ourselves. But we can be sure that whatever might be hidden, unknown, and unrealized within ourselves is in fact *working on us*, which is a better way to put it. Somehow we know—our instincts tell us—that the rest we've given ourselves so far, such as it is, has put us on the right track.

It's at this point, especially if our troubling or "deep dreams" occur longer than a few nights, that we probably want and need some guidance. It's not that we feel lost (although we might). Rather, we just need to talk. We may not want or need in-depth or lengthy counseling or therapy, as helpful as they might be. It's a basic knowledge of spiritual traditions and an understanding of how those teachings relate to our experience that helps us the most. We need a way to make sense of it all—a larger picture, a framework that puts our lives in perspective.

When I first reached this point on retreat, it just so happened that I received some assistance from a spiritual teacher, an Eastern swami who was also a Tantric master. I had hoped that he would help me with my tumultuous dreams. He had no intention of doing anything of the sort. Instead, he told me, repeatedly, to follow my instincts and "to relax." At first, I thought he was brushing me off, despite his gracious attitude toward me. Much later, I understood that he was offering the wisest possible advice. Not only that, his simple advice pointed to the very heart of his tradition: In the deepest part of our souls, we already know the answers we're looking for, and the way to find them is to learn "to rest in God."

Anyone would have to give some careful thought and prayer to appreciate the significance of what he said. It's not an intellectual puzzle, but a truth about one's own life and life itself that's always difficult to see. The realization of who we are and who God is arises naturally when we move through our fear of both— of ourselves and of God. Even more, he was saying that *there is nothing to be afraid of*. The problem that I faced was that I couldn't imagine that he was saying anything interesting enough to be of any real value, much less of relevance, to me. Think of it as a major lesson in humility.

After a few more days, he encouraged me to play tennis. I thought that was a great idea—I loved tennis. But I soon discovered that he meant playing tennis *with him*, which was an entirely different matter. I was a good tennis player, and so was he, but playing tennis with him was never just a game. In fact, it wasn't a game of tennis at all. There were no rules, no keeping score, no winners or losers. Anyone watching from the outside would think we were simply swatting the ball back and forth, getting exercise, enjoying some warm afternoons. That was true enough. But from the inside, a great deal more was going on.

Quickly, I found myself *playing out* any number of emotionally charged scenarios in my mind and through my actions on the court: frustrations and desires from my childhood, competitive streaks that I turned against him, the fear of losing, which I had no idea that I had—all kinds of things. I was transforming a leisurely afternoon of tennis into an exhausting, highly symbolic event very much in the manner of my dreams. In a very real sense, I was re-creating my dreams on the tennis court. He, on the other hand, remained uninvolved in my drama. Showing little or no effort, he simply returned each and every volley that I rifled across the net; and in doing so, he reflected my dramatic scenarios back upon me.

This, of course, provided me with the opportunity that I didn't realize I needed: to become aware of the very "busy" world that I was carrying around in my mind, whether I was at home or on retreat, whether I was dreaming when I was asleep or awake, and whether I was on the tennis court or anywhere else. The breakthrough occurred during one of those hot afternoons. After running myself ragged, I stood on my side of the net for a few seconds, motionless. It wasn't that I had any great insight into life's meaning, but I had become aware of myself in a deeper way. My awareness shifted to a place within that was separate from my emotions and the dreamlike world I had created on the court. I could see my fearful and busy mind for what it was. In that very moment, the "game" was over. He walked toward me, looked at me with a truly kind smile, and said "relax."

This was an exceedingly generous and helpful thing that he did for me. The "storm had been stilled," at least for a few days. He gave me the time, opportunity, and guidance to let the teaching "Just relax" sink to a place deep enough in my soul that I could catch a glimpse of what it meant. It was then that I began to understand that these simple words—"relax" and "rest"—touch the deepest heart of Tantric teaching: in effect, "let go of illusions about your self, and let the sacred energy of life flow through you."

Some followers of the Christian path, including me, would

call this "resting in God." The experience of "rest" in its deeper form is a sacred dance with the Spirit that, more often than not, we're deeply afraid of—despite the fact that the Spirit is alive and well within us every moment of our lives. In this sense, we really are afraid of our own shadow; but the shadow turns out to be the Spirit—and there really is no reason to be afraid, none whatsoever. Yet we've convinced ourselves that if we're *not* afraid of something, then life will lose all meaning and we won't know what to do next. How peculiar can we possibly be?

That's what I see in the image of Jesus "stilling the storm" on my desk. His disciples were terrified. They believed that they were "awake," attending to the storm, and that he was "asleep," oblivious to the danger. My instincts tell me that he wasn't asleep at all, not in the way we think of "sleeping." Rather, he was showing them what it means to be "awake" and "resting in God" at the same time, and asking us, "Why are you afraid of living?" Even better, "Why are you so afraid of the real world?"

I am grateful and fortunate to have witnessed, on more than one occasion, the impact that deep spiritual rest can have on a world that seems to be spinning out of control. I want to tell you about two of those occasions. One involved a meeting with some high-ranking leaders of the church. The other took place only two blocks away, under very different circumstances. They both happened in midtown Manhattan. I've known many people who are scared of city life, and Manhattan symbolizes their very worst fear. All I want to say in that regard is that Manhattan was my home for nearly fifteen years, and I loved it. It is, no doubt, a busy place; but despite the stories that I'm about to tell you here, which are true, I wouldn't call it frightening.

In the late 1980s, I was invited to attend a lunch and meeting at the Episcopal Church Center. Among those present were the Archbishop of Canterbury, the head of the worldwide Anglican Communion, and several colleagues with whom I frequently worked. Coincidentally, tensions were high in Manhattan during that week. The reason was not global terrorism, but a brutal incident of racial hatred that involved a few city policemen. This tragic, unjust, and hateful event occupied a prominent place in the media for several days, and it was discussed everywhere: from the numerous cafés all over town, to homes, places of worship, and community centers. People were justifiably outraged.

During our meeting, a security guard entered the conference room and informed us that the building was being evacuated. His concern was the possibility of a riot, and he advised us to leave the building immediately. For a few seconds, the room fell into complete silence. All of us were understandably worried about what this might mean. Almost in unison, as if it had been rehearsed, everyone in the room turned their heads in the direction of the Archbishop, who presided over the meeting. We wanted to know what our course of action would be. What we noticed was his response: The look in his eyes and his general demeanor had not changed in any way. He expressed utter calm and peacefulness. You might have thought that he hadn't heard one word the security officer said, although he had clearly been paying attention and the officer had directed his instructions to him.

No further comments about the possibility of a riot were made. We followed the Archbishop's lead by continuing to eat our lunch and completing the meeting in a more or less normal way— apart from a spirited discussion of racial prejudice. The agenda was followed just as it had been planned.

After a while, another person, who had just arrived, reported that the streets below were filled with people searching for taxis and heading for the subways. They were hoping to make their way home before the riot happened. Again, we returned to our business. A few minutes later, two people in the meeting spoke openly of their concern about remaining in the building much longer. The Archbishop replied only by saying that anyone who needed to leave could certainly do so.

The situation I've described so far was very much like that in the picture on my desk of Jesus "stilling the storm." I would like to claim that those of us at the meeting responded better than his disciples—we, at least, refrained from screaming—but I won't. We were unwilling to express openly the feelings that actually were in our minds. Of course, if the Archbishop had been asleep, or given that impression, then we might have been more forthcoming. Jesus' disciples, on the other hand, just spoke their minds: "Why aren't you doing something?" Or "Don't you care about what might happen?" Those are my words, but the minds of the disciples must have been working overtime along those lines. In fact, those were some of the same questions in the minds of those present at our meeting. No one actually put it into words, but you could feel it in the air. Of course the Archbishop cared; and of course, Jesus cared. Were they reckless or oblivious, or asleep at the helm? The answer is "definitely not."

As it turned out, no riot ever happened that day in Manhattan. And what if a riot had taken place? Would that have given his actions (or lack of action) a different meaning? I don't think so.

I'll share my experience of the second event, which had a very different outcome, because I want us to reflect on what overwhelming fear is like and recognize the possibility of it within ourselves. To acknowledge what this degree of fear involves—within ourselves—helps us to appreciate not only why it's so important to cultivate the instinct for rest (rather than ignore it), but also why learning to "rest in God" may be something that we really want to pursue. The event itself took place two blocks away from the one I just described, not in a quiet conference room, but on a busy street, three days after the attack on the World Trade Center.

Thousands of people had been killed. The Twin Towers lay in a smoldering heap. Fighter jets were still making their runs overhead. Most everyone in Manhattan was edgy, to say the least; others were in a state of shock and deep grief; some, but not very many, showed their outrage openly. People were doing their best to carry on with their lives, despite rumors about the possibility of further attacks. Their determination to carry on with "life as usual" was an expression of defiance, as well as duty and patriotism, but it was also a way to re-create a world that we wanted to share together.

During those difficult days, the difference between "rumor" and "news" was all but impossible to discern, which fostered a heightened level of anxiety that lasted for several weeks. People had second thoughts about riding elevators. Many could not get on them at all. For those who had jobs in midtown, the mere sight of skyscrapers could be unnerving. Tall buildings were an unavoidable and daily reminder of what had happened, and what might happen again.

It was not a second attack on New York City that came, but panic. I was in midtown, again doing some work at the Episcopal Church Center. By mid-morning, the panic hit with full force. I never knew exactly what triggered it. People were streaming out of office buildings as quickly as they could, their minds set on leaving the city. During the early morning, I had overheard a handful of people commenting on Manhattan as "an island." Two comments were made on the subway. Later, I heard almost the same words in a pharmacy, and then again, in a small café where I ordered a cup of takeout coffee. The sound of their voices expressed claustrophobia. They gave the impression of feeling bound and trapped by circumstances of geography, and they wanted to escape. I assumed that they must have heard something along those lines on the radio or read about it in one of the tabloids. Wherever the fear came from on this particular morning (I never discovered its source), it originated ultimately with the terrorist attack a few days before, and now that same fear had been brought to the surface again.

A few hours later, it was obvious that not much real work was being done, so offices were closing for the day. I began walking the two short blocks from Second Avenue to Grand Central Terminal. Along the way, I noticed that large numbers of people were heading away from Grand Central, rather than toward it, which seemed odd. When I asked one passerby what was going on, she said that she didn't want to get on the subway. Instead, like hundreds of people ahead of her, she was heading on foot toward one of the bridges. Apparently, anything above ground was considered safer.

As strange and unsettling as all this had been, what struck me the most was a brief encounter with a man on the street only a few seconds later. I had met him on another occasion, but I couldn't recall the circumstances. Obviously, I didn't know him well, but from a distance I recognized his familiar face. As I walked toward him, he was looking upward at a skyscraper. I had noticed the very same building on many occasions, because I frequently walked along this street on my way to and from Second Avenue. It had an unusual design near the top. If you looked at the building from certain angles, it could give the impression that it leaned outward, over the street.

Until that moment, I had thought that the building seemed peculiar only in the sense of intriguing. But he was staring at it in a different way, mesmerized and clearly disturbed. I called out to him. He turned and looked at me with terror in his eyes. I asked if I could help. The first thing he said was that there had been an alert of some kind, or so he thought. Then he quickly pointed to the building and said that it was beginning to collapse. I told him that this wasn't the case, that the shape of the building was creating an optical illusion in his mind, and that everything was really okay. He wanted to argue with me. He almost did; but for whatever reason, he changed his mind. I told him again that the building was not collapsing, and there was nothing to be afraid of. I asked him to look up at the building with me. Upon closer inspection, anyone could easily see how the building was constructed. I laughed, hoping he would join me. He looked at me again and smiled politely, but only for a second. Before I had a chance to say anything more, he turned and ran in the same direction as the woman who was avoiding the subway.

In this chapter, we have explored two extremes in the struggle to find rest in a fearful world: on the extreme that we know the least, the spiritual fulfillment of rest known as "resting in God"; and on the extreme that's more familiar, the crystallization of fear in the form of panic. In different ways, both extremes bring us back to the image on my desk of Jesus "stilling the storm." You might recall that my wife, Asha, put it in a frame for me. When anyone—a spouse, a partner, a spiritual teacher, or a close friend—encourages us to get some rest, it should be rather obvious that they care about our well-being. There are times, unfortunately, when we hear it as a personal affront. But if we listen more closely—with more intent—then we realize that by neglecting to get the rest we need, we put ourselves and the people who love us at considerable risk. This makes people afraid, for good reason.

It's not just that we need rest. We need to cultivate this instinct thoroughly, from the ground up. To deny rest to ourselves and to others is to inflict punishment on everyone involved. We may tell

ourselves the exact opposite, for example, that overwork is virtuous. There's no doubt that having the dedication and tenacity to
get our work done is hugely important. But this should not suggest
or imply that it's right to throw the Book of Genesis out the window. I'm thinking of the opening chapters of Genesis, where God
instructs us to thrive, but to care for this good green earth, which
includes you and me. And I'm thinking of the last of the Ten Commandments, which completes them all: "Remember the Sabbath
and keep it holy." And the ancient tradition of Jubilee (Leviticus 25)
that sets aside not just a few days, but a whole year every seventh
year to give the earth ample time for rest and renewal. Rather than
taking these teachings seriously, what we have, in fact, done is to
throw the principle behind them out, as if "rest" doesn't matter. By
refusing to cultivate our instinct for rest, or to give God's creation
a rest, we're playing a game of roulette with our lives, with the lives
of those we love, and with life itself. Like I said, this should make
us afraid. It probably does make us afraid unconsciously, which
may account for a large part of our unacknowledged fear.

Perhaps we have neither the time nor the inclination to pursue "resting in God" in its fullest sense, but we can cultivate our
instinct for rest a little bit every day. Just that alone may be enough
to steer us in the right direction—enough to help us discern the
difference between real danger and the illusion of danger, especially when the storms "out there" seem to land at our doorstep
much more than they should.

But the whole point is that the vast majority of the storms in
our lives originate not "out there," but within us. It's the power
of our primal fear that would have us believe that the fear-ridden
world we routinely see, witness, and struggle with is all there is,
when, in fact, there is a great deal more going on too—and it's
good. We don't see it because our fear prevents us from seeing.

That's why those gentle (or not so gentle) helpful hints from those who love us have the same source as "the still, small voice" within. They're all telling us that getting some rest in the midst of our busy lives may save our lives. They're calling us home—to the real world—and reminding us that unless we slow down soon, we'll reach our "final resting place" way ahead of schedule.

I wouldn't set aside the parable of "stilling the storm" too quickly, and I would never throw it out the window because we don't believe it literally happened. As for myself, I really do wonder what Jesus' "sleeping" might have been like, his head on the cushion, apparently oblivious to everything going on around him. And I wonder about us in the same way. What happens when we sleep—apart from occasional teeth grinding and vivid or unusual dreams?

Some spiritual traditions believe that this is an important question. The Yoga Sutras, for example, teach that everyone experiences four states of consciousness: waking, dreaming, dreamless sleep, and another more unfamiliar state called *turiya*. In the fourth state, according to the Sutras, a part of our soul actually rests in the presence of God—while we're sleeping. We leave our fearful world, and sometimes our fearful dreams, and reach that holy place for a few moments every night. The purpose of prayer, meditation, community service, and living a respectful, moral, wholesome life is to bring our whole conscious awareness into this restful presence of God, whether we're waking or sleeping. But I'm getting ahead of myself. I'm too busy within myself, and I'm going too fast. I'll return to this important point again in the next chapter.

A Spiritual Practice in Rest

Everyone knows that rest is not something that we actually "practice," like the game of golf or tennis. Yet most everyone I know doesn't like to admit that they aren't very good at getting rest. Our doctors, who may be the absolute worst about getting rest, often prescribe it to their overworked, frazzled, frightened patients. Obviously, this suggests that we all have something to learn, whether we're in the role of doctor or patient.

This is the spiritual practice that I recommend. It has two parts. My first suggestion, which involves breathing, was mentioned in the introduction and again in the last chapter. We would all reap enormous benefits from learning to "breathe through" our ordinary fears and worries, much in the same way as we deal with panic attacks and full-blown anxiety. This can be a very practical and easy thing to do. It draws directly upon the contemplative Christian tradition and the yogic practice known as "pranayama."

Sit quietly in a comfortable chair or on the floor, relax, and let yourself breathe easily in one continuous motion of inhaling and exhaling. The effects are profound and immediate. We soon realize that we hold our breath, if only briefly and intermittently, rather than inhaling and exhaling in an easy, continuous way. This suggests the presence of some kind of fear: We're literally holding our breath, even when we believe that fear plays no significant part in our lives. It's also very unhealthy to do this, yet it can easily become our normal habit.

By simply drawing upon and, quite literally, practicing a completely natural instinct—breathing—anyone can take a huge step toward moving through their fear and reestablishing a vital connection with the instinct for rest. So again, sit quietly, relax, and let yourself breathe easily in one continuous motion of inhaling and exhaling. As peculiar as this seems, most of us really do need to learn to breathe in a healthy, restful way.

My second suggestion is to give some thought to the kinds of activities that actually make you feel restful and rested. This may not be so obvious. For example, it is entirely possible that some of our recreational activities—things we do "for fun"—are not all that fun or restful. I've known Saturday morning golfers, for example, who finally set aside their clubs when they realized how angry, frustrated, and viciously competitive they felt when they were supposedly "having fun." Of course, the exact opposite may be the case for their friends: They may have the same experience in a game of tennis. The point here is to reflect, genuinely and honestly, on what you actually like to do, and then to claim it as a spiritual practice tailor-made for you. You might also consider whether those not-so-enjoyable activities amount to some heavy baggage that could be left behind.

Along the same lines, the fact that we habitually use the word "work" to describe activities that are genuinely joyful and fun can be misleading too. Many people, for example, truly enjoy "working in the garden." It involves some "work," but, for them, it primarily offers true rest and relaxation. Or, you might have been telling yourself that you would like to have a garden, but you haven't taken the time to actually do it—not yet. In effect, what you're avoiding is an enjoyable way to get some rest and relaxation. Often, we rationalize in this way by saying that we probably wouldn't be good at it, despite the fact that we really want to garden. In situations like this, a little help from our friends—some encouragement and know-how—can go a long way. It also generates a collective atmosphere of friendship and mutual assistance that cultivates the instinct of rest in unexpected ways.

I'll give another example. Recently, I met someone who can identify virtually any variety of bird in the eastern United States by its song. He can also identify them by their flying silhouette, the form of their nests, and their color; but, as a rule, he likes to hear them first, and then follow their song. This is something he "does," but it's not a form of "doing" that anyone would describe as "work." For him, this is an immensely restful and joyful part of *his life. It gives him the opportunity to feel at home in the world and within himself at the same time. You can see the "rest"—the inner peace—in his eyes even when he talks about it. Because he has claimed this joy as his own, and it has become an integral part of the person that he is.*

I've given the examples of gardening and birding to emphasize that any number of "activities" can be restful in the deepest sense of the word. We wouldn't normally think of these activities as having any direct relationship with our fear, and in some sense, they don't. Yet they cultivate a degree of inner peace that cuts through our fear and allows us to move through it easily—without giving it much, or any, thought.

Speaking for myself, an especially good spiritual practice in rest is to cultivate the art of listening, rather than talking, in my everyday life. Priests are supposed to be good listeners, but we're also prone to talking more than we should. For better and worse, pulpits—of any kind—have a strange and not altogether positive impact on those who use them. This is not a particularly difficult habit to break. The art of listening encourages a restful atmosphere that has an unexpected effect on the world around us: It creates a sacred space that allows people to step in our direction, rather than to turn away—and that alone cultivates a sense of inner peace in everyone, ourselves included. And if we're carrying around a "storm" in our minds—worries, preoccupations, and full-blown fears—then listening helps to calm the storm. It takes us out of ourselves, and enlarges our perspective on life. While listening is part of "my job," I don't consider it to be "work." Rather, listening is one of the most important ways that I cultivate rest in myself and others in the midst of a stormy world. I highly recommend it to you.

9.

FAITH: THE LEAP INTO THE UNKNOWN

The only thing that counts is faith working through love.

—Saint Paul's Letter to the Galatians, 5:6b

A few weeks ago, a friend sat down in my office and said that she wanted to talk about her faith. On an impulse, I discreetly reached toward my bookshelf, found the dictionary, and looked up the word. While I was flipping through the pages, the thought of what I was doing—a priest looking up "faith" in the dictionary—struck me as totally absurd. Never mind that I just wanted to know what Mr. Webster had to say. In that moment, my overriding concern—my fear—was that by opening the dictionary, I might have thrown my credibility out the window.

As peculiar as my actions might have seemed to someone else, it was the definition given for "faith" that I found really peculiar—"unquestioning belief." I realize that this is the commonly accepted meaning. And there's nothing wrong with it, not *as far as it goes. Nevertheless, two serious problems quickly come to mind. First, it doesn't take into account the very faithful people who question their beliefs all the time—like the friend and parishioner who was sitting in my office. Nor does it suggest (as it should) that their "questioning" can be (and usually is) a very positive sign, both intellectually and spiritually. Some questioning (even doubt) among faithful people tells me that they're not only alive and well, but also reflecting on their lives and the world that they're a part of. They want to know whether their faith is faithful, which is a matter of ultimate concern. It should be a concern for every one of us.*

"Unquestioning belief" is also the kind of definition that can make a person feel vulnerable and possibly defensive, which brings me to the second problem. It conjures up images of unquestioned authority breathing down your neck. I couldn't help but imagine my friend hearing the definition, and then holding her breath, clenching her teeth, and closing her heart. That is to say, just the thought of it evokes fear. The very last thing that I want to do, as a priest, is to make my parishioners afraid, when the circumstances of their lives can be scary enough.

Rather than repeating the definition out loud, I just smiled and quietly put the dictionary back on the shelf. Having finally realized where my instincts had been leading me, I followed them with confidence: I turned and listened to all the questions about her beliefs that my friend wanted to discuss. That is, after all, why she came to my office. In fact, listening to her should have been my first instinct, rather than turning to the bookshelf; but it's easy to forget important things like that, even for a priest—especially for a priest.

The meaning of "faith" that should concern us here is not the one we find in the dictionary. The question that should be our ultimate concern is this: Have we cultivated our spiritual instincts enough to move beyond what our fear would tempt us into believing in the name of faith? More often than not, our answer will be yes, although we probably realize that the other possibility cannot be dismissed out of hand. "It might happen to someone else, but not to me"—that's what we want to believe. My friend, however, knew that she could not say "yes" with a clear conscience, and that was what she wanted to talk about. In no way does this negate the fact that she was and still is a faithful person or that she knows, hopefully better than before and as a matter of faith, that God will help her when her faith falls short.

Fear that pretends to be faith is a possibility that anyone who wants to be faithful must take very seriously, especially in times of crisis. When we make the effort to look within ourselves, we will find that deceptive kind of fear. But what we may also find is a soul-numbing lack of trust, which breeds another kind of fear: the fear that we're living a life (and creating a world) that's filled with an illusion of faith—where the word "faith" is heard all the time, so much so that all our spiritual instincts are pushed into the background.

This is the reason that I've saved faith for last, and it's why this introduction, like the last one, must be a bit longer than the others. In other words, I'm not suggesting that faith is the only spiritual instinct that matters. Honestly, I would like to say that faith is the most important. Large segments of the Christian tradition virtually demand that I say it. But faith is never quite that simple, nor is fear. Even the towering figure of Saint Paul, who makes a strong case for the priority of faith in his Letter to the Galatians, speaks with caution to this very point: "The only thing that counts is faith expressed through love." And then, in another letter, he says something different, making the case for love above faith: "Faith, hope, and love . . . and the greatest of these is love" (1 Corinthians 13).

Still, I hesitate. I often hear his famous words—"the greatest of these is love"—read aloud at weddings. I look out at the congregation and see people for whom the loss of love, through little or no fault of their own, has delivered a terrible blow. I know them. I know how much they struggle to put any kind of faith in love, and I know that a broken heart puts them in grave danger of losing their faith. But many of them have held onto faith, or its possibility, and love eventually fills their hearts again, stronger than ever. I've seen it happen again and again. The testimony of my friends should neither be denied nor overlooked: It was their faith that carried them through the loss of love.

That's why my instincts tell me to emphasize faith above all our spiritual instincts, and I will; but only with certain qualifications on what we mean by "faith." If "faith" only means "belief" or a set of beliefs, then I'm not so sure. I'll give another example. Some people I know memorize what they believe are the right things to say to a traffic cop. Their hope is to avoid a fine or accumulating points on their driver's license. Quite often, their strategy seems to work, and for that reason, they claim to have faith in their strategy. They "believe in" their belief. It works for them, or it seems to work. In any event, this kind of belief doesn't say much for their faith or their spiritual instincts.

What I want to emphasize—and what I want you to consider—is how we can cultivate a deeper, more genuine kind of faith. By now, it should go without saying that fear is rarely a good strategy to take. You might scare people into acting a certain way, for a while; but this doesn't make them faithful. Spiritual traditions say that faith is a gift of God, completely undeserved and given out of love. Faith cannot be earned, nor is it a reward for good behavior. All this is entirely true; but it's not enough to say that faith is a gift of God and leave it at that. Why? Because everything is a gift of God: the whole creation, every living creature, every rock, the stars, the sunshine, friends, neighbors, loved ones, strangers—and enemies. All our instincts, primal and spiritual, are a gift of God. Yes, faith is a gift, but it's also our birthright, as creatures made in God's image, to put the faith that we've been given to good use. And there lies our answer: The best way to cultivate our faith is to use all our spiritual instincts, faith included. Unless we use those instincts enough to move through our fear, then our faith will become an empty shell.

That's what a crisis of faith can look like, especially in our day and age. It's not that we give up on faith. We may look for it with real commitment and the desire for unquestioning belief. The crisis comes when we separate our faith from all our other spiritual instincts. This is the spiritual disaster that Saint Paul was grappling with in his time, and it remains with us still. Yet a crisis of faith does not mean that the world is coming to an end, nor does it mean that our faith is completely wrong. God is real, and we try to be faithful. What it means is that we're making a passage from the old to the new. An old way of living is coming to an end, just as a more viable way of being faithful might be born—if we move through our fear. That is why it's important to realize that faith is more than unquestioning belief. Faith is also our God-given capacity to leap into the unknown. To make this leap, we can no longer put our faith in the service of fear, or use faith to conceal our fear.

I realize that this definition—"faith is the leap we make into the unknown"—sounds like yet another reason to be afraid rather than consoled. But it could also be a description of "courage," which is a habitually neglected word in spiritual writing. This near omission is unfortunate, to say the least. It leads us to believe that faith is what we have when courage fails. There is, no doubt, some truth in this. We can and should believe that when all is lost, God will find us. But I would never want to equate faith with a failure of courage. Rather, faith blossoms when all our other spiritual instincts awaken, for whatever reason; courage is the gift of faith put into practice, whether it takes the form of doubt or unquestioning belief.

In times like ours, we must ask ourselves whether our faith has become an excuse to avoid our fear—especially the fear of unknown places in our souls where the Spirit is asking us to go. The only truly honest answer that we can give is "yes," at least to some extent. Faith is too often our excuse for remaining afraid. But this is no reason for discouragement. Fear is the single greatest obstacle in life and on the spiritual path; and it's the fear of what lives within us that scares us the most. I can't help but think of this when I read Jesus' enigmatic words in the Gospel of Thomas (saying 70):

> If you bring forth what is within you,
> what you have will save you.

Then, in the very next sentence, Jesus explains, in very blunt terms, why we must take this teaching seriously:

> If you do not bring forth what is within you,
> what you do not bring forth will kill you.

Jesus was not the kind of person, I believe, who would say that faith is what we're left with when courage fails—although I would be happy to have faith in a situation like that. Rather, faith is one form that courage can take (and should take) when our survival is at stake. It requires courage to have faith. Saint Thomas himself showed this kind of courage. I'll explain that.

The canonical gospels portray him as the "doubting" apostle: as someone who refused to "believe," until he could see and touch the evidence of Jesus' wounds for himself. He was the disciple who expressed the very opposite of "unquestioning belief." This is true and, at the same time, misleading. His insistence on "the facts" need not suggest a lack of anything, including belief or faith. He was using all his spiritual instincts to discover the truth, which tells me that he wasn't afraid of his fear. He wasn't afraid of the opinion of others. He wasn't even afraid of what Jesus might have thought. He wanted to know whether the resurrection was real. Who in their right mind wouldn't want to know?

I fully realize that "unquestioning belief" can be a supremely devout expression of faith. But this should not suggest that faith is found or lived by avoiding the questions that we surely have. The fear that should concern us the most is the fear we refuse to acknowledge and move through. That fear can be our undoing, and that is also the fear that crises of faith inevitably bring to the surface—and that the Spirit helps us to move through. We know this already. We know it because our spiritual instincts tell us that it's true. However our spiritual instincts might be expressed, to discover that we simply have them is to realize something important about how God works through us. This is when we begin to realize that a power greater than ourselves really exists. And if we can have faith in ourselves, even a little, then we can have faith in God many times over. Even more, we can trust in God, when, for whatever reason, we've lost all faith and trust in ourselves.

This brings me to my last two stories. The first is a story about waking up in the morning, struggling with fear and faith, and making sense of a world that God has given us to care for. The second involves finding faith in God and trust in something as seemingly ordinary as preparing and sharing a meal together. Of course, there's nothing "ordinary" about anything.

It was not until my late twenties and early thirties that I began to realize why I became an anthropologist and would later become a priest. It should have been obvious, but it's not always so easy to appreciate the spiritual instincts that others cultivate in us. In my case, those instincts involved the compassion and empathy for others (the instinct of love) that my parents instilled in my sister and me. We must have been using those qualities in younger years, without understanding what we were doing or why. As for me, I was just as likely to overlook or reject them then, as children often do. But when I reached—by the sheer grace of God—my late thirties, I had become settled enough inwardly to reflect on these things in a more serious way.

That was when I first observed something peculiar, and, as it turns out, important about how my spiritual instincts sometimes work: My very first thoughts of the day, in the first few minutes after waking up, can be especially trustworthy. Because those small, quirky, seemingly insignificant parts of our lives can reveal a great deal about life itself, they shouldn't be overlooked or ignored. I'm not talking about the obvious, routine thoughts, like "I'm going to be late for work" or "I'm hungry," but fully formed thoughts that have depth and meaning. For example, if I find myself thinking about a particular person or a specific situation, then I might call that person later in the day or follow up on what my instincts suggest. I don't actually tell anyone why I've done this. It would seem (and might actually be) attention-getting and off-putting, which would create an unnecessary distraction. But I take my good instincts seriously enough to follow their lead.

I have some ideas about why my early morning instincts are trustworthy. I'll tell you what they are; but in order to do that, I must begin with an exception—or what seems to be an exception. In the last few years, my first early morning thoughts often involve the earth and the ecological crisis that we face. This, in itself, is not in any way peculiar—not for me. What is peculiar is that I wake up thinking that the crisis might be a bad dream or that the peril we face may not be so serious.

At first, this whole situation was troubling and confusing. The feeling that I had about these dreams wasn't full-fledged fear, although a trace of fear was clearly present—which is the peculiar part: Why would I have any fear whatsoever about the possibility that we have no reason to be afraid? You have to admit that this is a strange question to ask yourself. Time and time again this happened—not every day, but maybe once a week, or more. Sometimes I would dream it and wake up with the memory vivid in my mind: "All is well with the earth, and there's nothing to be concerned about." This continued for several months before I finally realized that I might be experiencing an exception that upheld the rule. Something else was going on in the early morning that was, in fact, trustworthy, but in a way that I had not expected or taken into account.

So why did I feel so unsettled? I believed those would be the last kind of thoughts my mind would ever produce, at any time of day. I considered the possibility that something might be wrong with me. Why? The reason is that I know as well as anyone that the environmental crisis is both real and profoundly serious. I've given the greater part of my life to it. I've done this as an Episcopal priest who has received advanced degrees in cultural anthropology. I've read and reread the scientific studies, and I know how to read them. I know that great civilizations have declined and fallen in circumstances similar to ours: Their way of life followed a course that ran counter to the ecological and spiritual design of Mother Earth. Because they failed to foresee the consequences of their actions, they didn't make it—they died. I know how this works like the back of my hand. I've seen the accumulating evidence with my own eyes—in cities and in the countryside, on islands and mountains, and in tropical rain forests. I've written, taught, mobilized, organized, and prayed. I've worked on it at every level—internationally, nationally, regionally, and in small communities and congregations—and I've used all my spiritual instincts to do this work. I know.

So I had to ask myself: Why would I, of all people and after all this, find myself having rosy thoughts, even rosy dreams, about the environmental crisis? Why would I be wondering whether the crisis is really all that serious?

One possibility is that I had been influenced unknowingly— against my better judgment and common sense—by some of the extreme anti-environmentalist commentaries frequently heard in some parts of the media. I considered this possibility, but it seemed unlikely. Asha and I don't have television at home. We're not against television, not in principle. We just don't have the time. Another possibility is that the more you know about the environmental crisis—and the more you realize what the consequences are—the more unbelievable and frightening it becomes. "Frightening" is the right word: climate change, extinctions, deforestation, water shortages, and a lack of clean water. Just as frightening are the financial, economic, and corporate institutions that try to avoid any serious responsibility for it. Even the words we routinely use are involved in the evasion. Like I said before, "economics" now means "the financial system," which seems to have little relationship with real communities, real livelihoods, real people, or real ecosystems—that is, the real world. You get the impression (which is usually true) that environmental "costs" aren't figured into their bottom-line equations at all, despite the fact that they tell you otherwise. We need to get our heads and hearts out of the world that we create in our own image and back into the world where we actually live. Any rational person would know where we're headed if we continue on the present course.

I had no choice but to confront the situation head-on, which I did by asking myself some hard, very personal questions: Had I reached a stage in my life when my otherwise reasonable, rational, conscious mind no longer wanted to face reality? Was I no longer able to trust my instincts because the truth was too much to handle? And last, but not least, was I succumbing to the power of my own fear? Even the questions were scary to think about.

This line of thinking offered an explanation of sorts. Sometimes we just can't hear bad news anymore. No sane person, I told myself, would want to believe that the possibility of an environmental catastrophe is in fact possible. I know as well as anyone that the mere thought of it can seem unwholesome, even paranoid, despite the truth of it. So I wondered whether the pleasant content of my wish-fulfilling dreams was erupting into my waking life, simply because I could no longer accept the world as it is. I recalled the first words that my father spoke in the mornings of my childhood—"rise and shine."

I may have hated to hear him say it back then, but I always "rose and shone," at least the best that I could. I wondered whether I was responding, even now, to the memory of his voice. In other words, I'll not only rise and shine, but I'll also have "rise and shine dreams," even if the ship is sinking.

There may be some truth in this explanation. "Rise and shine" is part of my nature, and I have a strong instinct for intent. I "never give up" on much of anything, even when I should. Nevertheless, "some truth" is about as far as it goes. Rather than dismissing my early morning thoughts outright—because they contradict the objective facts (they do), or because they represent a form of denial (telling myself that the crisis may not be so bad), or because of some wish-fulfilling fantasy that the crisis is under control (which would be astonishingly poor discernment)—I settle on the more likely possibility that there must be another way of understanding the situation. There must be more going on within me, something that cannot be explained or explained away so easily.

I decide to ask myself a different set of questions: Could my peculiar early morning thoughts be good instincts after all? Could they be trustworthy? Yes, this is possible, but to understand why I would need to look at the nature of my life in a deeper way. I would have to examine *my life* as I actually live it, rather than making hasty judgments about *myself*. This involved an investigation, of sorts, that would take me into some unexpected territory, which I'll share with you now.

Hoping to be a good detective, I begin with the obvious—what I already know. The first thing that comes to mind is that I'm especially aware of my early morning thoughts at the very moment when I wake up. This is so obvious that it seems to have no significance; yet it turns out to be a major clue relating to the interplay between "waking" and "sleeping" in the gospel stories and the miracle of Jesus "stilling the storm" that we discussed in the last chapter. Two more questions, then, come to mind: What was the last thing I did before going to sleep? And what was I doing when I was sleeping? Yes, those are peculiar questions to ask, but life is peculiar, mysteriously so, in the most sacred sense of Holy Mystery. What's really weird is to believe that life is anything but peculiar, mysterious, and sacred; for example, the belief that God's green earth has no significance apart from how we exploit it—that it's not a body of life in and of itself.

The answer to the first question is easy. My habit is to meditate or pray before going to bed, which I do in a variety of ways. I either pray in spoken words (intercession), or I sit in silent meditation (wordless prayer). On occasion, I simply lie on the floor in a standard yogic position and do a systematic relaxation that's exceptionally restful for me. If it's done often and with intent, it can lead to the experience of inner silence and resting in God. Some people might regard this as peculiar in the sense of "weird." Others would see it as a "spiritual discipline." For me, it's not weird at all, and I steer away from the word "discipline," which could create an impression of overdone piety that doesn't fit my personality very well. A more accurate description of my life is that I do my best to pray, meditate, and/or rest every day—and almost always before sleeping.

There's no doubt that faith and intent play a large part in this. I don't feel so good when my daily life departs from this pattern. I know that I've overlooked or ignored something important, which generates a healthy degree of guilt. The importance of praying before sleeping was a spiritual instinct (rest) that my parents cultivated considerably more in my childhood than they realized at the time, perhaps more than they intended; but I accepted it without resistance. In no way was this imposed or forced. Our home wasn't like that. In fact, very little was actually said about it, but it's what I learned. It made me feel peaceful inside, and I slept well. I remember the words of the prayer that they taught me. Most people I know remember them. They appeared in *The New England Primer* of the eighteenth century:

> Now I lay me down to sleep,
> I pray the Lord my soul to keep,
> And if I die before I wake,
> I pray the Lord my soul to take.

I've always been struck by the straightforward, matter-of-fact tone of that prayer. The words still feel comforting to me, just as they did fifty years ago. But now, the phrase "die before I wake" seems bluntly realistic, as if the prayer goes out of its way to make a point. Many people today might say that it's too realistic for a child's prayer. I wouldn't say that it was too realistic for me. I'm only commenting on how much we've changed in the last fifty years. Have we become so afraid of our mortality that we would erase it from our prayers? Do we believe that we can or should censor ourselves and our children from this one inevitable and perfectly natural part of our lives? It didn't seem too realistic when I was a kid. I wasn't afraid of the prayer. Quite the contrary! It made me feel safe and serene. The prayer was my lifesaver: It helped me overcome my fear of monsters waiting in the closet to gobble me up.

Perhaps that traditional bedtime prayer is an artifact of a way of life that has already disappeared. Traces of it still exist, in our memory, but the world we're creating now is based on a different set of assumptions. Not long ago, we taught metaphysical prayers to children, spoke openly about death, and we didn't talk about sex at all. Today, it's the reverse. I like sex and have no qualms about saying so; but I have to face the fact that this is a peculiar turn of events: Some of my friends today, whom I dearly love, organize their relationships around sex, won't go near a funeral, and absolutely refuse to think that they "might get old" someday. I can't help but notice the mute silence that follows any discussion or mention of death. There's nowhere to go with the thought, no refuge, and no rest. What I hear in the silence is fear and a cry for help.

Getting back to my story, I broke the habit of saying this particular prayer before bed during my teens and early twenties. Of course I did—it's a kid's prayer. That's what I told myself back then. I didn't want to be a kid anymore, but the intent and the faith remained. In its place, I took up the habit of silent meditation. As a matter of practical experience, I knew that almost any form of prayer before sleeping was good for me. The instinct had been cultivated, and I kept it. I slept better. When I woke up in the morning, I was more relaxed and refreshed.

The significance of this became all the more apparent later in life, when I noticed that so many people, including close friends, keep their televisions turned on all night. I can't sleep with the noise. They can't sleep without it. On a few occasions, when I've slept in their homes, I've gotten up and turned the television off. In the morning, they told me that the silence was disturbing. It made them anxious and a little afraid.

This makes me think that when we reject or lose one pattern (praying to God before sleeping), we replace it with anything that seems even remotely similar (listening to television while sleeping). Could we, as a people, have actually replaced our connection with the eternal, transcendent realm with a never-ending, counterfeit version of the "now" in the form of television? You have to wonder if a significant step toward cultivating our spiritual instincts would simply be to turn off the TV—especially when we're asleep. We might get some real sleep that way, some real rest, and a lot more faith. *It helps me understand that "waking up" in the spiritual sense, "resting in God" in the prayerful sense, "stilling the storm" that exists within us and in the world, and "moving through our fear" are all different ways of talking about exactly the same thing.*

By now, I'm sure that I'm on to something with regard to my early morning thoughts, so I turn to the second question: What was I doing when I was sleeping? I'll admit that this is an odd way to put it, but it seems right. I believe in the existence of the soul, which makes me wonder what the soul might be doing when our waking minds are asleep—that is, when we're, hopefully, not listening to television. Is it possible that some part of us might return to God or somewhere close to God: the power greater than ourselves, the ground of our being, the Holy Mystery, the source of everything that exists?

This brings us back to the Yoga Sutras that I mentioned at the end of the last chapter. Keep in mind that the Sutras are not a set of religious beliefs or doctrines as we understand them in the West. Rather, they are sacred teachings about consciousness based on direct, firsthand experience. Once again, according to the Sutras, every one of us, each and every day, experiences four states of consciousness: waking, dreaming, dreamless sleep, and another state, called "turiya," when and where we return to God. We all reach that "place" for a few moments while we're sleeping, and a part of us (the soul?) is somehow aware of it. It's not usually the "me" that we know in daily life that experiences God in this way. Rather, it's the deeper "me," the true self. Whether we realize it, or believe it, this is one of the Holy Mysteries that enters into our faith too—when we're sleeping.

My instincts tell me that the deeper reason that we were taught (or were once taught) to pray before bedtime was not just to make us feel comforted and restful within ourselves. The deeper reason was that we might reach that sacred but unknown place more easily, and stay there longer. We don't usually say things like that in the Christian tradition, but perhaps our forefathers and mothers retained it in their memory of the distant past, and passed it on as practical spiritual wisdom.

I can't prove this, but I come to the conclusion that my morning thoughts are neither a delusion nor the product of wishful thinking. I can't prove this either, but I believe that the ancient Yoga Sutras and the more recent Christian tradition are both right: We are in God's presence for a few sacred moments when we're asleep, *and* God is with us whether we're asleep or awake.

I'll explain. When we give ourselves even half a chance—by saying our prayers and getting some rest—the Spirit will help us remember the difference between the way things are and what the world might become if we cultivate our spiritual instincts. That's what my early morning thoughts were trying to tell me. Praying and meditating before sleeping, which is what the Eastern and Western spiritual traditions encourage us to do, really do cultivate faith; and that helps us to perceive God's presence in the world while we're awake. We learn, firsthand, that the Spirit is alive and well on this green earth, and that no one can destroy God's Providence.

The Spirit gives us reasons for hope—even in the form of rosy dreams about dire situations—rather than making us either lose faith in God and ourselves, or doubt, in the name of faith, what any reasonable, wide-awake person would know to be true. That's what the Spirit was trying to tell me through those unexpectedly pleasant early morning thoughts: Do not surrender to fear; do not give up; have faith; use your spiritual instincts. If I hadn't confused myself with my self-doubt, then I would have realized it sooner.

This is what the whole story means to me. First, the environmental crisis, which is also a crisis of faith, is a reason for serious concern and for fear. This kind of fear is good, because it puts us on alert to a real threat. The truth of it is overwhelming. It goes beyond what our minds can normally comprehend. Second, faith is not and cannot be opposed to truth. Faith is not meant to be a rose-colored version of the world that denies the very truth before our eyes. And third, the issue is not whether we can trust in God—we can. The issue is whether we will learn to cultivate our spiritual instincts enough to move through our fear and to do what God is calling us to do. If we do that, then all will be well.

Let me say it again: It's not the truth about life that undermines faith, but our fear of the truth—the fear that would tell us to have faith, while setting aside our spiritual instincts. This is the same fear that keeps us from getting the rest that we need, including a good night's sleep. And I wouldn't underestimate the importance of a good night's sleep. There's more going on when we sleep than we realize—more than in our wildest dreams. If all goes well, we might eventually realize that we really do live in a great body of life, filled with Spirit every minute of the night and day, whether we're awake or sleeping.

. . .

In addition to getting a good night's sleep, there's something else we can do when we suspect (or know) that fear shapes our faith and our lives too much. I want to tell you about what has worked for me, how it works, and why it works. You could adopt it as a spiritual practice. In fact, I hope that you will, but this is not a substitute for the spiritual practice at the end of this chapter.

This is what I do. I remember the most wholesome, seemingly ordinary, everyday activities that make me happy; I seek them out; and I do my best to make them a basic part of my life. Although cultivating faith in the "familiar" and "everyday" is the exact opposite of faith as a leap into the unknown, I can't think of a better preparation for making that leap. It puts life in the perspective we need, brings our souls back into our bodies, keeps our hearts and minds open, and helps us to cultivate and renew all our spiritual instincts, including faith.

The best example of a suitable ordinary, everyday activity that I know is the sharing of a meal. The preparation and sharing of food occupies an important place in spiritual traditions, and I'm not only talking about ritual meals. Every meal that we have ever eaten and ever will eat is sacred. Looking back, I can plainly see that my childhood was filled with this understanding, although it was never formally taught or spelled out in so many words. It was taught by the way we lived and by the fact that we lived the truth of it—which, ironically, is also the reason I learned to take this form of sacred knowledge for granted. In a manner of speaking, it was supposed to be taken for granted, but only in the sense that it's not something anyone would ever consider ignoring or forgetting.

It was no coincidence that all the disparate pieces of this ordinary, but sacred knowledge fell into place when I was old enough

to look back and remember *the way things were*. I reached the
point of realizing how much I admired a good cook; and as you
might expect, this process of remembering began about the time
that I was no longer eating at home; that is to say, when my
mother was no longer putting food before me at the dinner table.
Great food that I ate in my childhood—I could trust that it would
always be there. What I didn't quite understand was that it didn't
come out of nowhere. I should have known. In a way, I did know.
My grandfather had a small farm. I picked corn and strawberries.
I slopped the pigs, dug potatoes, and sometimes helped to wash
the dishes after we ate. I learned in my flesh and bones the lessons
that failed to penetrate my thick head and wandering heart.

Soon thereafter, a ray of light burst forth in my consciousness: My admiration for a good cook was no reason to think that
I couldn't learn how to cook myself! This, of course, is one of
many humbling lessons we all learn in how to "take care of yourself," which is part of the larger set of teachings in how to "know
yourself." Sacred knowledge, by the way, appears in this form
when it's perceived and understood from the standpoint of the
individual person—that is to say, when it involves self-knowledge.
But from the standpoint of food, which is equally important, this
same sacred knowledge tells us that the significance of a single
meal goes far beyond the individual person—it symbolizes and
actually is knowledge of a whole way of life and of the great body
of life on which our individual lives depend.

In other words, I was beginning to realize two crucial truths.
The first was how deeply sacred ordinary meals actually are;
the second was that it is my responsibility to create the kind of
life that I want to live. It isn't my mother's responsibility, or my
father's, grandfather's, and grandmother's responsibility.

I am responsible for my life; and the fact that this is true of
everyone makes it "our responsibility" too. Our "life together"

is our responsibility. None of this works unless we all play our part, which is why knowledge of spiritual traditions is a matter of survival.

After waking up in the morning (hopefully to the memory of pleasant dreams) and giving thanks for life itself, eating is the third most important thing we do at the beginning of the day. I know that a lot of people don't bother to eat breakfast; but there are some things we shouldn't overlook. We used to say that the soul needs nourishment as much as the body—on the reasonable assumption that we neglect the soul. Now, we have no choice but to say that they both need nourishment, having apparently decided to neglect the health of our bodies too. For example, who really believes that cardboard and fructose qualify as nourishment? Apparently, we do. We're on a sugar high and frenetically busy at the same time. It shouldn't be difficult to make the connection.

Of course, the times being what they are, we often have to eat and run, or so we believe. The problem with that is that breakfast time is no time just to run. The only time that it's advisable to break camp, running, without eating is when we're facing the threat of imminent danger. Even then, we would stop and eat as soon as the opportunity arises. And the only time I can think of when it's morally right to refuse food, especially when we need it most, is a fast—let's say for the purpose of religious and/or political protest. Otherwise, refusing or neglecting to eat is ridiculous. It makes us a danger to ourselves. Whatever the financial cost of our skipped breakfast might be, we should send it to the great many people who sorely need the food and want it. It's the only right thing to do. They're terrified of starvation, while we have more than enough of virtually everything, except the time and good sense to take care of ourselves. We may claim that we have faith, which is no doubt true in the narrow sense of the word, but we neglect to put our other spiritual instincts in the service of faith. What, in God's name, are we running from—and so afraid of?

So having given my obligatory sermon, let's reflect on a full-fledged meal and all that it involves, beginning with some of the ingredients and the sacred knowledge that go into it. I'll mention some of the highlights, beginning with the cook: a knowledge of how to collect and purchase the right food and seasonings, how to clean and prepare them, how to blend all the ingredients in just the right way, how to use cold, heat, and the transformative magic of fire—not to mention tender loving care, a watchful eye, a good sense of taste, smell, sight, and touch, a reliable sense of time, and, last but not least, patience. And that's only a snapshot of what happens in the kitchen.

Expanding the picture, we find farmers, farmworkers, ranchers, and fishers—all people who engage in backbreaking, often dangerous work to make a living. They rely on knowledge of the soil, water, the seasons and weather, rainfall, daylight and night, seeds, insects, predators, and pests. All these people and their sacred knowledge should never be taken for granted in our prayers and pocketbooks.

Then, after the cook performs his or her sacred act, a crucial threshold is reached when the "cooking" phase is completed. The food is served, shared, and eaten in an atmosphere of hospitality, good manners, and respectful thankfulness that creates a world that many people, including myself, would call a symbolic yet lived representation of the real world. By "the real world," I mean everything involved in the meal, from Mother Earth—all the plants, animals, birds, and fish—to the farmers, the food marketers, the cooks, and everyone who eats. And I'm thinking of all that we talk about around the dinner table too: the decisions we make, our fears, worries, and joys, our jokes, and how we help each other to make sense of it.

It is then, and only then, that "the great work," to borrow some important words from the great medieval alchemists, has been accomplished. This is faith and work, the Spirit and our spiritual instincts, our individual lives and the lives of friends, neighbors, and strangers, all coming together as one. And the fact that "the great work" has been accomplished at any given meal does not mean that it comes to an end. The "great work" is always a work in progress.

By now, we should all realize that the whole can (and does) break down at any point along the way, which is one of the reasons that spiritual traditions have always emphasized watchfulness, discrimination, and discernment. Our most basic sacred responsibility is to live the kind of lives that contribute to the greater whole. That's what the real meaning of words like "livelihood," "work," and "religion" actually involve. And that's why something vital about the condition of our spirit can be discerned by the quality of the water we drink and of the air we breathe; and that's why caring for our souls is directly tied to whether and how we care for the soil. We must be watchful of our spiritual lives in every respect, because the great body of life that God created is a sacred trust.

It's not difficult to see how important watchfulness, discrimination, and discernment are in the simple act of eating a meal. For example, consider the poisonous pesticides, wasteful packaging, harmful additives, industrial-scale agriculture gobbling up smaller farms, genetic modifications, exploited laborers, depleted soil, deforestation, stolen land, animals housed in deplorable conditions, and the vast amounts of greenhouse gases that go into the growing of our food. Of course, none of this seems to matter if we tell ourselves that faith (or reason) is separate from awe, love, intent, conscience, community, and rest. I don't think we've really gone that far; but we're walking farther down that very road with every passing day. We already know that the logical outcome—the consequence—will be utterly devastating: and along the way we will have surrendered our spiritual instincts to fear and sold our souls for what we believed was an acceptable price. We absolutely cannot let this happen.

The picture that I'm painting here should be obvious enough. We're all born with spiritual instincts—every one of us. It is our birthright to cultivate them; it is our responsibility to use them; and our survival depends on how well we use them. We're all in this together; we're all our sisters' and brothers' keepers, and our lives are meant to be a feast in preparation. We all have our part to play.

That's why I admire a great cook, but "admiration" is not a strong enough word to describe the depth of my feeling. "Awe" is better, and what begins with awe culminates in faith. A cook draws upon a power greater than we are, which makes every cook something like an artist, a healer, a priest, or anyone who really cares about the kind of life we create together. How "the great work" turns out depends on trust—the trust that everyone will play their part by using the spiritual instincts that they've been given, the best that they can. From this trust, a faithful life emerges. Unless we give ourselves the chance to find the source of that faith within ourselves, we probably won't find it—although where the Spirit is concerned, which is everywhere, anything is possible.

Concerning my part in all this, I should tell you that I've never become a great cook; but I'll never take for granted what a great cook does, or anyone else who is involved in the preparation of a meal. What I first learned, years ago, when I left the home of my childhood and my mother no longer cooked for me, is that the great body of life is woven together by sacred threads—which means that one thing always leads to another.

For example, my admiration for a cook eventually led to my decision to become a beekeeper. Once, I was in awe of beekeepers, so much so that I never considered the possibility that I could be one myself. As it turned out, I put my first hive in the backyard several years ago without deliberating very much at all. If I had deliberated too much, I might have found a reason to be afraid, either of the honeybees or of what I believed I couldn't do. I might have convinced myself that I didn't really want to become a bee-keeper. If that had happened, I would have been letting my fear deceive me.

We all have to be watchful about giving ourselves yet another reason to be afraid. This is not a lesson or a skill that anyone can actually teach. It's helpful to talk about it, if that means remember-ing that the answers we're looking for are found within ourselves; and we must cultivate and use our spiritual instincts to make any headway at all. But our teacher really is the Spirit, speaking through each and every one of us and through the great body of life. The inner confidence that a great feast not only can happen, but also will happen—even in the face of the worst unknown—is what I mean by "faith."

A Spiritual Practice in Discernment and Faith

Our lives are a process of growing in faith that happens through all our spiritual instincts. Those instincts are a precious gift. We're born with them like seeds planted in our soul. Our responsibility is to cultivate them in each other, so we can develop the capacity to use them well. Above all the others, the seed of faith is nurtured by how well we use our gifts of awe, love, intent, conscience, community, and rest. Whether we want to find faith, to under-stand it better, or to strengthen it, we must take into account these spiritual instincts too. What we find says a lot about our faith, how well we're doing in becoming who we want to be and whom

God wants us to be—and moving through the fears that prevent us from becoming that person.

This last practice involves an examination of the spiritual instincts that we've discussed so far as they relate to issues of faith and fear. The practice reviews and reflects upon what we've previously done, while taking it a step further: through and beyond our fear; that is to say, in the direction that our souls want to go.

Awe and Faith

I'm awestruck by the pictures of far distant galaxies and nebulae taken by the Hubble telescope. For me personally, they evoke a feeling of God's presence and, at the same time, provoke questions about whether God is really there or what kind of God we're talking about. I don't necessarily see a tension between religion and science in these images. Rather, they make me reflect on some of our ultimate concerns: who we are, what really are our deepest fears, and how we might move through them. Most important, I wonder what kind of "power greater than ourselves" we're turning to—or looking for—in our lives every day. What are we, in fact, in awe of?

Although those photographs of deep space are awe-inspiring, we could ask the very same questions by looking much closer to home. First and foremost, am I taking the opportunity to experience awe in nature? Do I let myself know what humility, reverence, beauty, and wonder mean in the world around me every day? Nature is not God, but it reveals God's presence and hand in the lives that we live together.

We should also take into account the fact that many people experience awe in other ways; for example, through entertainment, sports, and media stars or political and religious leaders. Obviously, this kind of awe is very "close to home" too. It is important to *ask ourselves what kind of ideas and assumptions about "reality" this kind of awe creates. What kind of "power greater than ourselves" are we really giving our attention to? Questions like these, especially when corporate interests shape or control the media and when the media itself occupies so much of our attention, should be given a great deal of prayerful reflection. The impact that this kind of awe has on our faith is greater than we realize.*

Love and Faith

When most of us think of love, we have "who" in mind. "Who" are we in love with? That's what comes to mind first, as it should. But as Saint Augustine put it centuries ago, we have all kinds of "loves," and most of them are better described by the word "what." What are our loves? In the larger picture of faith and life, the question of "what" we love often matters a great deal more than we might believe—or want to believe.

Only honest soul-searching will give us the insight into ourselves that we need to answer questions like this. Jesus, who set the mark for any answer we might give, said that he would "lay down his life for his friends." I think we all understand the depth of love that he's talking about. Hopefully life won't test us to that extent, but his statement raises a good question nonetheless: "What am I willing to give up for the people that I love?" To examine ourselves in this way may not be easy. It raises issues of fear: What am I most afraid of losing? The love of money, career, and lifestyle might come to mind. The answers that we give reveal a great deal about the strength of the bonds for the people we love, on the one hand, and our other kinds of love, on the other. The nature of our love always tells us, directly or indirectly, about the content of the faith that we actually live.

Intent and Faith

One of the most important expressions of intent relates to how we use our attention in everyday life, and that relates to our "intentions"—whether our intentions are good, whether we have agendas and motives that manipulate others, and whether we are transparent and clear about our goals in life.

One of the best ways I know to gain insight into how we use our intent is by reflecting on trust. For example, I might consider how much I trust myself. If I tell myself that I'm going to do something, how likely am I to follow through? Do I give up easily or create excuses? How distracted am I likely to be? What does it feel like when I follow through on my goals and keep my promises?

But the better questions concern others: How trustworthy do other people consider me to be? What reasons do I give them, through my own behavior, to put their trust in me? It should go without saying that a world where trust is called into question eventually creates a crisis in faith. But lurking behind that lack of trust and faith are our fears. Rather than judge ourselves too much or too harshly about this, it's better to work on our intent in everyday life, by saying what we mean and meaning what we really want to say. If it turns out that we're afraid of what others might think, then that is the fear that we need to move through.

Conscience and Faith

Usually, when we hear the word "conscience," our thoughts quickly turn to anything that we might feel guilty about. I'm not the kind of person who likes to make people feel guilty. However,

I also realize that a healthy capacity for feeling responsible and taking responsibility can be a very positive sign—and not because we should feel responsible or guilty when bad things happen. The reason is this: It tells us that our moral compass is in good working order, which is good to know.

As a rule, the outcome of a thorough examination of conscience will have some mixed results. We may have a relatively clear conscience in some areas of life, and a not-so-clear conscience in others. Perhaps our conscience will be clear at home, but less clear at work—or the other way around. Let's say, for example, that in our home life we're not happy with the way we've put off some important financial decisions that affect our whole family, or that we've been eating too much unhealthy food, despite the warnings of our doctor. In both cases, our not-so-clear conscience suggests either the denial of fear or a fear that's powerful enough to prevent us from doing the right thing. Put another way, our guilty feelings should not suggest that we're "bad people." Rather, they suggest the presence of the very fear that we need to identify and move beyond.

The very same principle applies to our awareness (or lack of awareness) of the living and working conditions of the people who have contributed to the lives we have. What about the people who made the clothes that we wear or those who harvested the food we eat? Do we know anything about them? Do we care about them? Why should we care? The answer to the last question is that their lives are present with us—not only at the dinner table, at home, and at work, but also with every step we take. And even if their lives weren't present, they are human beings who need our help. Why would we be so afraid that we would ignore their suffering? Why are we afraid of them?

Community and Faith

Trouble in our economic system has put tremendous pressure on all forms of community, which triggers a fear response in us—as it should. We should be concerned about the well-being and future of our communities. Yet our response to this fear is often to create communities based on fear. They may magnify and solidify the fears that we already have, rather than help us to move through them.

Although the kind of self-examination we need in this regard may be relatively straightforward, we may resist it. For example, we should be asking ourselves questions like these: What part does fear play in the communities that we're a part of? Are those communities a refuge from fear? Or do they make me afraid? Communities that offer refuge are absolutely necessary and good. They give us a space to breathe and a place to receive comfort and support. At the same time, they can also isolate us too much from the realities of life and prevent us from discovering the truths about the world that we need to discover.

We might also ask ourselves whether we're aware of the communities that we already have, but may not be a part of or participate in to the extent that we could. It is important to participate in face-to-face communities where we can look each other in the eyes, smile, shed a tear, and offer help and assistance when needed. The very last thing we want to do, in our day and age, is create the kind of communities where we might be wary or afraid of our neighbors, simply because we don't know them.

Rest and Faith

At this very moment, many people that I know are close to exhausted. There are times when we have no choice but to put in long hours for much longer than we would wish or than our bodies can reasonably endure. Life is like that sometimes. But without rest, we risk losing our perspective on life, our capacity to use our other spiritual instincts well, and our ability to fulfill the responsibilities that really are ours. Contrary to what we may believe, an unwillingness to take care of ourselves suggests the presence of some deeply rooted issues with fear and faith that we need to examine closely.

It is necessary and, sometimes, good to go beyond our limits— but only for a time. Friends tell us what we could hear from our own conscience, if we would take the time to listen. When we don't listen, we're headed for trouble. It makes them afraid, as it should, because they know that we might put ourselves at risk— and them. If anything, working more, when rest is what we need, only makes matters worse: We become more susceptible to harmful fear and to making the mistakes in life that we would otherwise avoid.

Perhaps more than anything else, ignoring the instinct of rest is not very faithful to the One who set aside a whole day of rest, blessed it, and called it "holy." The secret to rest is, in practice, a sacred truth: By giving ourselves some rest now and again, we give the world around us—and the people we know and love— the opportunity to renew and replenish the life that they have within them. Rest and work, in their proper balance, create the sacred space where our souls can embrace the kinship and communion on which our mutual survival depends.

IN DEFENSE OF JOY

This final chapter is no mere afterthought to what you've already read, and I chose its title for a very specific reason. I want to raise the question of whether joy needs defending. I believe that it does, for exactly the same reasons that faith needs defending and our spiritual instincts need to be cultivated. Yet, with the realities of life being what they are and the power of fear having such a contaminating influence on our lives, it turns out that a defense of joy is the best of all possible defenses.

Years ago, when I was going through a difficult time— struggling with life, dissatisfied with myself, and afraid of who knows what—I spent some time searching for the most joyful people I could find. Although I did this on a whim, it was one of the best things that I've ever done. I didn't announce it, nor did I drop everything and devote all of my time and energy to it. Rather, I pursued it in the midst of everything else. "In the midst of" included that part of Cajun south Louisiana where the *joie de vivre* was a fact of everyday living. I lived there for ten years or so, long before Katrina and the oil spill. How they understand joy and life's meaning now is something that they—and we—will have to work out together in the years ahead. What I can say is that south Louisiana was an excellent place to begin my search, and what I learned there and from them applies to everywhere and everyone.

I discovered, early on, that searching for joyful people is not all that difficult. The hard part is in finding them, which is not to say that joyful people don't exist, especially in south Louisiana. There are plenty of them around—maybe not in the vast numbers that you might think or like to believe, but enough—and they aren't hiding. For example, at the beginning of my search, when I believed that I had found one or two and then made their acquaintance, it turned out that I was wrong. I had been telling myself that joyful people would be those who laugh more than anyone else; in effect, they would stand out in a crowded room or a group. Not so. Joyful people might be serious, or silly, or quiet—or perhaps not. To make a long story short, the first lesson that I learned was really simple: The reason that I had so much trouble finding joyful people was that I couldn't see them; and the reason that I couldn't see them was that I was looking through the eyes of a wary and frightened young man—rather than a joyful one.

In those days, I could almost see them, but not quite. The only reason that I eventually learned to see them is that they—joyful people—taught me how.

This "gift of sight," for which I am eternally grateful, was entirely dependent on the good spiritual instincts, the insight, and the goodwill of the very people I was looking for. My guess is that you might be in a similar fix. Think of it this way: After all that I've written, you probably still wonder whether fear really is that much of an obstacle in life. Yes, it is true that there are terribly good reasons to be afraid and that some kinds of fear focus our attention in ways that ensure our survival. I couldn't agree with you more. Nevertheless, I still say that fear is the single greatest obstacle that we ever face. I'm sure; you're not so sure; and here we are.

On top of that, you might wonder whether this defense of joy is really worth reading, on the assumption that I might be wrong about the whole thing, which would make taking it seriously too much of a risk. Let's say, for example, that I couldn't find joyful people, not because I couldn't see, but because they simply weren't there. This is a cynical view, in my opinion, but let's go with it anyway. I would come back by repeating essentially what I've already said, that "I learned to find them because they taught me how to see." And, I would go a step further—I would also say "seeing is believing." Now it's your turn. You say, "That's all well and good, but the results of 'seeing is believing' can't be proven." Why? The reason is that believing is a matter of faith rather than fact. This, of course, is exactly my point: Seeing lives in the eyes of the beholder; beholding is seeing through the eyes of faith; and fear is the greatest of all enemies of faith. In other words, I couldn't recognize the simple joy of life, when it was all around me, precisely because I was seeing life from the standpoint of being afraid.

So, here we go again, going in circles. Let's make an agreement: Rather than get stuck in all that, let's move ahead with what I learned from and about them—joyful people. Yes, I am defending them. I like joyful people; I admire their courage; and I feel called to defend them. Even more, I'm defending the spiritual principle on which their very existence depends: that the joy of life gives us a much better, clearer, and more reliable perspective on life than does fear.

So now, I'll spell out what I learned in some detail. First, I should tell you that in all this time, from my mid-twenties until now, I've never met a joyful person whose life was ruled by fear.

Not one. Despite any preconceived notions that you or I might have about joy or the joy of life, joyful people have their bouts with frustration, anger, and rage; and like everyone, they have their fears. They're neither completely fearless nor joyful every minute of the day. Moreover, I wouldn't say that they have a "Come what may" or "Ignorance is bliss" attitude toward life, or that they live with their heads in the clouds, having no interest in work or getting things done. They're not, in any way, pretending to live somewhere over the rainbow. As a rule, they're involved in the world more than most people I know, and in the issues of the world.

Second, being a priest, I would like to say that joyful people are exceptionally religious. But if I said that I would be lying, and I don't believe in lying for a good cause—not usually. The fact of the matter is that joyful people may or may not be particularly religious, at least in any big or public sense of the word. If they think of themselves as religious, then we realize it gradually—like a bright sunrise that lifts above the horizon in the early morning. This may take us by surprise, if only because our first impressions, which were mistaken, led us in a dreadfully wrong direction. When joyful people don't think of themselves as religious, which is just as likely, any first impressions (or second, third, and fourth impressions) that we might have should be thrown out the window immediately. I'm not saying this because of them— nonreligious but joyful people. Rather, the problem comes with our usually mistaken impressions about how the Great Mystery, the Spirit, actually works within us. Either way—this is the point I really want to make—joyful people are intimately aware of a power greater than themselves. They just think of it in different and unexpected ways. Although they're not likely to put any of this into words, they're aware of this one thing probably more than anything else.

It took a long time to let all this sink in to a point where I could put two and two together: The miraculous and courageous thing about joyful people is that they refuse, as a matter of courage and conviction, to let fear rule their lives. Their courage is the stand they take in a world where fear would like to rule the roost. Like I said, they have their share of fear, but they know what lies beyond it, and they simply will not let fear stand in their way. Once they discover that this can be done and that they can do it, then the world never looks quite the same. Their conviction is that they have absolutely no desire to turn back—ever.

The deeper secret held within the hearts of joyful people is simple: They've realized that there is a real world—in the here and now—and the fact that there's nothing obvious about any of it may be the most peculiar thing about the world most people know. As I said, these are not people who are likely to ignore the way things are. They are better than most at dealing with the world as it is, and they're not likely to feel resentful or disappointed because life doesn't meet anyone's idealized standards. The extent to which this may be surprising and confusing to others depends solely on the power that fear has on their perception of things.

I realize that I may be losing you, so bear with me—I haven't finished explaining what you need to know. Joyful people insist on creating and living the kind of life that they believe we are all meant to have. They're not pushy about this. I don't think the word "proselytizing" exists in their vocabulary. This is another way of saying that they're as "wise as serpents, and innocent as doves" (Matthew 10:16). They're not so worried and afraid that they freeze up inside, and they're not so foolish as to become uncaring or oblivious to the world around them. Neither denying their fear, nor turning a blind eye, they unmask the power of fear for what it is, reveal the joy, and move ahead—knowing full well that tomorrow will be another day too.

Here again, their courage is astonishing: They know that unless they draw upon their spiritual instincts (the very same ones that we've all been given), the serpent will suffocate their joy in its coils and devour the dove in one quick motion. They would surrender their souls to a world ruled by fear, lose their eyes of faith, and thereafter see the world from the standpoint of being afraid.

The soul and the integrity of faith are a lot to lose, and that's why I want my last words to you to drive this point home as clearly as possible. Don't ever let anyone tell you or convince you that fear gives a clearer perspective on life than joy. To let that happen is to surrender every one of our spiritual instincts to the power of fear and to put our very survival in jeopardy. People with the best survival skills are those who have discovered the joy of life and make their stand there. They know what they've found; and for dear life, they're going to defend it.

I like what Saint Paul said to the Galatians (5:1) about this: *"For freedom, Christ has set us free, Stand firm, therefore, and do not submit again to a yoke of slavery."* What I'm saying is that all the parables in the Bible that describe what "the kingdom of God" is like and how to get there are about the real world. If we weren't so compromised by the way things are, and disabled by our fear, we would know this already. We would call "the real world" by its right name, having taken our stand for the great body of life and the joy of life. For now, we're letting our fear live our lives for us; and that, my friends, is living somewhere else.

As for me and, I hope, for you, we always have a choice. Fear would lead us to believe that we have no real choice at all, but fear is a skillful deceiver. We always have a choice. Our best choice will be to say "no" to a world ruled by fear, to live in the real world the best that we can, and to become the people that we're meant to be. If that's the choice we make, then the Spirit, always present, will help us find the joy that the great body of life bestows on those who live here.

ACKNOWLEDGMENTS, REFERENCES,

AND SUGGESTIONS FOR

FURTHER READING

This book originated during a leisurely lunch with Joel Foti-
nos, my editor at Tarcher/Penguin. He suggested a book on
fear; we both knew that the idea was good; and I soon began to
write. Toward the very end of the process, Joel's assistant, Michael
Solana—working under severe time constraints that were no fault
of his own—accomplished the unglamorous but skillful and necessary task of helping me make some difficult points more clearly.
Long before the book was an idea in anyone's mind, Susan Peter-
son Kennedy set the whole process in motion by the indomitable
nature of her fearless spirit. And never, under any circumstances,
would I want to forget my copy editor, Leda Scheintaub. Her tire-
less labor, by its very nature, is supposed to go unnoticed, which
makes it all the more worthy of gratitude.

Many other people have also helped to bring this book into the
light of day. They, in all likelihood, would never guess that they had
anything to do with it. I have no choice but to guard the privacy
of some, but a few others I would like to thank by name: Linda

Johnsen, Minka Sprague, Madeleine Mathiot, Jim Morton, Chris Harp and Grai St. Clair Rice of HoneyBeeLives, Darrell Posey, Hellen Grace Akwii Wangusa, Andy Dietsche, John Osgood, Richard Sloan, and Val Stelchen. I would especially like to thank Peter Mann, who informed and inspired my thinking on food and sacred meals.

Several quotes found at the beginning of the chapters are part of larger bodies of work that are worthy of exploration and study. I want to list them here, acknowledging their references, while also encouraging you to discover these writings for yourself, if you haven't already. You'll notice that none of these works deal especially with the subject of fear; but as I've emphasized throughout this book, fear and the movement through it are not what they seem to be.

I'll begin with C. S. Lewis. I am told that his provocative *Mere Christianity* (New York: Macmillan, originally 1943) has become popular again among a new generation, which is no surprise. Marvin Meyer's *The Gospel of Thomas: The Hidden Sayings of Jesus* (San Francisco: Harper Collins, 1992), with an interpretation by Harold Bloom, offers a thoughtful introduction to this enlightening text. The works of Theodore Parker have been generally overlooked in favor of Emerson; nevertheless, his impact on American life has been profound. Dr. Martin Luther King, Jr., referred to Parker's idea of the moral universe "bending toward justice" in one of his speeches, which was recently quoted by President Barack Obama. See "Of Justice and Conscience" in *Ten Sermons of Religion*, by Theodore Parker (Boston: Crosby, Nichols, 1853). *Rilke's Book of Hours: Love Poem to God* (New York: Riverhead, 2005), translated by Anita Barrows and Joanna Macy, is a great book that shouldn't be missed. Then, read everything else that Rilke wrote. The same can be said for the paintings and writings of William Blake. Try *The Complete Poems* (London: The Penguin Group, 1977) to get a feel for the depth of his creative imagination. Finally, among references to quotations found in this book, J. R. R. Tolkien's *The Lord of the Rings* (New York: Houghton Mifflin, originally 1954–1955) is, in my opinion, one of the all time best sacred stories involving the movement through fear. The quote at the beginning of chapter one here is from the last of his three volumes: *The Return of the King.*

For adventurous readers who like academic writing, I recommend *Phenomenology and Social Reality: Essays in Memory of Alfred Schutz*, edited by Maurice Natanson (The Hague: Martinus Nijhoff, 1970). This volume gives a general impression of how philosophers have understood "intent," and it includes Eric Voegelin's famous essay called "The Eclipse of Reality," which I especially like.

Let me also add that many books can be found on the life and teachings of Saint Francis of Assisi. My popular favorites are those written by Murray Bodo, specifically, *Francis: The Journey and the Dream* (St. Anthony Messenger Press, 1972) and *The Way of St. Francis* (St. Anthony Messenger Press, by arrangement with Doubleday, 1995). I would also recommend any of the writings of Desmond Tutu and Nelson Mandela. I have not referred to them here, but they have lived the movement through fear as few people have.

Biblical quotations have come from *The New Oxford Annotated Bible* (New York: Oxford University Press, 1991). Quotations from the Episcopal marriage service and the hymn "Amazing Grace" can be found, respectively, in *The Book of Common Prayer* and *The Hymnal 1982*, both published by the Church Hymnal Corporation, New York, the Church Pension Fund.

Finally, my heart turns close to home, where all our paths eventually lead. The Cathedral of Saint John the Divine and the General Theological Seminary, both in Manhattan, are wonderful places that have fed my soul, as has the Himalayan International Institute in Honesdale, Pennsylvania. The Third Order of the Society of Saint Francis has been a constant source of inspiration. The people of St. John's Episcopal Church in Ellenville,

New York, have always been compassionate and kind, as all really great congregations are; and the staff of Ellenville Public Library and Museum provided helpful assistance in the preparation of this book. The support and encouragement of my family, Bob and Sally Golliher and Wendy and Joe Worrell (and their children), have no limit; and no one has a greater gift of love and patience than my wife, Asha, to whom I am eternally grateful.